THE LIFE OF SOLITUDE

THE LIFE OF SOLITUDE

(*De vita solitaria*)

Francesco Petrarca

Translated by
Jacob Zeitlin

Edited with an Introduction by
Scott H. Moore

BAYLOR UNIVERSITY PRESS

© 2023 by Baylor University Press
Waco, Texas 76798

Cover and book design by Kasey McBeath
Cover art: Unsplash/okeykat

Paperback ISBN: 978-1-4813-1712-2
Printed case ISBN: 978-1-4813-1809-9

The Library of Congress has cataloged this book under ISBN 978-1-4813-1712-2.

Library of Congress Control Number: 2023932147

"My object in living is to unite
My avocation and my vocation
As my two eyes make one in sight.
Only where love and need are one,
And the work is play for mortal stakes,
Is the deed ever really done
For Heaven and the future's sakes."

Frost, "Two Tramps in Mud Time"

Yet I hold that the contemplative life of the Christian is not a life of abstraction, of secession, in order to concentrate up ideal essences, upon absolutes, upon eternity alone. Christianity cannot reject history. It cannot be a denial of time. Christianity is centered on an historical event which has changed the meaning of history. The freedom of the Christian contemplative is not freedom *from* time, but freedom *in* time. It is the freedom to go out and meet God in the inscrutable mystery of His will here and now, in this precise moment in which He asks man's cooperation in shaping the course of history according to the demands of divine truth, mercy, and fidelity.

Thomas Merton, *Seeds of Destruction*

CONTENTS

CHRONOLOGY OF PETRARCH'S

INTELLECTUAL WORLD

Year	Event
BC	
753	Traditional date for the founding of Rome by Romulus
509	Traditional date for the founding of the Roman Republic (Brutus ends Roman monarchy by overthrowing Tarquin the Proud)
c. 428–348	Plato
399	Socrates is tried, convicted, and executed in Athens
384–322	Demosthenes
384–322	Aristotle
264–241	First Punic War between the Romans and the Carthaginians
c. 235–183	Scipio Africanus
218–201	Second Punic War, perhaps the deadliest war in ancient history. Scipio's defeat of Hannibal will be for Petrarch an exemplary event and evidence of Rome's virtue.
149–146	Third Punic War, in which Carthage is decisively defeated and the city destroyed
106–43	Cicero
70–19	Virgil
45	Cicero retires to Antium and writes the *Tusculan Disputations* after the death of his daughter in childbirth
44	Assassination of Julius Caesar

Year	Event
29	Probable date for Virgil's *Georgics*
29–19	Virgil writes the *Aeneid*
27–25	Livy begins writing *The History of Rome* (*Ad Urbe Condita*—"From the Founding of the City")
27 BC–AD 14	Reign ("Principate") of Caesar Augustus (Octavian)
4 BC–AD 65	Seneca the Younger
c. 3	Birth of Jesus of Nazareth in Bethlehem in Judea

AD	
c. 27–30	Public ministry of Jesus of Nazareth
c. 30	Crucifixion and resurrection of Jesus
30–c. 60	Events of the Book of Acts
54–68	Reign of Nero
54–62	Seneca is a senior advisor to Nero. Writes *On the Happy Life*.
56–120	Tacitus
68	Nero commits suicide
70	Roman legions sack Jerusalem
79	Mount Vesuvius erupts, destroying Pompeii, Herculaneum, and surrounding area
312	Battle of the Milvian Bridge, in which Constantine, having seen a vision of the Chi-Rho and the words "in hoc signo vinces," defeats Maxentius
313	Edict of Milan, which established religious toleration for Christians in the Roman Empire
354–430	St. Augustine of Hippo
476	Traditional date for the fall of the (Western) Roman Empire
477–524	Boethius
480–547	St. Benedict of Nursia
482–565	Justinian I
c. 524	Boethius writes *The Consolation of Philosophy*
529	St. Benedict establishes his first monastery at Monte Cassino

Year	Event
1095–1099	First Crusade, in which the Crusaders retake Jerusalem and establish the Latin Kingdom of Jerusalem (which will last until 1187)
1096	Pauper's Crusade, led by Peter the Hermit
1115	Florentines overthrow the Marquise of Tuscany—nominally part of the HRE—establishing the Republic of Florence
1147–1149	Second Crusade, in which the Crusaders attempt, and fail, to recapture Crusader States in eastern Anatolia (including Damascus)
c. 1181–1226	St. Francis of Assisi
1187	Saladin retakes Jerusalem
1189–1192	Third Crusade, in which Crusaders recapture Cyprus, Acre, and Jaffa, but fail to recapture Jerusalem
1194–1250	Life of Frederick II, HRE, king of Sicily and Jerusalem, "stupor mundi"
1202–1204	Fourth Crusade, in which Venetian and Latin Crusaders sack and occupy Constantinople
1221–1274	St. Bonaventure
1225–1275	St. Thomas Aquinas
1265–1321	Dante Alighieri
1282	"Sicilian Vespers," in which Sicilians overthrow French king Charles I of Anjou
1293	Establishment of the Ordinances of Justice in the Florentine Republic
1302	White Guelphs, including Dante and Petrarch's father, condemned to exile from Florence
1304	Francesco Petrarca born in Arezzo
1305	Clement V crowned pope in Lyon, France
1307	Petrarch's brother, Gherardo, is born
1308–1321	Dante writes *The Divine Comedy* in exile from Florence
1308	Henry VII crowned king of the Romans in Aachen
1309–1343	Robert of Anjou ("the Wise") reigns as king of Naples
1309–1376	Avignon "Captivity" of the Papacy initiated by Pope Clement V and King Philip IV (of France)

Year	Event
1310–1313	Henry VII's "Italian Campaign," in which he attempts (and fails) to unite the Italian city states under Imperial rule
1313	Henry VII dies at Buonconvento. Pope Celestine V is canonized by Clement V.
1313–1375	Giovanni Boccaccio
1315	Petrarch's father takes a position at the papal court in Avignon and the family moves to Carpentras
1316–1320	Petrarch studies law in Montpellier
1320–1326	Petrarch studies law in Bologna
1321	Dante dies in Ravenna
1323	Thomas Aquinas canonized by Pope John XXII in Avignon
1327	Petrarch meets Laura at the Church of St. Claire in Avignon
1327	Marsilius of Padua's *Defensor pacis* ("The Defender of Peace"), which rejected papal claims to "plenitude of power," is condemned as heretical by Pope John XXII
1330	Petrarch accepts the position of household chaplain to Cardinal Giovanni Colonna
1333	Petrarch buys a home in Vaucluse and becomes friends with Philippe de Cabassoles
1336	Petrarch ascends (or claims to have ascended) to the summit of Mont Ventoux
1337	Petrarch's son, Giovanni, is born (mother unknown)
1337–1339	Petrarch begins work on *De viris illustrium* ("On Famous Men") and his epic poem *Africa*
1337–1453	Hundred Years War
1341	Petrarch requests to be examined by King Robert in Naples and then is crowned Poet Laureate in Rome
1342–1343	Walter (VI) of Brienne exercises tyrannical rule in Florence
1343	Petrarch's daughter, Francesca, is born (mother unknown)
1343	Gherardo enters the Carthusian monastery in Montrieux
1346	During Lent, Petrarch writes the first version of *De vita solitaria* ("The Life of Solitude")
1346–1353	Peak years of the second Bubonic Plague in Eurasia
1347	Petrarch writes *De otio religioso* ("On Religious Leisure")
1347–1380	St. Catherine of Siena

Year	Event
1347	Cola di Rienzo overthrows the rule of Rome by the barons, proclaiming the Roman Republic "restored." He would be forced to flee Rome merely seven months later.
1348	Plague devastates Italy and western Europe. Petrarch's Laura, Giovanni Colonna, and more than half the population of Florence die.
1348	Narrative date for *The Decameron*
1349	Boccaccio begins *The Decameron*. First dated circulation is 1360. Boccaccio will continue to revise the text through the 1370s.
1349	Petrarch's friend Mainardo Accursio ("Simplicianus") is killed by the Ubaldini clan while journeying from Avignon to come to Petrarch. In response, Petrarch will urge Florentine officials to wage war against the Ubaldini. This conflict will persist until September 1350.
1351	Boccaccio invites Petrarch to join the university in Florence. Petrarch declines.
1353	Petrarch moves to Milan to serve under the Visconti
1353	Probable date for final revisions to Petrarch's *Secretum* (perhaps begun 1346, revised in 1348)
1353–1361	Petrarch serves as an ambassador for the Visconti
1367	Petrarch writes "On His Ignorance and that of Many Others" from Padua
1374	Petrarch dies in Arquà
1375–1378	War of the Eight Saints fought between Florence and the Papacy over control of Tuscan regions near Florence. Pope Gregory XI had stipulated that papal control was a condition for the Papacy's return from Avignon. War ended in treaty.
1377	Gregory XI returns the Papacy to Rome, intending to end the Avignon papal court. In the aftermath of his death in 1378, the "Great Schism" will begin.

Introduction

Scott H. Moore

Francesco Petrarca ("Petrarch" in English, 1304–1374) is universally regarded as one of the greatest Italian poets and is frequently described as the "Father of Renaissance Humanism" and sometimes as the founder of the Renaissance itself. Petrarch is best known for his poetry, especially the sonnets that he composed in the vernacular Italian dialect of his home-land. But Petrarch was also the author of an extraordinary body of prose works in Latin, including numerous books, essays, and multiple volumes of his letters that, with Cicero as his model, he collected, edited, and pre-served for posterity—including a quite famous, though incomplete, letter written to Posterity itself.

Included among these Latin prose works is *The Life of Solitude* (*De vita solitaria*, DVS hereafter), which Petrarch began during Lent of 1346 and after twenty years of reflection, addition, and correction, sent to its dedi-catee in 1366. Book I contains an argument for why a life of solitude and contemplation is superior to a busy life of civic obligation and commerce. Book II contains a long enumeration of exemplars of the solitary life drawn from history and literature (and occasionally, mythology). Included in Book II are provocative digressions on whether one has an obligation to serve a tyrant and on the failures of contemporary monarchs to recover the holy sites in the East.

Petrarch's vision of solitude is not monastic solitude. It is not even "solitude," if solitude must entail the absence of all companionship. Petrarch says explicitly, "I never persuaded those for whom I said sol-itude was advantageous that, in their desire for solitude, they should despise the laws of friendship. I bade them fly from crowds and not from friends" [1.7.19]. These friends, however, will be few in number and will

2 The Life of Solitude

be committed to a life which is both contemplative and conversational, a life which is informed by both religious and secular learning and the cultivation of virtue. James Hankins has called Petrarch's ideal a "fundamentally new form of life . . . a life of *otium litterarum*, or literary retirement."[1]

DVS itself is a beautiful but uneven work in which moving reflection and staggering hyperbole sit side by side. The illustrations that are enumerated in Book II occasionally seem to demonstrate a special pleading that sometimes undermines, rather than supports, the thesis for which they have been put into service. For instance, Petrarch claims that if Caesar Augustus cannot actually be named among the exemplars of solitude, he was certainly one of its admirers, because "he was constantly longing for the restfulness of this kind of life" [2.13.2]. Petrarch's treatment of city dwellers, businessmen, women, Muslims, and many more besides, is often offensive and discourages some readers from taking seriously the remainder of the text. Many of these instances are simply artifacts of the historical and cultural milieu from which he wrote.

Why has DVS been neglected? Almost all of Petrarch's Latin works, both poetry and prose, suffer a similar fate in comparison with the extraordinary vernacular poetry of the *Canzoniere* ("Song Book"). In the English-speaking world, it was always the sonnets that made Petrarch's fame, and translating and retranslating his love poetry has been a hallmark of English literature since the Elizabethan period. The Latin works were never as popular, despite the fact that some of these works were, at one time, among the most important works to Petrarch himself. Today it is often difficult to find new translations or editions of this work. For instance, his unfinished epic poem *Africa* (on Scipio Africanus and the Punic Wars) has not been retranslated into English in almost half a century, and long portions of his compendium on the *Lives of Famous Men* (*De viris illustribus*), including his appraisal of Julius Caesar (*De gestis Cesaris*), have yet to be translated into English and published on a wide scale.

It is much the same with DVS. Even the original translator of the only English translation a century ago seems to think that it is not an especially significant volume. Jacob Zeitlin described it as a defense of "peaceful brooding," which "reflects the same confusion of tendencies, the same

---

[1]   James Hankins, *Virtue Politics: Soulcraft and Statecraft in Renaissance Italy* (Cambridge, Mass.: Harvard University Press, 2019), 176.

medley of contradictory ideals that is evident in Petrarch's other writings."[2] According to Zeitlin, "The *De Vita Solitaria* is an elaborate and redundant book. Its argument winds and wanders and sometimes forgets itself altogether."[3] Perhaps we should not be surprised that the only English translation (from 1924) has long been out of print and is now available almost exclusively through online digitized services.

In truth, both the form and content of much of Petrarch's prose work have largely fallen out of fashion. DVS, and its companion volume, *On Religious Leisure*, are often seen as "too religious" or, as Zeitlin described, possessed of an "affectation of envy"[4] of both an academic and monastic life Petrarch was unable to enjoy. Moreover, Petrarch is accused of both misrepresentation and self-deception. When it suited his interests, he spent much of his life involving himself in both regional and international politics, and when these efforts inevitably did not work out (so the accusation goes), he self-indulgently retreated to his life of contemplation and reflection. These accusations were directed at Petrarch even during his life, and he vigorously (and repeatedly) defended himself and his way of life. Nonetheless, this is perhaps the "medley of contradictory ideals that is evident in Petrarch's other writings" that Zeitlin finds throughout DVS.

If this is the case, why then should DVS be recovered and re-presented today? The reasons are numerous. To begin, there is much about the historical narrative which is now contested by Renaissance scholarship. The figure of Petrarch himself, and the questions surrounding his political activities and motivations, the vitality of his theological beliefs and commitments, and his role in the birth and rise to importance of the concept of "the individual" and "Renaissance humanism" are all very much open questions today.

But even if the broad contours of the narrative above were to be accepted, it would not constitute a reason to ignore this important, and frequently forgotten, volume. Common as such an *ad hominem* like this may be, Petrarch's political and contemplative lives represent less of a contradiction than yet another exemplary instance of the struggle between the communal move outward and the personal move inward. This phenomenon is on display in history over and over again. The same Seneca

---

[2]   Jacob Zeitlin, introduction to *The Life of Solitude*, by Francesco Petrarca, trans. Jacob Zeitlin (University of Illinois Press, 1924), 55.

[3]   Zeitlin, introduction, 67.

[4]   Zeitlin, introduction, 67.

who adored and longed for the tranquility of mind also found himself the advisor to Nero—and paid dearly for the privilege. The same Thoreau who went to the woods to live deliberately wrote the essay on civil disobedience, and the same Wendell Berry who finds solace in the woods at twilight took down Earl Butz, Nixon's secretary of agriculture, for all the world to see and remember. Petrarch's alleged contradictions are not so unique as we might imagine.

DVS needs to be recovered and (re)read today because it offers insight into numerous pressing questions and areas of inquiry. It is an historically significant text which helps us understand better precisely those questions above about Petrarch's life and his role in the changing intellectual, political, cultural, and religious worlds of the notoriously "calamitous" fourteenth century. But DVS is of more than merely historical value.

DVS can contribute to reflection and inquiry on at least two different contemporary philosophical fronts. First, the revival of philosophical virtue ethics in the second half of the twentieth century invites us to reconsider Petrarch's understanding and proposals for virtue and its formative role in personal and communal life. This is especially interesting in light of his well-known opposition to the received scholasticism and popular pseudo-Aristotelianism of his day. In our day, the revival of virtue ethics in the work of Elizabeth Anscombe, Philippa Foot, Alasdair MacIntyre, and others has usually entailed a return to both Aristotle and St. Thomas Aquinas. Petrarch's appeal to the centrality and significance of virtue and its relation to both contemplation and human flourishing bear far greater affinity with the Aristotelian and Thomistic traditions (though not with the Scholastic distortions of those traditions) than is often appreciated.

Second, the connection to human flourishing and to a vigorous and vital humanism also gives rise to another set of philosophical inquiries. In the middle of the twentieth century, the question of humanism returned to a place of prominence in the debates surrounding the work of philosophers such as Martin Heidegger and Jean-Paul Sartre. In recent decades, the English-speaking philosophical world has awoken to the vitality of a contemporary Italian philosophy which, in its attempts to come to terms with that debate, revived the contested legacy of Italian humanism. Italian humanist reflection inevitably finds itself returning to Petrarch and the rise of Renaissance humanism. DVS is, in my opinion, a crucial text for adequately understanding what Petrarch inaugurated and what his legacy entails.[5]

Beyond these important historical and philosophical questions, there are numerous issues that arise much closer to where most of us live. At the most obvious level, our world of consumerism and social media makes us desperately in need of models of solitude, retreat, and reflection. DVS is one of the great defenses of just this solitude, and it should be read with Thomas Merton, Henry David Thoreau, Max Picard, the Carthusians, Cardinal Sarah, Annie Dillard, and Wendell Berry, to name only a few. In *Persuasion*, Jane Austen famously laments that Anne Elliot's sister Mary had "no resources for solitude." Petrarch (both in DVS and beyond) provides marvelous resources for just such solitude.

Turning to the political stage, we today are especially needful of learning how to live under tyrants. Petrarch knew that tyranny can come in many forms. It is perhaps less obvious to many of us that we also live under tyrants—be they political, commercial, or technological. Nonetheless, we also need to cultivate the virtues necessary to resist the tyranny which corrupts our communities, our bodies, and even our souls. In Petrarch's words, the one who has given in to such tyranny has betrayed that which is most important: "I call him wasteful of life and doubly dead, since he has thrown away at once his body and his soul, at once his temporal and eternal life" [2.9.22].

Solitude becomes an essential component of the flourishing individual and of a genuinely authentic humanism. This is a humanism which seeks to understand the essential relation between work and leisure, the nature of community, the interaction of the active and the contemplative lives, the role of virtue in public and private life, and the reflection on the role that solitude should play in such an understanding. All of these reasons bring DVS to the forefront and justify making this remarkable text available to a larger English-speaking audience again.

Perhaps most importantly, we need DVS to help us learn how to respond to one of the besetting challenges of our (and every) day: *acedia*, "the noonday devil" or the spiritual despondency occasioned by our inability to make sense of our lives in a world in which getting and spending have become equated with happiness. *Acedia* is often mistranslated

---

[5]   Eugenio Garin, *Italian Humanism: Philosophy and Civic Life in the Renaissance*, trans. Peter Munz (New York: Harper and Row, 1965); Rocco Rubini, *The Other Renaissance: Italian Humanism between Hegel and Heidegger* (Chicago: University of Chicago Press, 2014).

as "sloth"; Petrarch understands the subtle dangers of *acedia* and recognizes the need for the contemplative leisure of solitude. Zeitlin's failure to understand the serious danger Petrarch found in *acedia* is justification in itself for the need for a new edition of DVS.

Acedia is one of the traditional "seven deadly sins." Benedict, Augustine, Cassian, Climacus, and many others recognize the danger of *acedia*. For Aquinas, it is one of the vices contrary to charity, undermining the joy which is an internal effect of charity.[6] *Acedia* also leads to despair, one of the vices contrary to hope and traditionally understood as an (unforgivable) sin against the Holy Spirit. For Dante, the *accidiosi* in Hell, having rejected "the sweet air that is made glad by the sun" (*Inferno* VII:123), are submerged with the Wrathful in the swamp that is the river Styx. And on Mount Purgatory, they are the runners of the Fourth Terrace, encouraging one another to overcome their lukewarm loves (*Purgatorio* XVIII).

Petrarch picks up this theme and devotes a substantial portion of the *Secretum*, his "secret book," to a discussion of *acedia*. In this private reflection and dialogue with an imaginary St. Augustine, he confesses his struggles with *acedia*. He describes it as "a dreadful sickness of the spirit"[7] and a "dejection which, like a noxious cloud, kills the seeds of virtue and all the fruits of the intelligence."[8] In DVS, he recognizes that within the solitary life, one can find the origins of *both* the cause and the cure of *acedia*, but such cannot be overcome through busyness and distraction.

Because Zeitlin is committed to understanding Petrarch as "the first modern man," he misunderstands Petrarch's struggle with *acedia*. Zeitlin describes Petrarch's yielding to Augustine as "not to the pressure of conscience compelling him from within, but to the dead hand of tradition whose weight he is powerless to shake off." According to Zeitlin, *acedia* is merely the name Petrarch gives to his "melancholy obsession."[9] For Zeitlin, to be modern is to shake off the "dead hand of tradition" and only be compelled by the conscience within.

Petrarch's point, reiterated in both form and content throughout DVS, is that the conscience is in fact formed through its engagement with the

---

[6]   Thomas Aquinas, *Summa Theologiae* IIa–IIae, q. 35.

[7]   Francesco Petrarca, *My Secret Book*, trans. Nicholas Mann, I Tatti Renaissance Library (Cambridge, Mass.: Harvard University Press, 2016), 2.13.1.

[8]   Petrarca, *My Secret Book* 2.16.10.

[9]   Zeitlin, introduction, 85.

sources of authority: the compelling witness of Scripture, the writings of the church fathers, and the works of Roman and Greek literature and philosophy that illustrate the authentic love of wisdom and the pursuit of virtue. And they can only be known through repeated and sustained reflection. Or, in the words of his imaginary St. Augustine, "implant them deep in your memory and make yourself familiar with them through close study; in that way whenever and wherever there is an outbreak of disease which allows no delay, you will, like a skilled doctor, have remedies which are, so to speak, engraved on your mind."[10]

Petrarch certainly felt the thrill of the idea of liberation. He kicks against the goads of false authority whether it be political or ecclesiastical. But he is convinced that he can only know true freedom when he knows the *end* or *telos* to which he as a human being is ordered. "How then should they love life when they do not know what it is good for?" [1.9.3] Petrarch believes that if he does not have a definitive end which is beyond the pleasures and satisfactions which the self can provide, then he will live only "for those things which we have in common with brute beasts." On the contrary, this brief life of "active rest and restful work" [1.7.8] is best spent "in better thoughts, in the contemplation of God, or the study of nature, or the practice of virtue" [1.9.4].

Petrarch's Vision of Solitude

In 1337, Petrarch returned to Avignon after his first visit to Rome. He found the noise, bustle, and corruption of Avignon unbearable, and he retreated to a small estate in the "sheltered valley" of Vaucluse ["Valle Clausa"], twenty miles outside of Avignon. Though he would come and go from the "sweetness" of this isolated, hidden valley, it remained a source of respite and inspiration to him for the remainder of his life. In his letter to Posterity, he says that "almost any work I ever happened to write was either completed or begun or conceived there."[11] In a letter to Giovanni Boccaccio from 1351, he acknowledged that though his rustic life in Vaucluse may lack "many things which pleasure requires and in which the city abounds," nevertheless, he chose to live out his

---

[10]   Petrarca, *My Secret Book* 2.16.2.

[11]   Francesco Petrarca, *Selected Letters*, vol. 2, trans. Elaine Fantham, ITRL (Cambridge, Mass.: Harvard University Press, 2017), ITRL, IX, 2, p. 553; *Sen.* 18.1.

life here because it offers that "which most greatly delights me: liberty, leisure, silence, and solitude."[12]

During his third stay at Vaucluse (1346), he began DVS during the liturgical season of Lent. It was addressed to his bishop Philippe of Cabassoles, one of his most beloved friends and confidants. From the opening words of the introduction, we see that Petrarch understands the life of solitude to be about overcoming the deceptions and self-deceptions of the age. He begins with an appeal to truthfulness, including truthful self-examination. "Every secret is in time disclosed; the shadows depart and the natural color remains. It is a great trouble to keep very long in concealment. No one lives long under water; he must come to the surface and expose the face which he had been hiding" (Preface, 1). The task before him is a battle for self-control. Scipio had only to vanquish a foreign people and rule a restless army. "Do we think that there is any government more restless than the state of the human mind? Do we believe that our enemies there are weaker than those of Scipio in Numantia? He attacked a single city and a single people, we are engaged in a struggle against the world, the flesh, and the devils" [1.10.6].

One of the great tensions in Petrarch's life was his movement between a desire for a life of solitude and his (overly optimistic) belief that in conquering his own demons he could instruct public officials and cultivate within them the virtue necessary for the public good. He began DVS in 1346. In 1347, he was an enthusiastic supporter of Cola di Rienzo, who in the span of a few short months seized control of Rome, claiming to restore the ancient Republic, and then, in part because of his own intemperance, was driven from it—almost as quickly as he took control. Petrarch's letters to Cola show his great excitement and enthusiasm followed just as quickly by his disappointment and disgust in Cola's behavior.[13]

Beginning during these years, and continuing until perhaps 1353, Petrarch was also writing the "secret book" [*Secretum*, cited above], in which he imagines a lengthy dialogue with St. Augustine on the subject of his spiritual discontent and his failure to overcome the pride and lust

---

[12]   Francesco Petrarca, *Selected Letters*, vol. 1, trans. Elaine Fantham, ITRL (Cambridge, Mass.: Harvard University Press, 2017), ITRL, II, 7, p. 117; *Fam.* 11.6.

[13]   Francesco Petrarca, *The Revolution of Cola di Rienzo*, 3rd ed., ed. Mario Emilio Cosenza (New York: Italica Press, 2008).

which he believes has so thoroughly consumed him. It is, quite frankly, an exercise in the contemplation and reflection of solitude. Petrarch omitted this text from his lists of writings, but during these very years (the early 1350s) he went to the court of Milan to serve archbishop and ruler Giovanni Visconti, believed to be a tyrant by Boccaccio and most Florentines. Throughout these years, despite the fact that DVS was probably mostly complete, Petrarch remained unsatisfied with it as he continued to wrestle with the conflicting temptations which variously called him toward the public and the private spheres.

It is important to understand that Petrarch is not prescribing the solitary life for all. He is making an argument that the solitary life is a better route to happiness and contentment. The great majority of people think that happiness and contentment will be found in the rush of the cities and in "the applause of strangers." Petrarch believes that this is the way to destruction, disappointment, and failure. "Happiness consist[s] not in sounding words, but [in] quiet deeds, and in the inward possession of truth rather than in the applause of strangers or in fragile reputation" [1.3.13].

> My counsel to other men to take account of their condition is precisely what I have employed in arriving at an understanding of my own. I heartily embrace and cling to solitude and leisure, about which I have conversed with you so much today, as if they were ladders to the level toward which the mind strives to ascend, and I dread crowds and busy cares as though they were bolts and bars to my freedom. [1.4.5]

As noted above, Petrarch distinguishes crowds of strangers from a small circle of close friends; true friendship is no impediment to solitude. "It will never be my view that solitude is disturbed by the presence of a friend, but that it is enriched. If I had the choice of doing without one or the other, I should prefer to be deprived of solitude rather than of my friend" [1.7.24]. And later, "No solitude is so profound, no house so small, no door so narrow but it may open to a friend." And speaking of the discovery of a friend, Petrarch exclaims, "then it seems to me that I have found not another, but myself somehow duplicated. Surely they are not two who have a single mind" [2.14.3]. Did C. S. Lewis have this Petrarchan sentiment in mind when he wrote that "The typical expression of opening friendship would be something like, 'You too? I thought I was the only one.'"[14] Or is it more likely the case that both authors are merely describing an experience most of us know all too well?

Obstacles to Reading DVS Today

If indeed there are some moments in DVS that we seem to know all too well, there are certainly numerous oddities in the text which are likely to trouble and astound us. In some ways, these arise from the common challenges that come from any engagement with a text written in a distant time and culture. There are at least three principal obstacles to reading Petrarch's DVS today. If we take our own time and culture as the standard for assessment, then we might be inclined to think DVS is unreasonable, elitist, or even offensive. It will appear to be unreasonable to those who simply assume that the city and an active urban life of commerce are obviously that which is most necessary for success and happiness in a world of technocratic prosperity. DVS might seem elitist to those who imagine that a preference for solitude and reflection is merely a "lifestyle" for certain "personality types" or the province of those wealthy few whose days are not consumed by the mundane tasks of survival. And it will seem offensive in its treatment of women, Muslims, and those who disagreed with him on other pressing matters of the day.

Perhaps no feature of our contemporary life is more obvious than the increasing march of technology, commerce, and urbanization. In the fourteenth century, Petrarch would have lamented what he perceived to be the same phenomenon—the extraordinary growth of cities, commerce, and industry as the vitality of rural life seemed to diminish. Petrarch's protest against and ridicule of city life will strike many as unreasonable and thoroughly impractical. Indeed, the hyperbole with which he presents the differences between the busy life in the city and the quiet life of solitude might seem too exaggerated even to make his point. Beginning with the second chapter of Book I, Petrarch compares the lives of two imaginary men and how they go about their days differently. The "hapless dweller of the city" sleeps fitfully and awakes to thoughts of how he will swindle his customers and betray his friends. In contrast, the man of leisure sleeps moderately under the sound of the nightingale and begins his quiet day

---

[14]   C. S. Lewis, *The Four Loves* (New York: Harcourt Brace Jovanovich, 1960), 96.

with prayers of gratitude. Petrarch follows this comparison as he works his way from dawn to nightfall.

How to interpret the hyperbolic contrast between the occupied man (*occupatus*) and the solitary man (*solitarius*) has long fascinated Petrarch's readers. A contemporary audience misreads Petrarch and DVS if it assumes that Petrarch's intent is to put forth an "objective" or "dispassionate" comparison of the occupied life of the city versus the quiet life of retirement and thus fails in the attempt. Petrarch is giving a defense of his own way of life, and it should not be surprising that he makes his comparison in a forceful, polemical way. He makes it clear in the introductory dedication to his bishop that one should not be surprised that he has taken up the subject that is most important to him. "What now do you expect of me other than what I have always had in my mouth and in my heart, and what is preached by the very place I am now looking on—the celebration of a life of solitude and leisure" [1.1.8].

Contemporary readers who cannot separate their understanding of happiness from the opportunities afforded by the hustle and bustle of technocratic urban life will have a difficult time seeing the joy and fulfillment which Petrarch finds in the silence and the solitude of his rural retreat. At the heart of Petrarch's presentation is his understanding that solitude offers a liberty and self-determination that is simply unavailable among the crowded masses. However unreasonable this may appear to be, any charitable interpretation of DVS begins with an acknowledgment of Petrarch's assumptions about the nature and source of true liberty.

Second, some will dismiss Petrarch's arguments for the solitary life as elitist, suggesting that his recommendations are only for the rich who can afford a life of solitude or are only suited for those specific personality types which find comfort in being alone, say, Enneagram Fives or Myers-Briggs's INTPs. On this latter consideration, an attachment to solitude is understood merely to be a source of personal comfort or satisfaction. This is not the case. Petrarch is clear, of course, that he is not prescribing a life of solitude for everyone. "Let each man decide according to his own preference, for it is impossible that it should suit all men to follow a single road in life, even if they were all bound for the same ultimate destination" [1.3.18]. But he does believe that if one has no occasion for solitary reflection and contemplation, one will be at the mercy of crowds, and true happiness cannot be found when one's life is dictated by the oppressive demands of others. According to Petrarch, those whose lives are ordered by others "are ruled by the power of another man's nod and learn what they must do from another man's look. They can claim nothing as their own. Their house, their sleep, their food, is not their own, and, what is even more serious, their mind is not their own, their countenance is not their own" [1.3.2].

Petrarch's affirmation of the centrality and significance of solitude is not, however, merely for those whose personality might incline them toward retreat and reflection. In our own day, personality and trait studies are immensely popular, and many such studies offer important insights into human behavior and how various types of people respond to challenges and opportunities. To the extent that various personality types help us understand our own (and others') strengths and weaknesses, our inclinations and our avoidances, then they can be quite helpful. When they condone those weaknesses and inclinations under the banner of a typology or deny the necessity of certain virtues and practices for human flourishing, they can become dangerous. In DVS, Petrarch demonstrates that a certain pursuit of busyness and distraction is actually an avoidance of the self-knowledge which can only come through silence and solitude.

The charge that Petrarch's vision of the fulfilled, solitary life is only possible for a wealthy elite presents a more complicated case. On the one hand, Petrarch's solitary life is available to anyone with the temperance necessary to remove himself or herself from the madding crowd. Some of the most memorable and persuasive examples that Petrarch presents are found in the joys and opportunities for solitude that come through nature, amidst the woods and the meadows or on solitary walks or quiet evenings with friends. These opportunities do not require great riches, but they do demand the time, freedom, and inclination for such a retreat. Moreover, Petrarch is insistent that "great wealth is a hindrance rather than an aid" to the endeavor of the solitary life. "Riches never come alone, but bring with them many divers ills and endless burdens and occasions of strife" [2.14.17].

On the other hand, there are necessities that the solitary life demands, and some of these will require the resources to make it possible. He acknowledges, "Nothing is heavier than gold, nothing more binding; except so far as it contributes to our necessities, it is neither to be desired nor liked" [2.14.17]. What counts as a necessity? According to Petrarch, we should be like sailors who "save their ship by sacrificing their cargo."

Riches should be "thrown away if they are excessive, until they reach the measure established by nature and virtue" [2.14.18].

And what is the measure established by nature and virtue? It would seem that nature refers to that which is in harmony with creation, and virtue is that which contributes to *eudaimonia* or flourishing. For Petrarch then, there is the need for the time and space to be alone or with a few friends, the financial resources to fulfill one's obligations, and the education to avail oneself of the seeds of contemplation. While many may have difficulty meeting these demands, it is clear that Petrarch saw his life at Vaucluse as simple and modest in comparison to the bustling, avaricious world of Avignon just twenty miles away. And for Petrarch, one's infatuation with the pleasures and false satisfactions of the city is a far more difficult obstacle to overcome than that modest measure of wealth, established by nature and virtue, which makes the solitary life possible.

Of course, it is never easy to distinguish necessities from luxuries, and some of Petrarch's examples do lead us to conclude that however modest he believed his vision of the solitary life to be, it was nevertheless a life of substantial privilege. A country retreat, a library to be envied, lengthy visits with beloved friends, with a few servants to attend to their needs—all of this seems to confirm the charge that only a privileged few could have partaken in his life of solitude. Petrarch was not unaware of his privilege, but he maintained that one's commitment to the solitary life was not dependent on great wealth. Indeed, such wealth was more a cause for concern, since that which might make the solitary life possible is also that which most endangers it. From the very beginning, he emphasizes that the goal for solitude is not solitude itself, but rather the freedom that dwells within in it [1.1.7]. And this cannot be bought.

Perhaps the greatest obstacle to our appreciation of DVS lies in how Petrarch treats those he deems an impediment either to the solitary life or to what he takes to be the requirements of faithfulness. This is especially true with his (quite diverse) treatment of both women and Muslims, which will strike many contemporary readers as absolutely inexplicable, and for many, will justify their ignoring the text. His reflection on women is particularly problematic and, taken in isolation, can appear misogynistic. "There is no virus as fatal to those who would follow this [solitary] life as the company of woman. For the attraction of women, the more fascinating it is, the more dreadful and baleful. . . . Whoever you are that desire peace, keep away from woman, the perpetual source of contention and trouble.

Peace and a woman rarely dwell under the same roof" [2.4.3]. But passages such as this should not be read in isolation. Petrarch also identifies numerous women in DVS as stellar exemplars of the solitary life, including (among others) St. Paula of Rome, Melania, Mary of Bethany (whom he, following a common medieval mistake, identifies as Mary Magdala), and of course, St. Mary, the mother of Jesus.

Petrarch was, of course, the author of some of the most extraordinary love poetry in the Western canon. He was enthralled by women, especially his beloved "Laura," whom he claims to have first seen on Good Friday (April 6) 1327 at Sainte-Claire Church in Avignon. Traditionally, Laura has been identified as Laura de Noves, a married woman with children who did not reciprocate his affections. Today there is some ambiguity about Laura's identity, with some scholars even doubting that "Laura" names one particular historical figure. Nevertheless, Petrarch wrote more than three hundred sonnets in praise of Laura, including more than one hundred after she died in 1348. Petrarch, who never married, fathered two children out of wedlock with women who are unknown to us today.

How should one understand these matters? It is quite possible that he was enthralled by women but treated them badly and harbored disrespectful views of them, especially of their intellectual abilities. Given the totality of the Petrarchan corpus (both poetry and prose), this view seems highly implausible. I think the more likely interpretation is that Petrarch was simply undone by women; it is not that he loved them too little but rather that he allowed himself to love them too much. Many of the sonnets that praise women, and Laura in particular, turn inward and demonstrate his own wretched state of being in love. We see this feature throughout the poetry.

And it is present in the prose works as well. One of the dominant features of the *Secretum* is his struggle with lust and intemperance. In his dialogue with the imaginary St. Augustine, he confesses his confusion and struggle with love: "I think that love, depending on its object, can be considered the most abominable of passions or the noblest of actions."[15] His cautionary comments about women in DVS merely underscore how weak and intemperate he was when it came to women. As the comments above make clear, the more fascinating a woman was to him, the less able he was to pursue the solitary life, which he believed was required for happiness and flourishing.

---

[15] Petrarca, *My Secret Book* 3.2.4.

This view is illustrated well by his treatment of Juvenal's famous (or infamous) *Satire* VI against Roman wives and a passage from Virgil's *Georgics* in which Virgil is reflecting on how those managing the horses and the cattle (especially the bulls) must remove them from the females to a far pasture. [2.4.5] The larger context in the *Georgics* is that Virgil is arguing that "Every last species on earth, man and beast alike, / the vast schools of the sea, the cattle and bright-colored birds / fall helpless into passion's fire: love is the same for all"[16] (III:242–44). But Petrarch does not merely make this point. He extends the metaphor in a clearly self-serving (and, in my opinion, unpersuasive) way. If the bulls were taken away to the groves and meadows, men too would love the solitary life of the meadows and fields. But this was not Virgil's point; the bulls are not enjoying the meadows for their beauty and solitude. They are fighting one another for a chance at the heifers. Virgil writes, "The bulls tangle in battle with great force, blood so dark that its black drips from bodies, and amid deafening bellows, tossed horns are driven home in both contenders" (ll. 220–23, p. 47). Petrarch's relation with women is probably like his relation with public life. His affections and beliefs pulled him, variously, in contradictory directions, and the only sure solution was to remove himself from them. Of course, none of this makes Petrarch's comments any more palatable.

DVS might also be deemed offensive in Petrarch's treatment of Muslims and Islam. In Book II, Petrarch is also quite critical of Islam, the Mamluk Caliphate which held Jerusalem at the time, and the prophet Muhammad. These criticisms seem quite far afield from a defense of the solitary life, but in DVS this digression follows from Petrarch's praise of Peter the Hermit. According to Petrarch, when Christ wanted to inspire the recovery of the Holy Lands, he appeared first, not to Christian kings or even to the pope, but to a humble solitary, Peter. Petrarch's larger point seems to be that the solitary life enables one to hear the call of Christ more clearly than the busy, occupied life. On Petrarch's telling of the Pauper's Crusade, Peter's great "successes" could not be sustained because of the recurring sinfulness and faithlessness of Christian kings and princes.

This narrative leads to a lengthy digression on the errors of Islam, its practitioners, and the prophet Muhammad. Petrarch's criticisms are scathing and will be seen as offensive not only by Muslims but also by careful

---

[16]   Virgil, *Virgil's Georgics*, trans. Janet Lembke (New Haven: Yale University Press, 2005), 48.

readers who recognize Petrarch's lack of knowledge and his distortion of the historical record. He refers to Muslims as "thieves" who have stolen the sites most holy to Christianity. Muhammad is accused of a variety of vices and impieties, and the Mamluks are (inaccurately) accused of not allowing Christian pilgrims to visit the holy sites.

Throughout it is clear that Petrarch knows very little about Islam. He had no firsthand knowledge of either the holy sites in the East or of the particulars of the Islamic faith. In 1358 he was invited to make a pilgrimage to the holy sites with Giovanni Mandelli, but he declined out of his fear of sea travel. (Petrarch wrote *The Itinerary to the Sepulcher of Our Lord Jesus Christ* as his gift to Mandelli for his absence. There are few references to Islam in the text, including statements such as "In these places Saracen incursions are overwhelming . . . be careful not to be separated from your companions for any reason."[17])

He speculates about relatively simple matters and conjectures wrongly about the answer. "What does puzzle the mind is the reason of his [Muhammad's] love for Jerusalem and hatred of Antioch" [2.9.17]. Petrarch seems to think that Muhammad loved Jerusalem because "his adversary" Christ had been crucified there, not realizing how Jesus ("Isa") is venerated in Islam and not knowing of the significance of Muhammad's Night Journey from Mecca to Jerusalem and the "furthest mosque" on the Temple Mount.

Once again, it is important to see Petrarch as the product of his age. The last Crusader stronghold at Acre had fallen in 1291, not long before his birth. Not only had the Crusades largely failed, but those failures fueled the animosity between Christians themselves, especially with those in the Byzantine world. There remained throughout the West a strong sentiment to renew the attempts to recover the Holy Lands, and yet these desires were tempered by anxiety and fear of the Muslim East. It is some indication of just how seriously Petrarch took this imperative that he breaks off from his treatment of the contemplative life of solitude to argue for the necessity of the active life of the crusade.

Petrarch takes issue with numerous others throughout the texts, most particularly the papal Curia which had taken the Papacy away from Rome and instilled it in Avignon. Kings, princes, and other nobility who have failed to demonstrate courage, prudence, or fidelity are usually charged

---

[17]   Theodore J. Cachey, ed., *Petrarch's Guide to the Holy Land*, trans. T. J. Cachey (Notre Dame, Ind.: University of Notre Dame Press, 2002), 18.7.

with a similar failure to cultivate the solitary life. But these examples are far less likely to generate offense or opposition.

On the current text and its divisions

The current text uses the English translation made by Jacob Zeitlin and published by the University of Illinois Press in 1924. As should be clear from the comments above, I have chosen not to republish Zeitlin's lengthy and, in my opinion, misleading introduction to the text and to Petrarch's life. As to the translation itself, I have only retranslated or edited Zeitlin's text in cases of the most archaic usage and typographical errors, and in the occasional instance of his overly zealous rhetorical flourishes.

I have, however, made extensive corrections to the format and presentation of Zeitlin's text to bring it into line with the best renderings we have of DVS. There is no critical edition of the entirety of DVS. K. A. E. Enenkel produced a critical edition of Book I in 1990, published by E. J. Brill, complete with an extensive commentary (in German).[18] For Book II, I have used Christophe Carraud's fine edition with accompanying French translation (Éditions Millon, 1999) and the Martellotti and Bufano Latin-Italian edition (Einaudi, 1977).

Zeitlin took such generous liberties with the organization of the text that it is virtually impossible for English-speaking readers to cite or consult various passages of DVS with confidence. In fairness to Zeitlin, it is not entirely his fault. The manuscript and early print editions of DVS vary widely. As Enenkel points out, there are conflicting versions of how the text is divided. The earliest manuscripts show Book I divided into ten chapters. Later editions frequently, but not consistently, divide Book I into thirty-three chapters.[19] Enenkel's critical edition uses the ten-chapter division and merely divides the text into books, chapters, and numbered paragraphs. This is now the standard method of citation and the one that I have imposed on Zeitlin's English translation.

Printed editions presented new challenges. The 1554 edition, reprinted in Basel (and referred to as "Bâle" by Christophe Carraud and others), popularized themed paragraph subheadings grouped into sections and newly described as "chapters." As noted by Carraud, the Bâle edition had

[18]   Francesco Petrarca, *De vita solitaria: Buch I*, ed. K. A. E. Enenkel (Leiden: Brill, 1990).

[19]   K. A. E. Enenkel, foreword (Vorwort zur Textausgabe) to *De vita solitaria*, by Francesco Petrarca, 20.

a long history of popularity and use.[20] Though Enenkel discarded these subheadings, Carraud kept them as marginal notations. (There are no section headings in the standard Ricciardi edition of 1955 or in Bufano's *Opere Latine* edition [1975] or in Martellotti [1977]). Zeitlin attempted to maintain the subheadings but was forced to create "tractates" to correspond to Bâle's "sections." Nevertheless, Zeitlin still even departs from Bâle on occasion.

To keep the current edition as close to the form of Enenkel's critical edition of Book I as possible, I have dispensed with Zeitlin's "tractates," and denoted the marginalia groupings as "sections" [§], placing them in italics within the text. They are for general information purposes only and are not relevant for citation. With those references, I have kept the Bâle enumeration despite the fact that the numbered "sections" frequently do not correspond with the standard chapter and paragraph divisions. (For instance, Bâle's Fourth Section of Book I begins after 1.3.18, despite the fact that Chapter Four only begins after 1.3.21.) In the now standard editions, Book I has ten chapters, and Book II has fifteen chapters. These chapters do not correspond to the sixteen "sections" in Bâle (six in Book I and ten in Book II) or "tractates" in Zeitlin. Appendix A contains Bâle's division of the text into sections and chapters and may be used to correlate Zeitlin's divisions with the current edition. Since there are no chapter titles in the text itself, I have created titles for the table of contents based on the topics covered in each chapter.

In Zeitlin's edition, many sentences and paragraphs were also moved above or below the standard divisions as he attempted to integrate various subjects and subheadings or to create what seemed to him like a more cohesive flow of argument. The current text restores the order and numbered paragraphs of the best traditions of DVS, exemplified in Enenkel for Book I and Carraud for Book II.

The footnotes throughout are from Zeitlin. Any content notes that I have edited, or provided anew, are noted "—SHM." On several occasions I have utilized newer translations of ancient and medieval texts, and each of these is noted accordingly. Scripture citations in DVS present some unique problems. Zeitlin used the Authorized ("King James") Version [1611] for English translations throughout and ignored the traditional

---

[20]   Christophe Carraud, "Introduction," in Pétrarque, *De Vita Solitaria—La Vie Solitaire* (Grenoble: Éditions Million, 1999), 22.

Catholic numbering of the Psalter. It is frequently not clear which version of Scripture Petrarch was using or the extent to which later editions have redacted Petrarch's quotations from Scripture. Sometimes the text is from the Vulgate and sometimes the text appears to be from one of the Vetus Latina traditions, which remained popular and in (scattered) use prior to the Counter-Reformation. Unless there is something about the quotation that is deeply problematic, I have retained Zeitlin's rendering. I have corrected the numerical citations to the Psalter.

The current text also retains Petrarch's gender-exclusive language, which was translated literally into English by Zeitlin. To have retranslated the text into gender-inclusive language would have misrepresented both Petrarch's text and the historical and cultural milieu from which and to which he wrote. Among the many potential offenses of Petrarch's language and hyperbole, his use of exclusive masculine language turns out to rank rather low in the hierarchy.

THE LIFE OF SOLITUDE

Francesco Petrarca

Preface

Francesco Petrarca (Petrarch), Poet Laureate, begins the first book of the Life of Solitude, *addressed to Philip, Bishop of Cavaillon.*

1. Few, my faithful friend, are the men whose respect and affection for my works is as great as yours, I will not say seems to be, but genuinely is. For I cannot harbor the suspicion that there is anything feigned or simulated in the clear and pure candor of your breast, nor do I think that if there were any simulation it could hold sway there for so long. For while truth is eternal, feigning and falsehood are of brief duration, and simulation is quickly exposed. Hair, though most carefully combed, is disordered by a faint breeze, and cosmetics, though painstakingly applied, are washed away by a light perspiration; so, even a clever lie must give way to truth and become transparent to one who examines it at close range. Every secret is in time disclosed; the shadows depart and the natural color remains. It is a great trouble to keep very long in concealment. No one lives long under water; he must come to the surface and expose the face which he had been hiding.

2. These considerations, excellent father, induce me to believe what I earnestly wish—for we are easily inclined to believe whatever is agreeable—that my performances may give you pleasure, since I studiously aim that they should give pleasure only to the few. For, as you see, the matters that I treat are often novel and difficult, and the ideas severe, remote, and alien from the vulgar horde which regulates everything by its sensations. If I should fail to please the ignorant, I shall have no occasion for complaint; rather shall I enjoy good hopes of my talent according to my

ambition. But if I should also miss the approval of the learned, I confess I shall be sorry, though not surprised.

3. For who am I, or what is my claim, that amidst all the possible variety of judgments I should flatter myself and arrogantly look for what was not even the fortune of Marcus Tullius, for all his illustrious and divine eloquence? His book entitled *The Orator* (good God, what a work it is and how loftily inspired!) failed, as, he himself somewhere remarks in his letters, to meet with the favor of Marcus Brutus at whose entreaty he had composed it and to whom he dedicated it; yet Brutus was a scholarly person and friendly to the writer. I pass over the more grievous annoyances which that great man suffered from distinguished orators who were yet far below himself, men like the two Asinii and Calvus, who with excessive presumption abused the prince of eloquence and censured what the rest of the world admired and worshiped. Who will protest against a judgment on his writing such as even Cicero was subjected to?

4. With you, however, I have no such fear for myself. To meet with favor and liking from you is not a token of my merit, but the result either of a certain sympathy in our dispositions or more probably of your extraordinary and wondrous love for me, which is no slight enemy to a fair judgment. Who that loves strongly can judge properly? If love were able to perceive and distinguish the truth, why should the ancients have imagined it as blind? However, though it is blind, it is not mute, and acts as the best of pleaders, pointing out to others what it does not see itself, and often what does not exist. A father's generous indulgence stops at nothing and overlooks the errors of his son even to the point of taking a certain satisfaction in them. If then you are mistaken in my merit, I am glad, and would like to have you remain ever in this error, since it is a source of pride to me and of satisfaction to you and injures nobody.

5. But if your good opinion is not mistaken, which I may be allowed to wish rather than to hope, shall I not congratulate myself the more, and on the strength of such a verdict become more precious and praiseworthy to myself? Clearly, should I not have been a thoughtless steward of my time, if I did not have regard to one whom I consider the first admirer of my literary talent? The elder Cato is in this matter an important witness who, at the beginning of his book on *Origins*, says that men of great and unusual gifts must look with as careful an eye to their leisure as to their

business.[1] This is a saying which many have approved, but our beloved Cicero embraced it with particular fondness, and in his speech defending Plancius declared that it had always struck him as high-minded and distinguished. If I also must take thought for it, either because of my moderate talent or my immoderate desire for fame, seeing that I have not yet tamed the latter with the curb of a rational mind, ought it not to be my first aim to have my leisure as remote from idleness as my life is from active affairs? And if I am to write anything which may have a chance of enduring, shall I not preferably inscribe it to those, by the reflection of whose glory I may be able to shine and resist the approach of the shadows with which the dark abyss of time and the forgetful ages, devourers of all illustrious names, threaten me?

6. Whenever I revolve these things, your name occurs to my mind, so resplendent in itself and so linked with favors to me that, whether I look for glory or personal pleasure, I cannot pass it over without serious loss. Besides, being now, according to my old established custom, settled in your country, I feel that I owe you the tithe of my leisure and the first fruits of my labor, as others owe you the first fruits of their fields. And so it is my intention every year to pay something, whether it be more or less, in proportion to the fertility or sterility of my genius from one year to another, whereby, like one of your farmers, I may give evidence of my good faith, with such fruits at least as my little plot of ground produces. If I may trust my judgment, there is nothing safer than silence for such as wish to escape the tongue of detraction.

7. With this in mind, I confess that I often rein in my thoughts, often my pen; often I warn them in fear of all sorts of consequences; implore them not to betray me nor gratuitously to allege against me in evidence not only of my style but of my character, which is far more serious, a piece of writing that may reach distant readers and future generations. For our life will be judged by our conversation; when the proof of our actions is gone, only the evidence of our speech will remain. But what profit is there in many words? I might perhaps have persuaded people to spare themselves and me and my good name, if it were not, as they say, that the mischief is already done and it is no longer possible for me to seek concealment in

[1] Cato's *Origins* (on the history of Rome and the founding of Italian cities) is lost. Cicero quotes and commends this line from Cato in his speech *Pro Plancius* 27.66.—SHM

silence. I am already known and read and judged, already without hope of escaping the verdict of men and of hiding my talent. Whether I go out into the open or remain sitting at home, I must still be in the public gaze.

8. What now do you expect of me other than what I have always had in my mouth and in my heart, and what is preached by the very place I am now looking on—the celebration of a life of solitude and leisure such as once you made frequent trial of by yourself and recently tasted in my society for the brief space of two weeks? I say in my society, though it was I who was constantly seeking yours, and yet you declared, as much by your acts as by your speech, that you would not have come here except on my account nor have remained except for my sake. You proved, as is your wont with me, how great is the power of love in leveling inequalities.

9. In view of this it should have been easy to persuade you of what, even if I maintained entire silence, you know from your own experience. If, however, I proposed to commend this virtue to the crowd, I should be spending my efforts in vain. I speak not alone of the ignorant crowd but of many who think themselves educated and perhaps are not deceived in their opinion. But a store of learning does not always dwell in a modest breast, and often there is considerable strife between the tongue and the mind, between teaching and the conduct of life. I speak of such as being oppressed and handicapped rather than improved by their education, have light-mindedly united a thing beautiful in itself, like knowledge, with disgraceful morals. It would have been much better if they had never seen the schools, since the only thing they learned there was with the overweening arrogance of their education to become vainer than all other men. They go about airing their Aristotle at street crossings, while the common people crowd gaping about them. They scatter though the streets and arcades, counting the towers and horses and carriages. They measure the squares and walls of the city and gaze in stupid admiration at the dresses of the women, than which nothing is more transient and frivolous. They fix their eyes not only on living but on marble images, and when they come upon a statue they stop transfixed before it as though minded to address it. What gives the last touch to their madness is the pleasure they take in crowds and in noise. These are the men who carry their educated folly over the entire city like a vulgar and purchasable commodity. These are they who are averse to solitude and enemies of their own home; they leave it early in the morning and are with difficulty dragged back in the evening to their hated threshold. These are the men with whom it is proverbial to say that

it is a splendid thing to visit other countries and to mix with people. Surely it is much better to visit stones and trees and to mix with tigers and bears. For man is not only a base and unclean animal, but furthermore—I say it unwillingly, and I wish that experience had not made it and steadily continued making it so generally familiar—he is pernicious, unstable, faithless, inconstant, fierce, and bloody, unless by the rare grace of God he puts off his bestiality and puts on humanity, unless, in short, he learns to make himself a man out of a common creature.

10. If you ask those very persons why they are ever anxious to be in the company of others, they will answer, if they are in a mood to tell the truth, that it is only because they cannot endure being alone.

On this point I shall perhaps have more to say in the proper place; for the present I shall merely observe that it is not easy to remove with words errors that are deeply rooted, or to persuade persons of anything when they are naturally insusceptible of persuasion. Besides, people who are fond of silence are loath to waste their words. Let them therefore cease their clamor against the true idea, for I do not speak to such as they and do not greatly care if they read with a disdainful lift of their eyebrows matter that is not intended for them but for quite another type of mind. Let this suffice for them.

11. But you, beloved father, as I have already said, stand in need of no zealous pleader, since no one could persuade you of the contrary; and in your heart and brain, from which the errors have been long since uprooted, the true ideas are firmly lodged. Nevertheless, though I may not in speaking of a settled truth make the certainty greater, I may set it in a fairer light. Calling upon Christ our lover and asking, while I unfold these thoughts, for a truce of a few days from the greater and older tasks which beset me and keep incessantly ringing in my mind, I approach the execution of my design. Do you, father, I pray, likewise enter into a compact with your cares, withdraw yourself for a term from important affairs and accord your mind to me. It is not always the choicest things that give pleasure; as the rich sometimes find satisfaction in a change of food, so do wise men in a change of studies.

12. Attend, therefore, and hear what ideas I am accustomed to entertain when I reflect on this whole subject of the solitary life. I shall set down but a few of the many thoughts that occur to me, but in these, as in a little mirror, you shall behold the entire disposition of my soul, the full countenance of a serene and tranquil mind.

BOOK 1

1

Introduction

§I. What is needful for them that desire to enjoy quiet

1. I believe that a noble spirit will never find repose save in God, in whom is our end, or in himself and his private thoughts, or in some intellect united by a close sympathy with his own. For though pleasure be covered with the most entangling lime and full of sweet and alluring baits, yet has it not the force to detain powerful wings very long upon the ground. But whether we are intent upon God, or upon ourselves and our serious studies, or whether we are seeking for a mind in harmony with our own, it behooves us to withdraw as far as may be from the haunts of men and crowded cities.

2. That I speak truly, perhaps even they will hardly deny who find a charm in the stir and hum of many people, provided they are not so deeply whelmed and sunk in their false notions that they do not at times come to themselves, as it were, and return to the lofty path of truth, if only with a crawling motion. Would this were not the state of so many, and that men had at least as much concern for the cultivation of their minds as of their fields and many less important things; for the human mind teems with errors like a fat field overrun with brambles, and if these are not diligently uprooted and with studious toil cleared away, the fruit in both cases will equally perish with the flower.

3. But we sing to deaf ears.[1] Yet, however lightly people in general may regard these matters, men of learning, I am sure, will second me in thought and word; and even if all should oppose me, you at least will not—indeed you would be the first to confute my opponents. You will recognize your

---

[1] Virgil, *Ecl.* 10.8.

own thoughts in my words, and I shall appear to have attained the ultimate goal of all eloquence—to have moved the mind of the listener according to my wish, and that with no trouble. It is a sore task for the pleader when he is bent on dragging over to his own view a mind that resists persuasion; but what trouble is there for an argument when it enters the ears of a person whose own thought chimes with what he hears and who, having the evidence of his own experience, in order to yield his assent requires neither concrete examples, nor weighty authority, nor pointed reasoning, but in silence says to himself, "It is true?"

§II. On those who have written in praise of the life of solitude and whom the author in this work wished to imitate

4. I am aware that certain saintly men have written much on this theme. In particular the renowned Basil has composed a little book in praise of the life of solitude—from which I have borrowed nothing but the title. As I have met with it in some very old manuscripts sometimes thrust in among the writings of Peter Damian, I have been doubtful whether it was the work of Basil or of Peter.[2] But in this treatise I have in a large measure had my sole experience for guide, neither seeking any other leader nor disposed to accept one if he offered himself. For it is with a freer step, though perchance a less secure one; that I pursue my own route than I follow the traces of a stranger.

5. You shall learn more from those who have had greater experience than I or who have searched further into the experience of others; from me you shall only hear whatever the moment may suggest. For I have not applied myself to this undertaking in a fastidious way, nor have I thought it necessary to do so, hardly fearing that matter would be wanting in so fertile a theme—at least in its superficial aspects—especially as I have often treated of it previously and the subject is variously and intimately wrought into my life.

[2]   The work here referred to was printed by Jean Lambert in Paris, without a date, along with three other treatises on the solitary life, and entitled "*Libellus pulcherrimus sancti Basilii de laude Solitie vite.*" The editor of the collection, while he assents in the traditional ascription to Basil, mentions also the claims of Gregory the Great and of Pietro Damiano and concludes that it may be safest to share the uncertainty of Petrarch concerning the authorship. The non-Basilian character of the treatise is amply established by its unqualified approval of the life of solitude and its style of unrestrained rhapsody. The most that Petrarch could have derived from it is a few illustrations.—JZ

6. I have not composed my books with deliberation nor particularly polished my style, knowing that I am speaking to one who will like me even when I am tangled. Content with faithful and general observations and with a homely discourse, I have drawn forth what you here read partly from the present tenor of my life and partly from a past experience which is yet fresh in my memory. To you I appeal first as witness of these things, being frankly conscious that among the many causes which have won to you my all unforced affection, not the least has been that you were led by a love of solitude and the desire for freedom which accompanies it to flee what is called the Roman Court, now so near—almost adjacent—to you, where you might have attained no mean elevation if that Tartarean din and confusion had offered you as much pleasure as you always derive from blessed solitude.

§III. On the manner of treating the substance of this work, and the differences between a life of solitude and a life spent in crowds

7. It seems to me that I can demonstrate the blessedness of solitude by exhibiting the troubles and afflictions of a populous environment, reviewing the actions of men whom one kind of life preserves in peace and tranquility and the other kind keeps agitated and careworn and breathless. For there is a single idea underlying all these observations, that one kind of life is attended with happy leisure and the other with grievous worry. But if at any time some marvelous instance or some extraordinary concurrence of nature and chance, properly to be reckoned among miracles, should befall to change my opinion, I shall change it without shame and shall not be afraid to prefer the pleasant and reposeful assemblages of people to a pining and anxious seclusion. For it is not the mere name of solitude, but the good things which are proper to it, that I praise. And it is not so much the solitary recesses and the silence that delight me as the leisure and freedom that dwell within them. Nor am I so inhuman as to hate men, whom I am instructed by divine commandment to love as I love myself, but I hate the sins of men, especially my own, and the troubles and sad afflictions that reside among crowds.

8. These things, unless I err, can be treated more suggestively not by discoursing separately what can be said on one side and on the other, but by mingling both, touching now this aspect and now the other, as the mind is by turns directed toward either, and, with alternate shift of the eye, as it

were, from right to left, easily judges the difference between the very diverse objects which lie side by side. It is with intent that I have placed the bitter first, that I might follow it up with the sweet, and that the pleasanter taste, being felt the last wherever there was a division, should thereby prevail upon the mind. But what need of many circumstances? Let us get to the point and discharge our promise. Place now before your mind's eye two persons of contrary habits whom I shall describe to you, and what you observe in them you may apply in general.

2
The Misery of the Busy Man and the Happiness of the Solitary Man

§I. On the misery of the busy man and the unhappy dweller in cities and the happiness of the retired man, inferred from the actions of each

1. The busy man, a hapless dweller of the city, awakes in the middle of the night, his sleep interrupted by his cares or the cries of his clients, often even by fear of the light and by terror of nightly visions. No sooner is he up than he settles his body to the miserable bench and applies his mind to falsehood. On treachery his heart is wholly fixed—whether he meditates driving a corrupt bargain, betraying his friend or his ward, assailing with his seductions his neighbor's wife whose only refuge is her chastity, spreading the veil of justice over a litigious quarrel, or whatever other mischief of a public or private character he intends. Now eager with passion and aflame with desire, and now frozen with desperation, like a very bad workman, he begins before dawn the web of the daily toil in which he shall involve others with himself.

2. The retired man—a man of leisure—awakes in happy mood, refreshed by moderate rest and a short sleep, unbroken, unless when he is aroused at intervals by the songs of night-haunting Philomel. When he has shaken himself lightly from his couch and, banishing thoughts of his body, begun to intone in the calm hours, he devoutly implores the guardian of his lips to make a passage for the matin praises which should issue from them, and he summons the Lord to strengthen his heart, and implores him to make haste, trusting not at all to his own forces and tremblingly aware of imminent peril. His mind is set not upon weaving deceptions but on reciting with unwearied service of the tongue and pious humility of spirit the glory

of God and the praise of his saints, not only day by day, but hour by hour, lest the memory of the divine gifts should by chance fade from his grateful heart. Yet often, wondrous to say, without anxious fear but filled with tremulous hope, mindful of the past and thoughtful of what is to come, he overflows with joyful sorrow and with happy tears. No pleasures of the busy man, no luxury of city life, no pomp of kingdoms can match his state.

3. Looking up from his place to the starry heaven and sighing with all his heart for the Lord his God who has his dwelling there, with thoughts of his country from the place of his exile, he turns immediately to the study of some honest and agreeable lesson, and so nourished with the most delightful food, he awaits the coming of light with great composure of mind.

*§II. Of the wretched busy man and the happy solitary man
when the light of day has come*

4. The longed-for light has now arrived to their differing prayers, and the busy man's doorway is beset by enemies and friends. He is greeted, solicited, pulled in one direction, jostled in another, assailed with arguments, and rent asunder. The retired man finds a free doorway, and he has the choice of remaining where he is or going whithersoever his mind disposes him.

5. The busy man, loaded with complaints and affairs, goes in troubled spirits to the courts, and the beginning of his cruel day is marked by lawsuits. The retired man, with store of leisure and of calm, goes blithely into a nearby woods and enters joyfully upon the propitious threshold of a serene day.

6. The busy man, when he has appeared in the proud mansions of the powerful or before the dreaded bar of the magistrates, by mixing falsehood with truth, either injures the just cause of the innocent or fosters the insolence of the culprit. Or he directly plots something to his own dishonor and another's ruin, his conscience all the while tormenting him and fear frequently disturbing his speech as he intrudes one word in place of another, the truth instead of a lie, suffering sudden changes of color and chiding himself that he did not choose starvation in a desert before the reputation of eloquence and that he did not prefer the life of a plowman before that of an orator. Suddenly, with his business still unfinished, he returns home and with base concealments steals away from the view of his own followers as well as of his enemies.

7. The retired man, as soon as he has gained a flowery spot on some salubrious hill, the sun being now risen in his splendor, breaks joyously with pious lips into the daily praises of the Lord, the more delightedly if

with his devout breath are harmonized the gentle murmur of the rushing stream and the sweet plainings of the birds. He prays first for innocence, a bridle for his tongue to make it ignorant of contention, a shield for his eyes to protect them from vain shows, purity of heart, freedom from delusion, and continence which tames the flesh.

8. Soon after, during the third lauds, he worships the Third Person in the Trinity and prays for the visitation of the Holy Ghost, for a tongue and a mind that utter themselves in healing confession, and for charity burning with a heavenly flame and of power to enkindle one's neighbors. If he devoutly prays for these things, he already hath much, being happier in this rapture of mind than in any splendor of gold or jewels.

9. But now slowly retracing his steps, as the sun which in the morning had shed a fresh light on all objects climbs in its course and blazes in the meridian, he desires nothing more earnestly than the extinction of those contentious flames which the other seeks to feed and to fan with his breath, and while the latter is consumed with his passions, he entreats that all the noxious heats of evil desires be dispelled. Finally, he prays for that which the satiric poet teaches us is the one thing which may without peril be prayed for, the possession of a sound mind in a sound body.[1] Which of these two, I pray you, so far has spent his hours more honestly?

§III. Of the wretchedness of the busy man and the happiness of the retired man when the hour of the noon meal arrives

10. When the hour of the noon meal is at hand the busy man composes himself amidst his piles of cushions in a huge hall over which ruin impends. The roof resounds with a variety of noises while all about stand the dogs of the hall and the household mice. A crowded array of flatterers vies with one another in obsequiousness, and a troop of greedy menials sets the tables with bustling confusion. As the floor is swept of its dirt everything is filled with vile dust. Silver vessels wrought with gold flash through the room and goblets hollowed out of precious stones. The benches are covered with silk and the walls with purple, and carpets are spread over the floor, but the servants shiver in their nakedness.

11. Once the line of battle is drawn up, the signal of the onset is delivered by a trumpet. The captains of the kitchen rush against the captains of the hall. A great clatter is set up; dishes conquered by land and sea are

---

[1] Juvenal, *Sat.* 10.356.

dragged in, and wine trodden in ancient Cos. The vintages of Italy and Greece glitter in the ruddy gold; in a single cup are blended Gnosos and Meroe, Venusius and Falernus, the hills of Sorrento and Calabria. And they are not content till the Ausonian Bacchus, seasoned with the honey of Hybla or the juice of the oriental cane and perfumed with blackberries, artfully changes his natural flavor.

12. In another place may be seen an equal display of a different sort—horrible beasts, unknown fishes, unheard of birds, saturated in costly spices. Some of these, forgetful of their ancient home, show their origin only in their designation and preserve nothing but the name of the Phasian bird. There are smoking dishes which are a cause of amazement to the very banqueters, having been subjected to every wanton trick of the cooks. If a hungry man were to see in what a filthy and disgusting manner they were concocted, he would be sated with the view alone and go his way. In that place may be seen a mixed and mutual strife of the native with the foreign, creatures of the sea with those of the land, white with black, sour with sweet, the hairy with the feathered, the tame with the savage—the old Ovidian chaos renewed, as it were, and compressed into a narrow space, not in a single body but in one small dish:

> For hot and cold were in one body fixt;
> And soft with hard, and light with heavy mixt.[2]

13. Amidst such an impure mixture of divers and mutually hostile ingredients, amidst all these yellow and black and blue condiments, the busy taster not without reason looks for the suspected poison, though against hidden treachery another kind of remedy has been found. Between the wine and the food there shoot forth the livid crests of serpents cunningly twisted among golden branches, and as though by a voluptuary device Death itself wonderfully stands on guard against the death of miserable man. But the feaster sits with countenance overcast, eyes dull, forehead clouded, nose wrinkled, and cheeks pale, parting his sticky lips with difficulty, scarce lifting his head. Fairly overpowered by all the glitter and odors, he knows not where he is, being still swollen with the excesses of the previous night, dazed with the outcome of the morning's business, and already cunningly plotting where to turn next and what mischief to per-

---

[2]   Ovid, *Metam.* 1.19–20 (Dryden's translation).

form. He perspires, he sniffs, he belches, he gapes, nibbling at everything and nauseated by all.

14. But the retired man, content with few attendants or a single one, or even without any, quick-witted and alert because of the previous day's fast, adorns the neat board before his modest hearth with nothing better than his own presence. In place of tumult he has peace, silence instead of clamor, himself alone instead of a crowd. He is his own companion, his own storyteller, his own table guest. Nor is he afraid to be alone, seeing that in place of a mansion he has bare walls of rude stone, and instead of an ivory chair, a bench of oak or plain beechwood or fir. He loves to look not on gold but at the sky, and to tread on earth better than on purple. He is a pleasant musician, and as he sits down and rises up, his sweetest song is the benediction and the grace. His steward, if need be, is also his butler, cook, and domestic. Whatever is placed before him he renders precious by his good humor and refinement. One would imagine that his food was all conveyed from distant shores and forests and his drink pressed among the Ligurian and Picentian hills. Such is the countenance and such the mind of him who joys in this existence, so grateful is he toward God and man, so happy in the common, unpurchased fare, that not only, like the old man in Virgil,[3] does he liken his mind to the wealth of kings, but puts a far higher value on it.

15. He envies no one, he hates no one. Content with his own lot and inaccessible to the injuries of Fortune, he feels himself above all fears and all desires. He knows that no poison is poured into his vessels. He understands that a few things suffice for the life of man, that the greatest and truest wealth is to have no wishes, the greatest power to have no fears. He passes his life happily and tranquilly, with peaceful nights, serene days, and undisturbed recreation. He goes about freely and sits down without trembling. He neither contrives snares nor is on guard against them. He knows that he is loved for himself and not for his possessions, that his death will be of benefit to no one and that his life is harmful to no one. He thinks that it does not greatly matter how long he lives but how well, nor does he regard the time and place of his death of so much importance as its manner. On one thing only is his heart strongly fixed, that he shall round out with a beautiful close the story of a well spent life.

[3] *Georg.* 4.132.

§IV. Of the wretchedness of the busy man and the happiness
of the retired man when dinner is past

16. Gradually the hours fly and the day slips past, and now dinner is over. The busy man is distraught by the army of his hangers-on, the disorder of the tables, and the clatter of men and dishes. The roof groans with drunken jests and the hundred complaints of hunger. For it is not the least evil of the rich man's table that it is incapable of justice, and so there is hunger there and repletion, but moderation never. There is an unpleasant odor in the court and a disagreeable color, and the footing is uncertain. The whole floor of the kitchen is stained and reeking with the scattered refuse, and the place is slippery with wine and clouded with smoke, filled with nasty scum and tepid washings and decomposing fat, whitened with bones and red with blood. In short, to use the expression of Ambrose, one might call it a slaughterhouse rather than a kitchen. It may be, as the ancients say, that this early meal got its name because it was eaten by the warriors in preparation for battle; in this case, however, it was not a preparation but a complete action. Indeed, one might imagine a genuine battle there instead of a meal. The chieftain is wounded and tottering, and the whole army, overcome with drink, goes staggering away. The table is the line of battle, pleasure is the smooth and treacherous enemy, the couches are the tombs, and conscience takes the place of hell.

17. But with the retired man everything is different. His house is better suited for the feasts of angels than of men. Its sweet odor and color are the best index of his manners and witness of his refinement. His table is peaceful, innocent of luxury and disorder, an enemy to gluttony, and free from all uncleanliness, a place where pure joys dwell and whence foul pleasures are exiled, where temperance rules as queen, where the couch is chaste and untroubled, and conscience is a paradise.

18. The former gets up drunk or in ill humor, the latter serene and sober. The one is in dread of disease; the other, conscious of his abstemiousness, feels safe from all the ills to which the human frame is subject. The one is either surly or boisterous, the other refrains from both extremes and gives thanks to God. All the rest of the day is spent by one in licentious indulgence, in sleep, in anxious cares, and toilsome business, by the other in the worship of God and in noble studies, in learning new things and remembering old, while only a moderate part of the day goes for needful repose and innocent recreation.

*§V. The employments of the unhappy man of action and the
happy man of leisure at midday*

19. The sun now stands in the middle of the heavens, and the man of
action is agitated, fretful, excited, redoubling all his tricky contrivances lest
he should miss something on that particular day through lack of energy,
or lest any sluggishness in his evil deliberations deprive his fertile wit of
the hoped-for outcome, anxious that his hidden snares should take effect
before nightfall. For it is a characteristic of practically all evil designs that
they brook no postponement.

20. The wicked mind is impatient of delay; it cannot bear to put off
for a single moment the object of its craving. The observation of the satirist, that whoever wants to become rich wants to do so suddenly,[4] does
not apply to avarice alone. This is a trait which Cupidity shares equally
with her sisters, Wrath and Licentiousness, who being begot in hell of an
infernal father have not unlearned the confusion and rashness and horror which were the nature of their own origin. For these are the Furies
whom the poets properly have declared to be the daughters of Acheron
and Night because they bear with them the gloom of ignorance and the
stuff of repentance. And these very creatures of hell, from which men
say they have their origin, are also dwellers in cities and attendants upon
the busy man, and they are constantly inciting the blind and perverse
passions with their burning goads immediately to execute their worst
intentions lest, if there should be any delay, a reformation and healthy
state of mind should steal upon them. For vice dislikes all restraints, and
just as earnestness and deliberation are becoming in honorable affairs, so
unadvised haste is always the friend of evil designs.

21. The retired man, on the other hand, does nothing hurriedly, but
noting the passage of time in its flight and longing to be where there
is life without flow of time or fear of death, he turns once more to his
devotions, praying not only for the light of a single day but for the clear
evening of his whole existence and the glory of a never setting life, and
this he implores not as his right but as a reward for the sacred death of
Christ, knowing that it were more than man deserved if the earthly death
of one who had no sin had not been of such great efficacy that it could
procure immortal life for those who were by nature mortal and had perished through their sinfulness.

---

4   Juvenal, *Sat.* 14.176.

22. And so, soon after, as he contemplates the sinking of the sun and imagines himself also declining toward the ground, anticipating the descent of black darkness upon the earth, he supplicates the aid of the supernal light. And whether he begs with tears that his spirit may not be exiled from heaven for the weight of its offences or that he may be granted the pure light of faith, that his burning passions may be cooled, his vile thoughts cleansed, his wavering mind supported and its contentions pacified, he still prolongs his morning chants with evening praises from the inexhaustible fountain of his piety.

§VI. *Of the wretchedness of the busy man and the happiness*
of the retired man when evening falls

23. When the sun has set, the busy man is again compelled to issue from his house and to rove through the city, treading its dirty streets and colliding with people in his way, sweating, toiling, panting, burning; and after he has applied himself to every kind of fraud and cleverly untangled all his intricate snares, he returns at last, late and exhausted, and grumbling sorely about his practice, bringing home neither a name of good report nor a clear conscience, but perhaps a little gold and unquestionably a great deal of crime and hatred.

24. But the retired man, rejoicing that the day has passed without a blemish, seeks out a clear spring or grassy bank by the seashore, and before the light has faded he implores the unfailing mercy of his Creator to arm him with watchful sobriety, with the shield of prayer and faith against the dangers of the night to come, against the temptations and treachery and fury of the enemy who rages like a lion, and to guard him against dreams and pollution and the apparitions of night. And so, entrusting his spirit to the hands of the Lord and calling upon the angels to stand guard over his habitation, he betakes himself home, having no wrong to complain of nor any evil wish, but bringing with him the praise and satisfaction of a soul daily advancing in goodness.

25. In short, one man spends all his days in despoiling the living, the other in interceding for the dead; one in assailing the chastity of matrons and virgins, the other in reverent worship of the Virgin Matron. One makes martyrs, the other glorifies them; one persecutes saints, the other offers them homage.

§VII. Of the wretchedness of the man of action and the happiness of the man of leisure when night returns and it is time for supper

26. With the return of night the busy man returns to his potations. There is great pomp and a long array of attendants before and behind. One could imagine it to be the funeral of a living man. Lest the obsequies be lacking in any circumstance, the hired mourners and the pipes precede, then comes the corpse, still warm and still breathing, in sumptuous raiment and perfumed with rich odors, and is once more buried among cushions. He heaps a heavy supper upon his still undigested dinner and, obstructing the way for another meal, prepares disgust for the following day. The retired man, however, either persuades himself that he has already eaten or dines in such a way as to give point to Plato's saying, that he disliked to fill up twice a day.

§VIII. Of the wretchedness of the man of action and the happiness of the man of leisure when it is time for sleep

27. After this they both seek their beds in very different states of body and mind. One is full of troubles, replete with dining and wining, gripped by fear and envy, dispirited by the checks he has encountered or vainly elated by his successes, afflicted with melancholy, bursting with wrath, at war with himself, not master of his own mind. He is besieged by parasites, spied upon by rivals, deafened with outcries, importuned by letters and besieged by messages, held in suspense by a report and terrified by a rumor, stunned by omens and deluded by falsehoods, wearied out with complaints and harassed by contentions even at night. His life is like that of the fiends; he is hateful to his neighbors, oppressive to his fellow citizens, an object of terror or derision to his own people. He is suspected by all and trusted by none. For a long time he tosses about on his purple covered couch, sleepless and making trial of all sorts of wanton pleasures. And after his miserable body has been spurred to the enjoyment of immediate sensations and his imagination has wandered with a vague longing toward remote delights, he is finally overcome with weariness and his eyes are closed in sleep. But his troubles are still awake, and his distracted soul is on fire and gnawed by the worm of an undying conscience. Then he beholds his day's actions—the clients betrayed, the poor oppressed, the farmers evicted from their land, the virgins violated, the wards defrauded,

the widows robbed, the innocent tortured and slain, and along with all these, the Furies wreaking vengeance on his crimes. Often he cries out in his sleep or makes querulous moans, and often his sleep is broken by some sudden terror.

28. But the other is full of pure joy and sacred hope and inspired with a pious love, not frantic like that of Nisus but like the love of Peter for Christ. He is happy in the sense of a sound conscience, his trust in men, and fear of God. He is free from noxious food and superfluous cares, solitary, silent, serene, almost like one of the angels. He is dear to God, an object of fear to none, of love to all. Entering his chamber, which is contrived for sleep and not for unchaste pleasures, he enjoys sweet and undisturbed repose. His dreams, if he has any, mostly resemble the actions of his waking hours; or he beholds still fairer visions, being more blessed than the other even in this portion of his life. And his advantage is not only in greater happiness of mind but in greater health of body and in an easier command over the movements of his limbs. For the virtues of the mind, and moderation in particular, are of great benefit to health of body, and generally those who do most service to the body do it most mischief.

3

The Difference in the Lot of the
Busy Man and the Solitary Man

*§I. Summary of the discussion and transition to the unhappiness
of those who are engaged in other people's affairs.*

1. Behold, father, I have placed before your view a single day of an individual man of action and an individual man of leisure. It is the same with all individuals of the kind and all days, except that the trouble of one class grows more bitter, the peace of the other more delightful in proportion as their habit of mind becomes confirmed by the passage of time and earthly motions bear them on toward the state of eternity which comes ever nearer in life's steady course. For one class there is labor without end, for the other ease.

2. Perhaps you will think the condition of those persons happier who are taken up with other people's business. They, however, are ruled by the power of another man's nod and learn what they must do from another man's look. They can claim nothing as their own. Their house, their sleep, their food, is not their own, and, what is even more serious, their mind is not their own, their countenance is not their own. They do not weep and laugh at the promptings of their own nature but discard their own emotions to put on those of another. In sum, they transact another man's business, think another man's thoughts, live by another man's grace.

3. It is of these men the noble poet is speaking when he says:

And some with impudence invade the court.[1]

---

[1]   Virgil, *Georg.* 2.504 (Dryden's translation).

It is these men whom another poet rebukes more boldly and stingingly, in that satire in which he treats of life at court, when he says reproachfully to his friend,

> If,—by reiterated scorn made bold,
> Your mind can still its shameless tenor hold,
> Still think the greatest blessing earth can give,
> Is solely at another's cost to live—[2]

4. Between these men and such as are condemned to pass their lives in the dungeons of rulers and kings I know not what difference there is except that the former are bound with chains of gold, the latter with iron. The chain is fairer, the servitude equal, the blame greater, because they do of their own accord what the others are compelled to by force. To express my opinion of these men in a few words, I call them the most profoundly unhappy of all unhappy men of the world, because they are not even permitted to enjoy the brief reward of their evil practices. They have lived at the behest of another but are doomed to die at their own peril; they have toiled for the benefit of others but have incurred the sin for themselves. Happy would they have been if they had labored without sin and without thought of advantage, but now, while the offense is their own, the pleasant fruits, deceitful and fleeting though they be, serve for another's delectation.

5. We say that the farmer's lot is hard if he plants a tree whose fruit he is not destined to look upon. For who, the Apostle asks, "plants a vineyard and does not eat of its fruit?"[3] But he at least may find comfort in the thought that another generation will enjoy it, and though he knows to a certainty that what he makes will not belong to him, he does not on that account refrain from his work. When he is asked for whom he sows the seed, he answers in Cicero's words, "For the immortal gods";[4] it would be still better if he said, "For the one immortal God."

6. How much more unfortunate are those who sow that from which they reap only punishment while others gather pleasures that are deserving of punishment. They cannot blame anyone but themselves for the mischief they do. They cannot blame their own generation, for which, by working

---

[2]   Juvenal, *Sat.* 5.1–2 (Gifford's translation).
[3]   1 Cor 10:7.
[4]   *Sen.* 7.

[too hard] they often snatch away the liberty that had been taught to them,[5] nor posterity, for which they prepare slavery, nor God whom they offend in order to be pleasing to men. They cannot even charge their fault against the very persons whom they injure in pandering to them, for whom at the cost of their own eternal life they prepare a brief interval of sinfulness, which means the privilege, for these too, of eternal damnation. Stark blind they are and utterly mad, plunged into the world's light—it would be better to say its darkness—under hostile stars, since while they raise others aloft, they themselves lie prostrate, crushed, it may be, by the very persons to whom they have devoted their service. In the meantime, having procured many conveniences for their patrons and contributed much toward the indulgence of their desires, they have themselves had no advantage from their actions, and the only glory which they have reaped from their base zeal is to have fed the greed of princes and the lust of lords with their acceptable counsels.

7. What more shall I say? There is an imprecation current among our people that seems to me no less biting than one which is habitual with the Cretans; though neither is at all horrible in sound, there is a certain destructive venom wrapped up in both. The Cretans wish that their enemies may find delight in evil companionship while with us the curse is that they may never cease from employment and care. If one considers somewhat deeply—not the words themselves but the thought implied in them—one can scarcely find a sadder thing to say. I speak of those busy men whom we constantly see and of whom common life is full; a different species of this class does not exist, or it is so rare as practically never to be seen. Where the truth is sought, I am loath to spend my time on fictitious shadows.

And so, to dismiss the matter once for all, in my opinion practically every busy man is unhappy, and the man who is employed in the service of another is doubly unhappy because he has only his pains for his reward.

§II. Almost every busy man is unhappy, though there are
some few who are worthily employed

8. Now I am not unaware that there have been, and perchance still are, very active men of a saintly nature who themselves go the way of Christ and lead straying souls along the same path. When this happens, I acknowledge

---

[5]   The translator, Jacob Zeitlin, found the meaning of this clause (*cui saepenumero laborando praeceptam sibi libertatem eripiunt*) to be obscure. It is retranslated here by Alden Smith.—SHM

that it is a great and immeasurable good, a double blessing to be contrasted with the twofold misery of which I have said so much. For what is there more blessed, more worthy of a man, and more like divine goodness than to serve and assist as many as require help? Whoever is able to do so and does not, has repudiated, I think, the glorious duty of humanity and proved false to the name as well as the nature of man.

9. If it should be proved that this is possible, I shall freely subordinate my private inclination to the public welfare and, abandoning the place of retirement in which I consulted only my own humor, I shall venture forth where I can be of use to the world, following the advice given by our Cicero. "It is more in accord with nature," he says, "to emulate the great Hercules and undergo the greatest toil and trouble for the sake of aiding or saving the world, if possible, than to live in seclusion, not only free from all care, but reveling in pleasures and abounding in wealth, while excelling others also in beauty and strength. Thus Hercules denied himself and underwent toil and tribulation for the world, and, out of gratitude for his services, popular belief has given him a place in the council of the gods. The better and more noble, therefore, the character with which a man is endowed, the more does he prefer the life of service to the life of pleasure."[6]

So says Cicero, and I yield an unconstrained assent, if things are as he says. But it is my view of the matter that the force of a general truth is not destroyed by a very few exceptional instances. There are many who profess to believe that employment is of general advantage and holier than any kind of retirement. I know. But how many, I ask you, do we see who carry out what they profess? There may be a few or there may be a great many; show me one and I shall hold my peace.

10. I do not deny that there are learned and eloquent men who maintain the opposite view with great subtlety. But it is not so much a question of cleverness in arguing as of conduct. They go about the cities and deliver long harangues in public about vices and virtues. I could barely refrain from inserting here the satirist's biting tooth in a way which would be decidedly to the point, but I recalled to whom I was addressing myself and decided to sacrifice a vanity of style rather than be wanting in true respect.

11. Yet these earnest persons, you observe, say many useful things which often are of advantage to their hearers. I grant it, but the physician

---

[6]   *Off.* 3.5 (Walter Miller's translation).

is not necessarily in good health when he helps the patient with his advice; in fact, he often dies of the very ailment which he has cured in others. I do not disdain the careful choice and artful composition of words contrived for the salvation of men, and I honor the useful work regardless of the character of the workman, but this is a school of life and not of rhetoric, and our thoughts are now fixed not on the vainglory of eloquence but on the secure repose of the soul.

12. I am not unmindful of the sentence of Seneca: "Throw aside all hindrances and give up your time to attaining a sound mind," to which he promptly adds, "No man can attain it who is engrossed in other matters."[7] Now what I maintain is not that solitude develops such a mind, but that solitude is conducive to preserving and strengthening it, for I have not forgotten another observation of the same writer to the effect that the place in which one lives does not greatly contribute to one's tranquility.[8] Be it so, yet doubtless it contributes something. Otherwise why does he say elsewhere that "we ought to select abodes which are wholesome not only for the body but also for the character?"[9] And in still another place he exclaims, "I shall flee far from the very sight and neighborhood of the Forum."[10] For as a severe climate puts to the test even the sturdiest constitution, so there are some situations which are very unwholesome for a well-disposed mind before it has come to full maturity. Whence, pray, is the difference in the soundness of minds and habits of conduct if there is nothing in places? There is something in places, with Seneca's leave I would say a great deal, though not everything. I quite agree with his view that "it is the mind which must make everything agreeable to itself."[11] That is well said, after his fashion. But whence comes the light of truth and right reason? Doubtless from a source without.

What I have said about environment I shall affirm about the mind itself, that it is something, nay, a great deal, but by no means everything, and only that mind is truly reasonable which makes proper allowance for the influence of its environment. There is something great and veritably divine in a serene composure of mind which makes it an attribute of God alone, but it is a gift which he most frequently

---

[7]   *Ep.* 53 (Gummere's translation).
[8]   *Ep.* 55.
[9]   *Ep.* 51.
[10] *Ep.* 28.
[11] *Ep.* 55.

likes to bestow upon those who have fixed their dwelling in seclusion. Both these points I have for brevity's sake proved by general arguments and by a juxtaposed series of contrasts, and shall before long confirm with examples from illustrious lives.

§III. In praise of the serenity of mind which is granted to those who are confirmed in solitude, and that the mind cannot apply itself to a diversity of interests

13. If perchance a man capable of heeding truth should closely apply his inmost ear, not to the tongue but to the heart of one of those preachers at whom the credulous throng gapes in amazement, I believe that he would admit without cavil that he had heard his naked conscience honestly confessing that happiness consisted not in sounding words, but quiet deeds, and in the inward possession of truth rather than in the applause of strangers or in fragile reputation. And then he will hear many things quite at variance with the words which, along with the rest of the crowd, he admired in the pulpit, and he will understand that there is a difference between the external surface and the heart of things.

14. It is without question the nature of the mind that when it is earnestly applied to one interest it must neglect many others. Hence it is that those who cultivate eloquence are often so inept for action and that men engaged in important affairs are less accomplished in expression. In the same way those who aim at an ideal of sobriety avoid vulgar pleasures, while those who place a value on pleasurable indulgence scorn the notion of sobriety. Men who are possessed with a desire for augmenting their private wealth often make small account of their friends and the state and lead an ignoble kind of life, while those who are magnanimously devoted to the public interest are frequently seen to be neglectful of their domestic concerns. The same wind cannot be equally favorable to manners whose courses lie in opposite directions. This I say that you may not be surprised at finding the same truth applied to the matter under discussion. The busy life is fond of noise and finds pleasure in talkativeness, while contemplation is the friend of silence and retirement; and by the same token, the former hates silence, the latter hates disturbance.

Which mode of life is safer—this, my father, is what I shall examine in my discourse today.

§IV. How from the dangers of the shepherd's life it may be inferred that the busy life is less safe, and for that reason the author himself has chosen the retired life

15. Tell me, therefore, if I may take my example from the occupation which I have had to mention, how often does the shepherd lose his life in the course of his duties? How often does he fall into a trap while trying to find a sheep that has strayed, or tumble over a precipice while pursuing one that is running away? How often, do you think, does the healthy physician contract a mortal disease while he is making the round of his patients, or the gravedigger while he is burying the dead encounter the contagion which results in his own death? Let no one deceive himself that the contagions to which the mind is subject are less serious than those of the body; they are in fact more so. They afflict more heavily; they penetrate more deeply; they diffuse themselves more stealthily.

16. But it is commendable, people say, to be helpful to great numbers; it is praiseworthy to be of service to as many as we can. Who denies it? Yet we know where a well-ordered charity begins. Take my word for it, it is a matter of no small assurance to promise aid to the struggling, counsel to the perplexed, light to the blind, joy to the grieving, safety to the terrified, hope to the depressed, health to the sick, rest to the weary, comfort to the afflicted; to show the path to the straying, to place your shoulders beneath the falling and to extend the hand to those that lie prostrate. These are great things if they are performed, trifling if only promised; for a large promise is of no more consequence than a small one, it is only the fulfilment that is more impressive. But I am not so much proposing a rule for others as exposing the principles of my own mind. If it commends itself to anyone, let him follow its suggestion. Whoever does not like it is free to reject it and, leaving us to our solitude, to embrace his own anxious cares and live to his own satisfaction in scorn of our rural retreat.

17. I should not mind, I confess, to be of service to as many as possible or even, in Ovid's words, to be a bearer of health to the entire world;[12] but the first is in the power of only a few, the second of Christ alone. I would yield so far to persons of a contrary opinion as to admit that whoever is in

[12] *Metam.* 2.642.

a place of safety sins against the law of nature if he does not offer what aid he can to the struggling. But for me, who have myself been hitherto struggling as in a great shipwreck, it is enough to pray for the aid of him who is alone able to provide aid in our need. My prayers are far-reaching, but I shall be content if they are fulfilled to a moderate degree. I could wish to have everyone, or at least as many as possible, gain salvation with me. But in the end what do you expect me to say? It is enough for me, yea, a cause of great happiness, if I do not perish myself.

18. But for those who profess themselves guardians of the helpless sheep, alas, how much I fear that they are wolves eager to rend them alive. Let me not involve myself too long in reflections not pertinent to my argument, but let each man decide according to his own preference, for it is impossible that it should suit all men to follow a single road in life, even if they were all bound for the same ultimate destination.

§I. The retired life, especially to those unversed in literature, is heavier than death and seems calculated to bring on death

19. In this connection each man must seriously take into account the disposition with which nature has endowed him and the bent which by habit or training he has developed. For there are some for whom the life of solitude is more grievous than death and seems calculated to result in death, and this will happen particularly with persons who have no acquaintance with literature. Such men, if they have no one to talk to, are destitute of any resource for communion with themselves or with books, and necessarily remain dumb. And indeed, isolation without literature is exile, prison, and torture; supply literature, and it becomes your country, freedom, and delight. "What is sweeter than lettered ease?"[13] is a well-known saying of Cicero. Not less familiar is Seneca's sentence, "Leisure without study is death; it is a tomb for the living man."[14] Although I know full well that those two sweet solaces of philosophers, solitude and leisure, as I said at the outset, are at times annoying even to such as have an acquaintance with literature, the reason for it is evident. For with people of this class it sometimes happens that they are fettered by pleasure and in love with their prison or seek to make their living in traffic with the multitude and in sordid business, or aspire to climb up the slippery steps of honors through

---

[13] *Tusculans* 5.36.
[14] *Ep.* 82.

the windy suffrages of the populace. For these—and their number in our times is great—literature is not a means of giving cultivation to the mind and refinement to life, but an instrument for procuring wealth. Children are sent by their parents to study literature not as to an academy but as to a marketplace, at great expense to the family but with the hope of a much greater financial return, so that it need be no occasion for surprise if they make a venal and avaricious use of an education which they have pursued for purposes of sale and on which they have based the sinful expectation of a usury not of a hundred percent but a thousand.

20. All these things have to be carefully considered in selecting a mode of life, and so I would not invite to the life of solitude such as those I am describing, nor willingly admit them if they came of their own accord. You may infer from this how numerous a lot I should exclude. For what shall a fish do out of water or these fellows at a distance from cities?

21. That is what I formerly said to a certain enervated and effeminate lawyer who had begun to frequent this locality, not from any love of quiet, of which he had not the least notion, nor from any yearning after leisure, which he hated, but only from some itch of imitation. It is a question whether he was a greater nuisance to himself or to me, but he left suddenly, being overcome with the tedium of the place and the craving for the pleasures of the city. If I had not foreseen this outcome I should have withdrawn on my own part, so utterly destitute of conformity were our conditions and our ways of regarding things. It is true that he called himself my friend and that we had engaged since boyhood in the same studies, but our aims were far apart, as the event proved. I return, however, to my purpose.

4

Virtues of the Solitary Life

§II. Although it would be best that all should recognize in their youth what is the proper kind of life for them, nevertheless if one fails to do it in youth, it is wise that one should at least do it in old age

1. It would be an excellent thing if the need for good counsel, that unavoidable characteristic of youth, did not stand in the way, and that each one of us at the very beginning of our maturity should give careful and earnest thought to the selection of some particular kind of life, and never turn aside from the path we have once chosen, except for important reasons or for some grave necessity. Hercules did so on entering manhood, as is testified by Xenophon, the pupil of Socrates, and by Cicero. But because we fail to do it and live in most cases not by our own judgment but by that of the crowd, and are rushed along over tortuous paths, following the footsteps of others in the dark, we often emerge upon perilous and impassable roads and are carried so far that we have become something or other before we have had a chance to look about and consider what we wanted to be. And if one has not been able in youth to reflect on the role which nature or accident or some mistake has thrust upon him, let him ponder it in his old age, and like a wayfarer who has gone astray, let him, as far as he may, look to his safety before nightfall, being assured that the potentialities of his nature cannot be completely suppressed.

2. If a man has been illumined by the celestial light at his very entrance into life, when, as I have already said, not a spark of judgment is active, and has been able to find a safe road or one whose dangers are slight and easily avoided, he has reason for everlasting gratitude to God. For one whose fortune has been less auspicious, greater trouble is in store. Yet once he

has begun to open his eyes and to understand what a crooked path he is traveling, let him bend all his energy to correct, even though it be in old age, the follies and errors of his youth, and let him recall the old man in Terence,[1] an excellent example of reformation in old age and a source at once of profit and delight. Though the undertaking is not particularly easy, it is notably profitable and by no means impossible. No action should be considered as coming too late when it is recognized as wholesome.

3. For this view there are some authorities not to be despised. Augustus Caesar, the most philosophical of princes, says, "What is done well enough is done speedily enough,"[2] and Plato, the prince of philosophers, says, "Happy is the man whose fortune it is even in old age to attain wisdom and truth."[3]

§III. What course is to be kept in the order and plan of personal reformation

4. In every well-ordered plan for reforming one's life, it is especially important to keep in view that we are to be guided not by idle wishes but by our character and predisposition, and that we are to follow not the road which looks most attractive but the one which is best suited to our needs. In this connection I require that a man shall be particularly honest and exacting in passing judgment on himself and not prone to be led astray by the delusive temptations of eye and ear. I know that it has happened to some men that in their admiration for the qualities of others they have lost the consciousness of their own limitations, and attempting actions that are remote from their powers, they have provided matter of mirth to strangers. One admonition that I have derived from the philosophers is that each man should note the relation between his own character and habits and a given mode of life, whether it be the retired life or life in the city or any other manner of life, and understand which is best suited for himself. If this is advantageous to those who are just entering upon life, how much more so must it be to those who have advanced in it, since in addition to the trouble of choosing they are also faced with the task of destroying old and firmly rooted notions.

5. As for me, who, as far as I am aware, have nothing in common with the crowd and whose attainment in literature, while not so great as to puff

---

[1]   Demea in the *Adelphi*. See ll. 855ff.
[2]   Suetonius, *Aug.* 25.
[3]   *Laws* 653A. Quoted from Cicero, *Fin.* 5.

up the mind, is enough to give it pleasure and to make me a friend of that solitude in which I acquired it without the intervention of a wordy teacher and without obstinate laziness (would I could say without persecution from envy), whom neither sweetheart nor wife, neither bond nor interest nor guardianship nor chance of profit, neither the rostrum nor the bath, neither the tavern nor the banquet nor the public square could tie down to the city—as for me, I say, whose attitude, to tell the truth, was decided not so much by a deliberate resolve of my own or the advice of others as by a natural prompting of my disposition, my unusually retired life has been not only one of superior tranquility but also of conspicuous dignity and security. My counsel to other men to take account of their condition is precisely what I have employed in arriving at an understanding of my own. I heartily embrace and cling to solitude and leisure, about which I have conversed with you so much today, as if they were ladders to the level toward which the mind strives to ascend, and I dread crowds and busy cares as though they were bolts and bars to my freedom. But when some need compels me to dwell in the city, I have learned to create a solitude among people and a haven of refuge in the midst of a tempest, using a device, not generally known, of so controlling the senses that they do not perceive what they perceive.

6. Long after I had developed it into a habit by my own experimentation, I discovered that it was also the advice of a very brilliant and learned writer, and I committed it to memory all the more eagerly because of my joy at finding that a practice of mine was supported by the authority of antiquity. It is Quintilian, in that book in which with great elegance he has put the finishing touches on the education of the orator, previously set forth with such beauty by Cicero, who says: "Study by the lamp, when we come to it fresh and vigorous, is the best kind of retirement. But silence and seclusion, and entire freedom of mind, though in the highest degree desirable, cannot always fall to our lot; and therefore we must not, if any noise disturbs us, immediately throw aside our books, and deplore the day as lost, but we must strive against inconveniences, and acquire such habits, that our application may set all interruptions at defiance; for if we direct our attention, with our whole mental energy, to the work actually before us, nothing of all that strikes our eyes or ears will penetrate into the mind. Does a casual train of thought often cause us not to see persons in our way, and to wander from our road, and shall we not attain the same abstraction if we resolve to do so? We must not yield to excuses for idleness; for if

we fancy that we must not study except when we are free from all other cares, we shall always have some reason for self-indulgence. In the midst of crowds, therefore, on a journey, and even at festive meetings, let thought secure for herself privacy."[4]

7. I have quoted this passage from Quintilian the more gladly because it is not too well known. Seneca's letter on the subject is more familiar, and I shall therefore cite only its conclusion. After discussing at length the way in which the mind of the student should endure the disturbances of the crowd, he finally asks himself, "Is it not sometimes a simpler matter just to avoid the uproar?" And answering his own question, he says, "I admit this. Accordingly I shall change from my present quarters,"[5] as if all that he had previously said was only by way of consolation in cases of compulsory sojourn, while his final advice was for voluntary withdrawal.

8. And this is in fact the truth. For I also have found only this recourse in my need, that in the midst of the turmoil of cities I create for myself in thought, as far as I may, an imaginary solitude in some retreat and by an effort of the mind triumph over my situation. This manner of remedy I have often used hitherto, but whether I shall resort to it again I do not know, since the future is always uncertain. Assuredly, if my choice were free, I should seek solitude in her own retreat.

§IV. *The praise of solitude*

9. This I have done while I could, and you shall see how eagerly I shall continue to do it. Solitude is indeed something holy, innocent, incorruptible, and the purest of all human possessions. To whom does she reveal herself amid forests, for whom does she display her charms and thorns? Whom, unless it be the fishes, does she deceive with a bait? Whom, apart from wild beasts and birds, does she entangle in her nets and snares? Whom does she allure with song or graceful motion? Whom does she fascinate with her colors? For whom does she weave the purple, to whom does she sell the oil, for whom wreathe garlands of flowery speech? With whom, finally, does she ingratiate herself, whom does she seek to please, except the person who has penetrated the inmost recesses of solitude and for whom therefore there is no solitude? She aims to deceive no one; she neither simulates nor dissimulates; she adorns nothing, she glosses nothing, she pretends nothing. She

---

[4]   Quintilian, *Inst.* 10.3.27–30 (J. S. Watson's translation).
[5]   *Ep.* 56.

is utterly naked and unadorned, for she is averse to garish exhibitions and vulgar plaudits such as are poisonous to the life of the spirit and of all things. She has God for sole witness and puts her trust not in the voice of the blind and unreliable multitude but in her own conscience.

10. At times she even reposes small faith in her conscience and remains perplexed, recalling that it is written, "Who can understand his errors?"[6] and again, "If I am perfect, yet would I not know my soul."[7] Nor is she forgetful that "the Lord is good to all and his tender mercies are over all his works,"[8] that "the Lord upholdeth all that fall and raiseth up all those that be bowed down,"[9] that he is "nigh unto all them that call upon him,"[10] that "he has not dealt with us after our sins nor rewarded us according to our iniquities. For as the heaven is high above the earth, so great is his mercy toward them that fear him. As far as the East is from the West, so far hath he removed our transgressions from us."[11] Finally he looks upon us as a father and not as a judge, "Like as a father pitieth his children, so the Lord pitieth them that fear him. For he knoweth our frame, he remembereth that we are dust. As for man, his days are as grass; as a flower of the field, so he flourisheth," and his life is fleeting as a shadow. "But the mercy of the Lord is from everlasting to everlasting,"[12] since he has made us and none of the works of his hands is hateful to him.[13]

11. And so while the Scriptures breathe threats on the one hand and extend hope on the other, Solitude remains doubtful of her merit and does not know whether she is deserving of love or hatred, but trembles and hopes and comforts herself with the assurance of the mercy of her king. Thus watchful of the devil's wiles and with her mind fixed on one thing only, she looks about her, and leaning on divine support, she makes light of the danger. Thus she is happy and composed and, in a manner of speaking, a fortified citadel and a haven against storms. If anyone fails to take advantage of such a refuge, what result can he expect but to find himself without a haven, tossed about in a sea of troubles, live upon rocks, and perish in the waves?

[6] Vulgate, Ps 18:13 (KJV 19:12).
[7] Job 9:21.
[8] Vulgate, Ps 144:9 (KJV 145:9).
[9] Vulgate, Ps 144:14 (KJV 145:14).
[10] Vulgate, Ps 144:18 (KJV 145:18).
[11] Vulgate, Ps 102:10–12 (KJV 103:10–12).
[12] Vulgate, Ps 102:13–17 (KJV 103:13–17).
[13] Wis 11:25 (NRSV 11:24).

12. I am not, however, so unreasonable in my attitude or so narrowly attached to my view as to think all others foolish or to compel them to pledge fealty to my doctrine. Many may be brought to profess, but no one can be forced to believe. There is nothing more vital than independence of judgment; as I claim it for myself, I would not deny it to others. I grant you (for it is possible) that every man's purpose is honorable and sacred. I would not constitute myself the judge of the deep and hidden mysteries of the human conscience. All men with the grace of God may lead a good life; the infinite clemency spurns none, though it is spurned by many. Even in the practice of human philosophy there are gradations of virtue. Everyone cannot hold the highest place, otherwise all the lower ones would be unoccupied. But all who have determined to lead their life, in whatsoever calling, out of the reach of ill report, must at least keep free from the indecency and sordidness which are generally found in low conditions. To avoid indecency is a duty, to have high aspiration is virtue, to attain it is felicity.

§V. On the fourfold distinction of virtues introduced by Plotinus and approved by Macrobius

13. I am not unaware of the celebrated distinction of the virtues into four kinds introduced by Plotinus, the great Platonist,[14] and approved by Macrobius. Even with them, however, the political virtues occupy the lowest stage. These virtues may belong to busy men, but not to all of them, only to those the end of whose activity is their own virtue and, to a much greater extent, the welfare of the state. You see how with a single word the whole enormous host of busy men is reduced to a very small number.

14. The purgatorial virtues occupy the next step above. These are the embellishment of those who, freely forsaking cities, become men of leisure and true followers of philosophy; they eradicate from the mind the passions which are only moderated in the case of the former. The virtues of the third stage are higher than those that are termed the virtues of a purified mind; their property is freedom from those passions which the political virtues have mitigated and the purgatorial ones removed. These are the virtues of perfect men. Where such men are to be found I know not, but if they have ever existed, they have surely loved solitude, and if one of them

---

[14]   *Enn.* 1.2.

still survives, though with his virtues for a rudder he may sail the high seas in safety, I think nevertheless that he too loves the haven of solitude.

15. The fourth and highest is the place of the exemplary virtues, which are above the reach of man and dwell, as it is said, in the mind of God alone. It is maintained that the three other kinds of human virtue are derived from this fourth as from an immutable pattern, as its very name suggests, or, following Plato, from the ideas of the virtues which along with other ideas Plato fixed in the mind of God. It is not enough to say that these virtues do not exert the same influence on the passions as the others; to utter the word passion in connection with them is the height of profanity and sacrilege. I should have said nothing about them, for they have no connection with my theme, but since the occasion prompted me to say something about the political and purgatorial virtues I did not care to break and untwine the chain which Plotinus had woven with so much art.

Sweetness of the Solitary Life

§VI. The delight and sweetness of the solitary life and the spiritual conflict of the solitary man

1. Do you see how I have striven with a roundabout profusion of words to reenter into favor with the man of action? But it is now time to set a limit to these digressions. I shall return to myself and to solitude. I could wish that I had drunk more deeply of its true and intimate sweetness, that I might more confidently converse with you in this discourse. A worldly mind is ashamed to speak of sacred things. Who indeed is able to express in words what he scarcely realizes in thought? It is presumptuous for an earthly—I might say a mere earthly—creature to speak of a life celestial and truly angelic, having been ravished by the sole enchantment of its name and the bare report of its perfection, and, to speak truly, having but faintly smelled its aroma without getting a taste of its flavor.

2. It is exactly as if a shepherd who was born in the woods and brought up in the woods, accustomed to satisfy his thirst in the brook and his hunger on roots, to draw his food from the ground and take his rest in an overgrown cave, should blunder by some accident upon the walls of a vast and opulent city and, while he sits wearily at the entrance and turns his eyes eagerly in all directions and thrusts his gaze in to the city itself, actually seeing only the houses of the watchmen or some alley that lies close to the gate, should return to the woods and recount to his friends what he had beheld in that city, in its palaces and streets, its courts and public squares, in the shops of the artisans and the halls of the nobility, and the business that was being transacted in its public and private conferences. Or it is as

if one who has barely reached the threshold of some sacred temple should think that he knows in what secret recesses every vestment and holy vessel is kept concealed and understands all the forms of the books, the duties of the priests, and the whole sacred ceremonial.

3. In reality how do I differ from this shepherd, except that he has approached the city or the temple but once while I have paid frequent visits to solitude; he has stood on the outside while I have ventured within; he has departed promptly while I have lingered? And yet what greater certainty have I as to the inner nature of the life of solitude? Caves, hills, and groves lie equally open to everybody; no one blocks the way when you would enter or expels you after you have entered; the wilderness has neither porter nor watchman. But of what avail is it merely to go to a place or to be carried along winding streams? What advantage is there in strolling through woods and what delight in sitting upon mountains, if wherever I go my mind follows me, the same among the woods as in the city?

4. It is the mind that I must lay aside before all; it is the mind, I say, that I must leave at home, humbly imploring the Lord to make my heart pure within me and to establish an upright spirit in my body. Then at last shall I penetrate to the hidden recesses of the solitary life.

5. As for my present solitude—why should I boast of what I do not possess? It is not that solitary life for which I yearn, although outwardly it bears a near resemblance, being equally withdrawn from the human crowd but not equally emancipated from human passions.

6. Oh, could I but behold that ineffable sweetness which is felt by blessed souls at the remembrance of the struggles they have passed through and the prospect of the joys to come, whether by those who have triumphed over the enemy or by those who, while they have often got the upper hand, have not yet vanquished him completely. These are still called upon to stand in battle array but not without sure hope of triumph, and to fight, not alone, but aided by the company of angels. And when they have put on the armor of God, wearing, if I may imitate the language of the Apostle, "the breast-plate of righteousness," "the shield of faith," "the sword of the spirit," and "the helmet of salvation," they go forth repeatedly to wrestle "against principalities, against powers, against the rulers of the darkness of this world,"[1] with no mortal looking on, but before a great presence of heavenly spirits who favor them with their countenance while Christ

---

[1]   Eph 6:12–17.

himself presides over the combat. What a welcome peace to the exhausted mind is there in those sighs rising out of the depths of the soul to highest heaven! What secret relief in the tears gushing from the purest fountain of the heart! What watches and vigils of the soldiers of Christ on the towers of Jerusalem and the ramparts of Zion against the hosts of Babylon as they sing their psalms through the entire night and maintain the guard over their walled encampment, knowing that they are in a strong and well-fortified place where neither food nor drink is lacking, believing that while they may be assailed by the stratagems of the enemy, they cannot be overcome, and feeling themselves so exalted in grace that the fiercest onslaughts of the foe are a boon to them and a punishment to the assailants, as an action which is superfluous with regard to our safety may often be directed to the increase of our glory. And thus exercising itself, the army of Christ's champions, battling in the arena of this life, grows more wary, its victory becomes more impressive, its triumph more glorious.

§VII. The comfort and joy of hoping for the perpetual company of the angels as a reward for the brief withdrawal from men

7. What a comfort and delight it is to enjoy the present and yet look forward to a better state, in a place of a brief retirement from human society to partake of the perpetual companionship of the angels and the gaze of the divine countenance in which is the end of all holy longings and desires; instead of a few tears to have laughter without end, instead of earthly fasting eternal feasting, true and inestimable riches in lieu of self-imposed poverty, the freedom of the ethereal city in place of a forest habitation, the starry palaces of Christ in exchange for a smoky hut, the choiring of angels and the sweetness of celestial harmony in place of the silence of the woods, and, transcending all other melodies, to hear the voice of God as the faithful, trusted pledge of all these blessings when, after so many labors done, he calls his children to eternal rest! To reflect day after day upon what I have left and what I have gained, what I endure and what I look forward to, what I have sown and what I shall reap! To consider with what little waste of time—I should not say with waste but with what gain and escape from many irksome distractions, eternal felicity will soon be won, and that no sooner do we abandon the sickly appetites of men and the dangers of cities, in which exists that true hell of living men of which the Psalmist speaks, and hasten to our heavenly fatherland, than our happiness begins! Indeed, the end of unhappiness is the beginning of happiness, since the

nature of opposites demands that where one ceases the other should begin. Finally, there is the joy of having elevated thoughts, and conversing with comrades of the spirit, and beatific visions, and of often commanding the presence of Christ in intimate communion.

8. For he is always present, since he is always in all places. Is it not he of whom it is written, "If I ascend up into heaven, thou art there; if I make my bed in hell, behold, thou art there. If I take up the wings of morning and dwell in the uttermost parts of the sea—"?[2] He to whom it was easy to endow us with eyes and ears and understanding, surely finds it easier to see and hear and understand us. He sees us therefore and hears us even before we speak. For though Moses was silent, the Lord said to him, "Wherefore criest thou unto me?"[3]

9. He forestalls our wishes and anticipates the movements of our hearts. He knows our thoughts from afar, long before they are formed. He answers our prayers before they are uttered, and he beholds our needs before they appear. He sees the day of our death before we are born, but even though he finds us unworthy he regards us with pity, unless, which heaven forbid, we repel his mercy with headstrong contumacy.

§VIII. Having Christ for our faithful witness,
we need no imaginary witness

10. Having our Father therefore for witness and judge, we are not in need of that imaginary witness of whom I have written elsewhere and whom some philosophers have admonished us to seek. Epicurus, for example, who, though he stands in ill repute with some is nevertheless held in great esteem by others who are themselves estimable men, writing to a friend, bids him act in all things as though Epicurus were looking on. Cicero, in the letter which he addresses to his brother Quintus, after some impressive exhortations to virtue, ends as follows: "You will achieve this very easily if you think of me as being always with you and taking an interest in everything that you say and do, since it has always been your aim to please me more than all the rest of the world."[4] He must have had very great confidence in the advantage of his real presence to his brother when he could regard the mere recollection of it as having such an influence on the pursuit of virtue.

[2]   Vulgate, Ps 138:8–9 (KJV Ps. 139:8–9).
[3]   Exod 14:15.
[4]   *Quint. fratr.* 1.46.

11. In imitation of these examples Seneca admonishes his Lucilius to imagine the presence of some illustrious persons, not venturing to offer himself as a model. "There is no real doubt," he says, "that it is good for one to have appointed a guardian over oneself, and to have someone whom you may look up to, someone whom you may regard as a witness of your thoughts."[5] Shortly after he adds, "Act, in whatever you do, as you would act if anyone at all were looking on"; and a little further on, "Set as a guard over yourself the authority of some man, whether your choice be the great Cato, or Scipio, or Laelius—or any man in whose presence even abandoned wretches would check their bad impulses." That it may be clear that he is here preaching Epicurean doctrine, I shall cite a remark of Seneca's from another place to this effect. "'Cherish some man of high character, and keep him ever before your eyes, living as if he were watching you, and ordering all your actions as if he beheld them.' Such, my dear Lucilius, is the counsel of Epicurus; he has quite properly given us a guardian and an attendant."[6] Then, after inserting some examples in support of this advice, he adds, "Choose therefore a Cato; or, if Cato seems too severe a model, choose some Laelius, a gentler spirit. Choose a master whose life, conversation, and soul-expressing face have satisfied you."

12. You see that he names a number of persons and leaves us free to choose whom we like, provided our choice falls upon one whom we admire not for his family, his power, or his wealth, but for his virtue and conversation, for a face which is the witness of a noble spirit, and for words which move the mind to worthy deeds. While this advice of the philosophers about an imaginary witness of one's life is not without profit to people in their condition, it is not necessary for us. I have given it this place in the book that by what I have said it may become clear that a Christian does not need such a witness, that he does not have to imagine the presence of Epicurus or Cicero or Cato or Scipio or Laelius, since a good angel is provided for him as guardian and companion of his life, under whose gaze, if he has any sense of shame, he will not dare to do what he would not dare before a man. To say something even more impressive and awe-inspiring, Christ himself is present in all places and at all times, a faithful witness not only of our deeds but of all our thoughts as well, and thoughts could not be seen by Epicurus even if he were present in the flesh.

[5] *Ep.* 25.
[6] *Ep.* 2.

13. At this juncture I am inclined to arrest the current of my thought and reflect whether any person has ever been so close to the verge of madness and so abandoned in sin as not to put a tight rein upon his violent and careering lusts when he felt that he was in the presence—I will not say of Christ—only of some friend of Christ. And yet there is absolutely no Christian who doubts that Christ himself is always present in the most secret recesses of the soul, examines what goes on there and sees everything as though it were openly exposed, and who does not refrain from every unseemly act on account of the dread and veneration of such a witness.

14. What a delusion it is that, because we do not see with our eyes the presence which we acknowledge in our hearts, we should slip back into the error of which Cicero, who surely did not know Christ, arraigned the ancients when he said that they saw nothing with their minds but referred everything to their bodily eyes.[7]

15. And if we too fall into this case and look for counsel, we must give heed to the same Cicero, not because other authorities are lacking, even among writers of our own faith (seeing that Augustine composed his book *On the True Religion* chiefly from this point of view), but because there is an advantage in hearing what a stranger, if I may call him so, has to say on this subject, especially since in a single passage he both exposes the wound and applies the remedy. "It is in the power of a large intellect," Cicero says, "to free itself from the senses and draw our thoughts away from our prejudices."[8] Let us too, therefore, apply ourselves with all our strength, and having subjugated our senses and got the better of our habits, view things with the eyes of the soul. Let us open at last those inward eyes by which things invisible are beheld and clear away the mists that have obscured them, and we shall see that Christ is actually with us. If Cato was ashamed to die with a groan because one was by to see, how much greater shame shall we feel, if Christ looks on, to live badly and die badly, or to commit any base or dishonorable deed in so awful a presence?

16. But to bring the discussion back to the subject, Christ is in truth our infallible and perpetual witness, and though he is present everywhere he never deigns to grace us more fully with his presence, to listen and converse with us more intimately than in solitude. And no wonder, for there no one breaks in with his clamor and nothing distracts the mind from

[7]　*Tusculans* 1.16.
[8]　*Tusculans* 1.16.

its absorption, and so the human spirit accustoms itself to celestial contemplation, by continuous intercourse acquires confidence in its salvation, and from a guest and stranger becomes a member of God's household. For from great love and unremitting, faithful service there grows up an intimacy between God and man such as is not known between man and man.

17. Therefore, just as it is my faith that the restless men who are always entangled in worldly troubles and completely immersed in earthly affairs are already having a foretaste of their activities in the life immortal and of the labors of hell, so I believe it to be equally true that the solitary souls who are the friends of God and habituated to pious moods begin in this life to feel the delights of the life eternal. Nor should I say that it was beyond belief that any one of their number, to whom there clings no trace of the dust of this world, should be raised up with the assistance of the divine mercy to such a height that, though still confined to earth, he may hear the chorus of angels singing harmoniously in heaven and behold in an ecstasy of mind what he is unable to express when he comes back to himself.

6

Freedom of the Solitary Life

1. But what can I know or say about all these things, unhappy sinner that I am, dragging about with me the ball and chain of my iniquities? My love of a spot favorable to literary leisure springs no doubt from my love of books, or perhaps I seek to escape from the crowd because of an aversion arising from a discrepancy in our tastes, or it may even be that from a squeamishness of conscience I like to avoid a many-tongued witness of my life.

§IX. Of the freedom of the solitary man and the application of the mind

2. Therefore, let us pass over these considerations, although, beloved Jesus, we have been created by you to the end that we may find our peace in you; for this we were born and without it our life is unhappy and unavailing. How much value, my father, do you set upon these common things: to live according to your pleasure, to go where you will, to stay where you will; in the spring to repose amid purple beds of flowers, in the autumn amid heaps of fallen leaves; to cheat the winter by basking in the sun and the summer by taking refuge in cool shades, and to feel the force of neither unless it is your choice! To belong to yourself in all seasons and wherever you are to be ever with yourself, far from evil, far from examples of wickedness! Not to be driven along, not to be dashed aside, not to be tormented, not to be pressed, not to be dragged to a banquet when you prefer not to eat, or to be forced to speak when you would rather be silent, not to be held up at crossings with importunate greetings and handshaking, and with a crude and tasteless kind of urbanity to linger in torture for days at a time making obeisance to passers-by!

3. What fellow looks with gaping mouth upon you as though you were some monster? Who comes to a halt when he meets you? Who turns around and sticks at your heels, either whispering something hoarsely in the ear of his companion or questioning a passer-by concerning you? Who is there that offensively jostles you in a crowd or somewhat more offensively gives place to you? Who extends his hand to you or puts it to his head in recognition? Who sets himself to hold long talks with you in the narrow streets? Who signals to you silently with the eye but goes by with lips compressed?

4. Finally, think what it means not to grow old among objects of disgust, to squeeze and to be squeezed amid dancing throngs, to have your breath cut short or inflated with noxious mists, to sweat, though it is the middle of winter; not to unlearn humanity among men, and through satiety of feeling to hate things, hate people, hate business, hate whom you love, hate yourself; not to forget your own concerns that you may be free to serve the ungrateful many! Yet all this is without prejudice to the saying of the Apostle in his letter to the Romans, that "none of us lives to ourselves and none of us dies to ourselves, for whether we live, we live unto the Lord, or whether we die, we die unto the Lord."[1] And so you must live and die as if you lived and died unto the Lord and to no other.

5. To stand meanwhile as though on a high tower watching the troubled actions of men beneath your feet, to see all things in this world and yourself along with them passing away, not to feel old age as an affliction which has silently stolen upon you before you suspected that it was so close, as generally happens with busy men, but to expect it long in advance and be prepared for it with a sound body and a serene mind; to know that this life is but the shadow of life, that it is not home but an inn, not the fatherland but a road, not a chamber of rest but an arena; not to love fleeting things but to desire things that endure and to submit patiently to circumstances.

6. Always remember that you are a mortal but that you enjoy the promise of immortality. We have the privilege to travel back in memory and to range in imagination through all ages and all lands; to move about at will and converse with all the glorious men of the past and so to lose consciousness of those who work all evils in the present; sometimes to rise, with thoughts that are lifted above yourself, to the ethereal region, to meditate on what goes on there and by meditation to inflame your desire, and

---

[1]   Rom 14:7–8.

in turn to encourage and admonish yourself with a fervent spirit as though with the power of burning words—these are not the least important fruits of the solitary life, though those who are without experience of it do not appreciate it.

7. While I am speaking of these, however, let me not pass over in silence the more obvious pleasures: to devote oneself to reading and writing, alternately finding employment and relief in each, to read what those who have gone before have written and to write what later generations may wish to read, to pay to posterity the debt which we cannot pay to the dead for the gift of their writings, and yet not remain altogether ungrateful to the dead but to make their names more popular if they are little known, to restore them if they have been forgotten, to dig them out if they have been buried in the ruins of time, and to hand them down to our grandchildren as objects of veneration, to carry them in the heart and as something sweet in the mouth, and finally, by cherishing, remembering, and celebrating their fame in every way, to pay them the homage that is due to their genius even though it is not commensurate with their greatness.

§X. *How divine honors were awarded to the inventors of certain arts*

8. We hear that the inventors of certain arts after their death have been worshiped with honors of deity. This shows more of gratitude than of piety, for there is no piety in any act that offends God; but the ill-advised gratitude of mortals, not content with bestowing human honors to commemorate benefits to the human race, has committed the folly of sacrilege. The harp has made a god of Apollo, medicine has made gods of both Apollo and Asclepius, agriculture of Saturn, Bacchus, and Ceres, the forge of Vulcan. Egypt worships Osiris and the learned city of Athens worships Minerva because the former is reported to have discovered the use of flax, the latter that of oil as well as the art of weaving. It would be a long task to particularize, for there is no limit to this sort of vanity among the Ancients.

9. The greatest and most careful of their poets does not dare openly to condemn it, fearing perhaps the punishment that would be visited on him, but secretly he has not been afraid to mock it, and with no little refinement, since he has placed in the lower regions the souls of

"those who enriched human life by the arts they invented"[2]

---

[2] Virgil, *Aen.* 6.663.

and whose names the false multitude, the fountain of all errors, has raised to heaven in spite of the anger of the Lord of heaven. He recites specifically how the discoverer of healing himself was hurled down to the Stygian waters by the thunder of almighty God.[3]

10. But let this remain a question among the ancients; among us there is no talk of gods. And yet I can never cease marveling that men in all other respects so perfect should be so foolish in their superstitions, like very swift runners moving in the wrong direction and not seeing the good directly before their eyes. I marvel at their perversity, but I pity their blindness.

11. If in truth some honor is due to the discoverers of things of this sort—and I do not deny that great honor is due, provided it be human and reasonable—what glory shall be showered upon the inventors of literature and the noble arts, who have provided us not with a plow to make furrows, nor woven garments for our bodies, nor tinkling lyres for our ears, nor oil and wine for our gullets—though to be sure our ears and gullets take pleasure in the sounds and tastes—but have furnished us with nobler instruments wherewith to procure nourishment, raiment, instruction, and healing for the mind?

12. Moreover, I ask, where can this debt most effectively be paid? Who doubts that this pursuit of literature, by means of which we consecrate our own name or that of another, carving statues of illustrious men much more enduring than bronze or marble, can be carried on nowhere more successfully or more freely than in solitude? Here at least I speak from experience, for I know what spurs it supplies to the mind, what wings for the spirit, what leisure time for work—things which I know not where to seek save in solitude.

13. And if you do not take my word for it when I say that leisure or freedom, call it what you will, is the source of literature and the arts, you may trust Aristotle who in the first book of the *Metaphysics*, declaring the reason why the mathematical arts were so highly celebrated among the Egyptians, says that it was because of the leisure that was offered to the race of priests. Plato too has not omitted to note, speaking of these people in the *Timaeus*, that being entrusted with priestly functions they remain apart from the rest of the people in order to preserve their purity unpolluted from profane contact. One of our own priests, Cheremon the Stoic, a most eloquent writer, describing their mode of life as priests, says

[3]   Virgil, *Aen.* 7.770.

that they put aside all business and thoughts of the world and lived always in the temple, studying nature and its causes and making computations of the stars, that they never consorted with women, never saw their near kin or even their children after they had once entered upon the service of the divine cult, and regularly abstained from flesh and wine. He adds that they were accustomed severely to suppress and correct the bodily humors which might develop from idleness or inaction by not eating for two or three days, and he relates many other things about their food, drink, and sleep. By habits like these I can easily believe that they acquired a certain divine fertility of intellect.

7

Nature and Friendship in the Solitary Life

§I. Reasons why some people blame the solitary life

1. I am not unaware that I shall be violently attacked at this point by those who think solitude is unfavorable to literature and virtuous life. They maintain in the first place that in solitude the instructors are absent who are, as it were, the propagators of literature and, if I may use the expression, the nurses of tender minds, without whose continual help no striking talent was ever developed. But in saying this they assume that I am addressing myself to children instead of to those who have long dispensed with the schoolmaster's rod.

2. Still they insist earnestly and declare that even in learned men the mind is distracted by a view which stretches out in all directions and by too open a sky. No man of learning will deny that when some great work is in hand the energies must be reined in and collected as with a swift horse whom you are preparing for a great leap.

3. Quintilian is authority for this idea who, in the ninth book of his *Institutes of Oratory*, if I am not mistaken, agrees with me in saying that a private and secluded spot and the deepest silence are particularly suitable for writers and declares that no one disputes it. Immediately after he makes a remark which seems at variance with my opinion. "Yet," he says, "we are not therefore necessarily to listen to those who think that groves and woods are the most proper places for study, because the free and open sky, as they say, and the beauty of sequestered spots give elevation to the mind and a happy warmth to the imagination. To me, assuredly, such retirement seems rather conducive to pleasure than an incentive to literary exertion;

for the very objects that delight us must, of necessity, divert our attention from the work which we designed to pursue; for the mind cannot, in truth, attend effectually to many things at once, and in whatever direction it looks off, it must cease to contemplate what had been intended for its employment."[1] This is to all appearances spoken with sufficient clearness, and yet in order to make you understand how strongly he feels in the matter, he insists upon the point and repeats it. "The pleasantness, therefore, of the woods, the streams gliding past, the breezes sporting among the branches of the trees, the songs of birds, and the very freedom of the extended prospect, draw off our attention to them; so that all such gratification seems to me more adapted to relax the thoughts than to brace them."[2]

4. Here then a witness not to be despised comes in judgment against me, and as though he did not sufficiently trust his own authority, he brings forth in support of his opinion the practice of Demosthenes, a man not known to common fame but the unrivaled prince of Greek eloquence. "Demosthenes," he says, "acted more wisely, who secluded himself in a place where no voice could be heard, and no prospect contemplated, that his eyes might not oblige his mind to attend to anything else besides his business."[3]

5. O thou zealous devotee and worshiper of the woods, someone will remark, here is a man who thinks that woods and mountains, far from being helpful to the student, are a distinct hindrance to his activity. And what answer shall I make? Shall I deny either that Quintilian spoke correctly or that Demosthenes acted wisely? I should prefer, if I could not convert them to my side of the argument, to go over to theirs. To agree, indeed, would be safer than to dispute, for I could very easily turn aside the attack on the ground that they were both orators, though one was famous and the other supreme. It is quite true that there is no class of students to whom woods and all the things we are here talking about and solitude in general are less suitable (as I shall show more explicitly when I come to the examples), but I am not of a mind to avoid the issue. I am neither for flight nor for war; I look for concord.

6. And so, though I nowhere feel my mind working more happily than in the woods and mountains, though nowhere do great thoughts occur to me more readily—if indeed a great thought ever does occur to me—or words rise up so adequate to my ideas, I am nevertheless reluctant to set

---

[1] *Inst.* 10.3.22–23.
[2] *Inst.* 10.3.24.
[3] *Inst.* 10.3.25.

up what may be peculiar to myself as a truth for all and to condemn the practice of such great men as I have named, preferring rather to embrace both views and to demonstrate that neither is hostile to our purpose.

7. I do not require that students should write their books in the woods or mountains, but I permit them to withdraw their minds, after refreshing them with the sight of these, to some silent and concealed recess. Who is there, however partial he may be to cities, who does not recognize that such places can be found nowhere more conveniently than in solitude? I make no objection to those who command that a writer shall choose a dark and silent place, only let not him who works by the light of the lamp despise the advice given to those who work by daylight. In this particular both you and I, my learned father, have tested the profitable advice of Quintilian, and I shall communicate it to the reader. In praising this habit of Demosthenes, he closes by saying, "As for those who study by lamplight, therefore, let the silence of the night, the closed chamber, and a single light keep them as it were wholly in seclusion."[4] You will admit that none of these things, as I look at the matter, are at variance with the state of solitude, that they all, in fact, promote it.

§II. *Woods, fields, and streams are of great advantage to the solitary*

8. If therefore among such great authorities I too may be heard and new counsel is not despised, I shall both follow them and, going further, if the choice of situation is free, shall offer some original advice to such as circumscribe themselves within the example of Demosthenes. Let provision first be made that, after the prosperous conclusion of his mental toil, one may be enabled to put off the burden of his weariness by having easy access to woods and fields and, what is especially grateful to the Muses, to the bank of a murmuring stream, and at the same time to sow the seeds of new projects in the field of his genius, and in the very interval of rest and recuperation prepare matter for the labor to come. It is an employment at once profitable and pleasant, an active rest and a restful work, so that when he returns to that narrow and secret chamber favored by Demosthenes, he may eliminate all that is superfluous and give the desired perfection of expression to the germinating thought. In this way not a moment of time will pass with any waste or loss to the student.

---

[4]   *Inst.* 10.3.25.

9. This should apply particularly to those who compose oratorical discourses or histories, for I deem that those who ponder philosophy, and even more those who brood on poetry, whose minds are given to refined and subtle thought rather than to collecting many facts, must be left to their own devices. Let these follow the impulse of their genius, in the assurance that their minds will respond, no matter where place and time invite them, wherever they feel themselves strongly incited by the goad of their inspiration, whether it be under the open sky or the roof of a locked house, within the shelter of a solid rock or beneath the shade of a spreading pine. They have no need of turning over many books, for they can read in memory the books they have read before and often even compose in their minds what they have omitted to read, but they raise themselves aloft on the wings of their genius.

10. They need to be carried away with more than human rapture if they would speak with more than human power. This, I have observed, is without doubt achieved most effectively and happily in free and open places. Wherefore I have often looked upon a mountain song as if it were a frolicking goat, the most joyful and vigorous of the whole flock, and being reminded of its origin by its native grace, I have said to myself, "You, who have tasted the grass of the Alps, come from above."

11. But to make an end to this point at last, both Cicero and Virgil, the uncontested princes of Latin eloquence, adhered to this practice. The former on many occasions, but especially when he came to compose his treatise on the Civil Laws, sought out leafy oaks and delicious retreats for his labor, and I remember that he makes mention there of a shady bank and lofty poplars, and the caroling of birds,[5] and the rippling of waters,[6] and a little island very like this one of mine in the middle of a stream which it cuts in half.[7] And Virgil when about to celebrate in a pastoral poem his Alexis, whoever he may be, did it walking continually,

> Where, piles of shadows, thick the beeches rose,[8]

alone among the mountains and the woods. Both imitated Plato who carried on the discussion about his *Republic* and *Laws* amidst calm cypress

---

[5]   *Leg.* 1.15.
[6]   *Leg.* 1.21.
[7]   *Leg.* 2.6.
[8]   *Ecl.* 2, 3 (Caverley's translation).

groves and sylvan spaces. But I report matters that are doubtless of familiar knowledge.

12. Cyprian, a good deal after these men in time but before them in faith, illustrious for his martyrdom and not undistinguished for literary skill, seems to have thought and written the same thing. There is one passage from his many writings which his great admirer Augustine cited as evidence of his intellect and an example of his style, wishing to make it clear to us by this citation to what a height his eloquence might have reached if he had not been wholly concerned with the weight of his matter and neglected the ornaments of expression. Speaking in this passage of the employment of the mind, he does not ask for a chamber in a secret spot, girt about with walls, secured with locks, darkened and concealed by a marble vault, or any such thing, but "Come," he says, "let us seek this abode. The adjoining solitude provides us with a retreat, where the vines straying and drooping in pendulous coils, as they crawl over the supporting reeds, form a portico with their shoots and a house of leaves."[9] See what sort of porch and what sort of abode this holy and eloquent man asked for—vines and branches and leaves and reeds, and amidst all these the privacy ever dear to the studious. Surely he would not have desired this if he believed that the mind was happy in no retreat outside of walls and a roof. I might seek for the same evidence in other writers and establish my point with the testimony of many more, if I were not afraid of its being said that the smallness of my faith was proved by the number of my authorities and that I took more trouble than was need.

13. Thus far I have set forth my opinion with the idea that none who read it, if indeed there be any so rich in leisure as to read the product of my leisure, should think that I have been establishing a rule for their minds. Let them rather examine the truth of the matter in detail and not feel bound to take me or anyone else on faith but only trust the evidence of their own experience.

§III. The interpretation of the words of Seneca in which he seems to impugn solitude

14. But it seems now that those who believe solitude to be unfavorable to the virtues have Annaeus Seneca among others for their warrant, who in a certain passage of his Epistles says that "solitude prompts us to all

---

[9]   *Doctr. chr.* 5.14 (quoting Cyprian, *Ep.* 1, ad Donatum).

kinds of evil,"[10] and again that in solitude all wicked plots are fomented, all dishonest passions marshaled, insolence inflamed, lust excited, and violence provoked.[11]

15. If these things were spoken generally and at large, there would be no recourse but either to oppose Seneca or desert the cause of solitude. But this is not the situation, for it is clearer than daylight from Seneca's own words that he speaks only of those who are stupid and a prey to their passions. "When persons are in mourning," he says, "or fearful about something, we are accustomed to watch them that we may prevent them from making a wrong use of their loneliness."[12] You perceive that solitude is forbidden to such a one, but pay heed to the reason: it is probably because of melancholy and sickly fear, the most consuming of mental passions. Developing this point more at length, he says, "No thoughtless person ought to be left alone." Who does not see how entirely true this is? For as soon as a man who is not master of his will is left to himself, he is bound to come to grief.

16. But for such people I judge that it is not merely solitude that is dangerous; the city too is not a wholesome place for them, though in one way it is more wholesome. For the city, while it contains the agents of crime, also has its prosecutors and avengers, but solitude by the hope it offers of concealment and impunity banishes the fear of law and regard for honor. Solitude affords the privilege of shameless sinning while the city supplies the elements that promote crime, and therefore both are alike mischievous. But that is the perversity of nature and not the fault of solitude.

17. You may convince yourself that this is unquestionably true and that Seneca also was of this opinion. That very solitude which he forbids to the melancholy and morbid and witless, he not only in the same letter permits to Lucilius, he even recommends and enjoins it. "Yes," he says, "I do not change my opinion. Avoid the many, avoid the few, avoid even the individual. I know of no one with whom I should be willing to have you shared. And see what an opinion of you I have; for I dare to trust you with your own self."[13] An austere precept, if I mistake not, and a rigid one. "Avoid the many," he says: I assent to it willingly. "Avoid the few": I can bear it without distress. "Avoid even the individual": you can drive me no further; you

10   *Ep.* 25.
11   *Ep.* 10.
12   *Ep.* 10.
13   *Ep.* 10.

have hemmed me in within the narrowest confines of solitude. What now remains except that I should avoid myself? Yes, but then I should still be avoiding the individual. "There is no one with whom I should be willing to have you shared." Strange! But there is at least one with whom I would have you, my father, share yourself; perhaps there are several, but one there surely is.

18. If I were to give such counsel to a friend, the enemies of solitude and virtue would exclaim on all sides and call me stony and inhuman, but here is a great man like Seneca enjoining his very dearest friend to avoid even the individual, and he speaks to a man who has attained moral perfection. The last statement, however, I should with your good leave contradict no matter who made it. Seneca himself, if sworn in as a witness, will admit that Lucilius was one of those who were making progress in virtue rather than one who had fully attained it. For though he often praises him, as is the manner of those who love, yet he would not exhort him so continually nor rebuke him on occasion if he thought he was perfect. If it is only affirmed that his advice is for one devoted at least to the study and practice of virtue, I agree. But let me return to my purpose, for I speak only to those who eagerly pursue learning and virtue. For the rest I have no wholesome counsel, unless it be that first of all they change their manner of life; after that we shall see about the proper environment for them.

§IV. Those to whom solitude is advantageous should not be persuaded to despise the laws of friendship; they should fly from crowds and not from friends

19. Besides, I never persuaded those for whom I said solitude was advantageous that, in their desire for solitude, they should despise the laws of friendship. I bade them fly from crowds and not from friends. And if anyone thinks that he possesses crowds of friends, let him first see to it that he is not deluded. Some sudden need or change of fortune is well calculated to reveal the truth, and while this is not to be wished out of a mere craving for experience, yet if it so befalls, it contributes much to our enlightenment and the dissipation of our illusions. Moreover, if in his friendships as in other things one man should be richer than another, I should not be disturbed, nor should I admonish the solitary man so much to shun his friends as to wish that they should come to visit him singly and not in throngs, bringing comfort and encouragement to his leisure rather than annoyance.

20. Let his leisure be modest and gentle, not rude; let his solitude be tranquil, not savage; in short, let it be solitude and not barbarism. Whoever invades him in this retreat should have occasion to marvel that humanity, which is exiled from the cities, inhabits the wilderness and that while he has found bears and lions in populous places, in solitude he has discovered angelic man. Such is my feeling in the matter, and this I hold to be the middle of the road between the two extremes.

21. The man at one extreme is not happy unless he is in a crowd: he is deserving of pity rather than correction. The other says, "Avoid even the individual." To him I know not what reply to make. I confess, Seneca, you have me there and weigh me down with your authority. And perhaps I should be inclined to submit if it were not for the opposition of one who is not inferior to you—I think you will not be angry if I say greater than you. Cicero, discussing the conditions of friendship, does not address only those for whom friendship is the most agreeable thing in life after virtue. Even persons of a fierce and brutal nature, he says, and those who shun the company and assemblies of men, of whom he discovers hardly one example in the whole world, cannot endure existence if they do not find—he does not say a friend, for their character is in the way—but someone upon whom they may discharge the venom of their bitterness.

22. Taking this observation as his point of departure he cites the saying of Archytas of Tarentum that no one can be happy on earth, no matter how great his prosperity, nor even in heaven with the view of the stars spread out before him and the knowledge of the universe, unless he has someone with whom he may share these blessings. So averse is nature from complete solitariness![14]

23. In a still more famous passage he says, "If all that is essential to our wants and comforts were supplied by some magic wand as in the stories, then every man of first-rate ability could drop all other responsibilities and devote himself exclusively to learning and study." Then, to show that it was ironically spoken, he says openly, "Not at all, for he would seek to escape from his loneliness."[15] See how in a few words he seems to condemn all that we have said of solitude; and he would have done so effectively if he had not gone farther. It is not our concern so much to explain the saying of Cicero as to reject from the examination this evidence of an orator's

[14] *Amic.* 23.
[15] *Off.* 1.44 (Walter Miller's translation)

prejudice as suspicious, although it occurs in his philosophical writings. For if you note what he adds, it will appear quite clearly that he is speaking only of the extreme and inhuman kind of solitude (and if one seeks escape from this one is surely not escaping from the society of a chosen friend) and not passing judgment on my view but on another, and that in escaping from solitude he does not mean to rush into a crowd but only fears that in the pursuit of solitude one might flee humanity. For when he says, "He would seek escape from loneliness," he does not say from associates too, but he does say that he would seek a companion in his studies and would wish to teach and listen and learn.

24. Since solitude, though it is furnished with such great advantages, without someone to share it seems unendurable even to savage minds and such as hate human intercourse, what must it seem to the gentle and refined? And if the conversation of a single companion is supposed to afford such great comfort to persons incapable of friendship, what must be the pleasure for its true followers, engaged with a faithful friend in whom they see their own image reflected, from whose lips they hear truth spoken, in whose presence, according to Cicero, "they dare to talk of all things as though they were talking with themselves,"[16] of whom they harbor no suspicion, in whose heart there is no deception, for whose sake every toil is sweet, without whose company no repose is soothing, from whom comes our defense against adversity and the crowning joy of our prosperity! I should be austere indeed if I thought that a friend like this was to be excluded from our solitude. It will never be my view that solitude is disturbed by the presence of a friend, but that it is enriched. If I had the choice of doing without one or the other, I should prefer to be deprived of solitude rather than of my friend.

25. And so in embracing solitude I do not reject friendship, and I do not fly from any individual unless haply he be of the sort whose character I should shun in cities also, if I gave heed to the dictates of a serene life. The whole matter then comes to this, that I would share my solitude like everything else with my friends, believing that Seneca spoke with true humanity when he said that "no good thing is pleasant to possess without friends to share it,"[17] and being assured that solitude is a great and sweet possession.

---

[16]   *Amic.* 6.
[17]   *Ep.* 6.

26. But I should hold at arm's length from it not merely the wicked, but the idle and ignorant as well. Abominable is the retirement of Tiberius by which he stained with everlasting disgrace the innocent isle of Capri where, savage and wicked old man that he was, he established a brothel for his cruelty and licentiousness. Ridiculous is the solitude of Servilius Vatia who grew old in obscurity not far from that island on the Neapolitan shore near Cumae in Campania famous for his wasted opportunity, buried rather than living within the walls of his country house. I suppose there are a great many people like Servilius everywhere, but he occurs first to the mind because a noble writer[18] has made him known by his mockery and delivered him over to us that we may be free from the necessity of inflicting upon our contemporaries the injury of a truthful exposure and the annoyance of serving as an awful example.

27. You now understand to whom I apply all that has been said or is to be said on the subject of solitude. It is not given to all men to excel by holiness of life or by literary achievement, or by noble use of leisure to earn the love and acknowledgment of posterity, hence it is neither present glory nor hope of future fame (for which many have willingly poured out their lives) that spurs on the others, and for that very reason they are held illustrious. How much does it mean to you—if I may return at last to the subject—that this minute portion of time belongs to you, which, as soon as it has run by, there remains no hope of ever recalling or replacing? Besides, no man, though he be but moderately learned, is prevented from acquiring by reading and meditation a mind that lives on calm thoughts and is liberated from the chains of circumstance, submissive to God and reason but free in every other way, and a body also released from its heavy yoke, serving the mind alone. And if sometimes he should rebel in his insolence, he will before long return to his allegiance, and being saved from a thousand toils, a thousand dangers, a thousand tricks of fortune, he will be able to go about at will, to sit, to stand, to speak, to be silent, to think, and not be subject to disturbance from those busy, agitated fellows who are not content with their own unhappiness unless they can add the unhappiness of others to the general sum.

---

[18]   Seneca, *Ep.* 55.

8

Joy of the Solitary Life

§V. Of the singular joy of the solitary in their freedom from earthly cares

1. What shall I say of the pleasure of the past which comes as though at our back? There is that well-known expression of Virgil,

> This too with joy will be remembered.[1]

and the less familiar one of the same poet,

> Glad to have 'scaped so many Argive towns
> And through the midst of foes our flight pursued.[2]

These two expressions differ in the language, but they are both spoken by Aeneas with a single idea in view. You observe that while he is still in the midst of his trials he uses a verb in the future tense, but when he has once passed through them, he uses the present; whereas he first said *iuvabit meminisse*, he afterward writes *iuvat evasisse*.

2. For it is sometimes sweet to recall what was in experience bitter, and dangers when they have receded into the distance have a power to soften the mind. For prosperity too has its dangers, which are neither fewer nor less serious and certainly more treacherous than those of adversity. The anxious father in Virgil says:

> What fears had I lest Libya's realm should prove thy bane.[3]

---

[1]   *Aen.* 1.203 (James Rhoades's translation).
[2]   *Aen.* 3.282–83.
[3]   *Aen.* 6.694.

3. How great therefore is the joy and the sense of safety in the solitude of one who has passed through everything that was to be dreaded and counts all evils behind him. How pleasant it is to feel that one has escaped calamity unhurt and has held to the right turn at the crossroads when death lay in wait at the left, especially as the balance was inclined on the other side. For it is a natural effect that where the danger recollected was greater and more imminent, the joy at having escaped from it is the greater. The truth of this can be judged with particular force after a critical illness, a terrible shipwreck, a harsh imprisonment, or dreadful wars; and that is why you may often hear those who have been restored to health or have gained the harbor or escaped unexpectedly from their chains or returned victors from the battle recounting joyfully the stories of their dangers. But how sweetly the mind returns to worldly blandishments that have been rejected, to earthly honors despised, to riches well distributed, to pleasures scorned, to menaces evaded, to misfortune high-mindedly overcome, or to whatever had power to betray and did not betray. And the pleasure in these reflections is all the greater when you have so fairly escaped that there remains no fear of danger to come.

Boredom and Vulgarity of City Life

*§I. Of the boredom and dullness suffered by busy
men and those who dwell in cities*

1. I may seem to be referring to very trifling things—yet is it a small matter
to escape that daily boredom from which the dweller in the cities is hardly
ever free and which is the result not only of what man does to man but
what the sick mind at strife with itself inflicts upon itself?

2. Everywhere in the squares of cities crowds of fools may be encountered in whose mouths no words occur more often than the familiar ones
of the grammarian's formula, *piget, taedet, paenitet*—I am troubled, I am
weary, I am sorry—or the phrase from Terence, "I don't know what to
do."[1] I believe them in every particular, especially the last, for if they knew
what to do, all their complaints would be immediately hushed. Of what is
it that you are weary, I ask you, if not of your very ignorance and folly? It
is Seneca's saying that "folly is ever troubled with weariness of itself."[2] They
do not find life agreeable, and not without ground, for they have no fixed
purpose, no firmness, no unshakable determination. Seneca adds in the
same connection, "Only the wise man is pleased with his own."[3] They do
not know what to do, and not knowing that they do not know, they make
no effort to know. The result is that they do not know to what end they
are alive. How then should they love life when they do not know what it
is good for?

---

[1]   *Eunuchus* 1.1.28.
[2]   *Ep.* 9.
[3]   *Ep.* 9.

3. They generally live as if they thought they were born for no other purpose than to serve their gullet or belly, unhappy servants indeed to be subjected to such base masters. Lest there be any doubt that I have described their condition correctly, I will mention what is a frequent subject of discussion among them. If nature by some kind indulgence granted life to man without dependence on sleep or carnal desire, or food, or drink, and if without any of these things a man enjoyed rest and offspring and a temperate and steady satisfaction of his desires, would such a life, they ask, be more desirable than this of ours which is constantly exposed and enslaved to so many wants? And whenever by some chance I have been present at their disputations, a silent listener to the end, I seldom have heard one among them who did not audaciously maintain that our present state of misery was to be preferred to the other state of blessedness.

4. Exulting in their own madness, they are in the habit of saying, "If you take away sleep and carnal pleasure and food and drink, what are we going to do? And what will life be when it is stripped of life's gifts and employments?" So completely do they expose their natures and acknowledge without the least sense of shame that they live only for those things which we have in common with brute beasts, as if that lost time, in which we share this brief space of life with sleep and pleasure, could not be spent in better thoughts, in the contemplation of God, or the study of nature, or the practice of virtue. To rouse your indignation still more strongly and to dispel every hope of their wholesome reformation, I call God and my memory to witness that I have heard these things more often from the lips of old men than of young.

§II. Of the error of some busy old men and dwellers in cities

5. Such is the gravity and ripeness of our old men that they think it a misfortune to be torn from their lusts, though death stands before them ready to snatch their miserable souls from the decaying and ruinous habitation of its members. The name of pleasure beloved by youth is still so dear to them in old age that even when pleasure is exhausted, they neglect to regard the outcome of pleasure, and they do not care to reach the object of their desire except by a foul and muddy path—unhappy and mistaken wayfarers who hate the destination and love the road even when they are approaching their journey's end. If any of them should appear later to make confession of these things, you will hear him wavering and arguing

in such a way as to make it quite clear that he is withdrawn from the false path only by a sense of shame and is not embracing the truth in response to his reason.

6. Writing of these men in his book *Of the True Religion*, Augustine says, "Those to whom the health of their body is of small account would rather feed than be free from hunger, and rather indulge their passion than not feel its excitement; there are even found those who prefer sleeping to not sleeping. And yet the object of all these pleasures is to secure freedom from hunger and thirst and fleshly desire and bodily fatigue."[4] A little later he adds, "Those who wish to be thirsty and hungry, and to burn with passion, and to feel exhaustion in order that they may eat and drink and copulate and sleep with greater satisfaction"—he does not say of such men that they are in love with wretchedness and sorrow, for no one is so indifferent to his welfare as to like the names of wretchedness and sorrow, but he does say of them that they "are in love with poverty which is the beginning of the greatest sorrows."[5]

7. For it is clear that as the effects are generally inherent in the causes, so the love of the effects is implied in the love of the causes, and therefore Augustine concludes terribly, "What they love shall be fulfilled in them, so that their portion shall be wailing and gnashing of teeth."[6] You see how he deduces the effect from the cause: because they loved poverty, they shall gain sorrow. He says many things besides in his divine style on this subject, but the point is obvious by acknowledgment of the general voice.

8. And so, as he says, we are able to declare that many may be found who prefer this form of life, and some few who would like another kind but who, when they try to lift up their eyes a little higher, are unable to do so because they are blinded by the general dust and smoke, and when they would offer their ear to those who summon them to better things the din and tumult of popular errors hinders their purpose.

9. And so the greater number, whether of their voluntary accord or constrained by bestial habit, with abject bearing cringing to their body but careless of their soul, without the charm of virtue, without any knowledge of it, drag along their spirit in ignominy and distress, and though their better nature at times pricks them and reminds them of its claims, yet the obstacles which I have mentioned remain in the way.

---

4   *Ver. Rel.* 53.
5   *Ver. Rel.* 54.
6   *Ver. Rel.* 54.

10. Hence the hatred of life, hence the beginning of weariness, hence that restlessness of mind than which man can suffer nothing worse while he is alive. What wonder is it then if they waver in their actions and designs, if they find no pleasure in whatever they undertake? For they cannot gain what they desire if they desire nothing with conviction. To have a single aim sure and steadfast is the mark of a wise man; inconstancy of purpose is the most certain proof of folly. I shall never tire of citing Seneca to you. To one who asked him what port he should seek, he replied that no wind would favor him.[7]

11. Such men keep constantly going and returning, and they do both with loathing. You have seen sometimes how they hastily remove from a place, how they issue forth in flocks, how they suddenly scatter. When one wants to go here, another wants to go there. How indeed shall so many agree with one another when each one is so much in conflict with himself? I like to linger on this point. The man whom you have seen a moment ago you no longer recognize, and in a little while you will have to be told who the person is whom at this moment you know well. Now they are happy, now sad; now downcast, now elated; now oppressed with care and inert, now aflutter with childlike frivolity. The play of evenly matched instincts, the thoughtless gathering of wrath and its appeasement, the hourly mutation of feeling which Horace attributes to children[8] is in reality the peculiar quality of old men. Their instability is the more pernicious insofar as it is under less compulsion, rejects advisers, shields itself with authority, and works mischief by its example.

12. For though a man's nature may have enough vices of its own, most evils arise from a spirit of emulation and a hankering to imitate. And what imitator has ever been content with limiting himself to the error of his guide? We are anxious to excel and be conspicuous and to leave in our rear those whom at the start we followed.

13. I admit that Quintilian advised students of eloquence that they should enter into equal competition with their models rather than follow tamely in their wake, on the ground that by this attitude, even if we do not succeed in getting ahead of a rival, we may at least be able to come abreast of him. For no one who thinks he has to follow in another's footsteps can ever catch up with him, since he who follows must needs always remain

---

[7]   *Ep.* 71.
[8]   *Ep.* 2.1.99–100

behind. Besides, he says, it is generally easier to do more than to do precisely the same.[9] He advances further proofs in this argument which, while they are very admirable in their place, it would be a waste of time to reproduce here. Anyway, what is advantageously taught in the art of oratory, the art, that is, of speaking with propriety and elegance, has in our time been mischievously applied to the art of wicked and disgraceful living. We have carried out the instructions of Quintilian, we have emulated, we have rivaled, we have excelled. From followers we have become leaders; doubtless we shall be overtaken by those who come after us. The same idea may be put in different ways: whether proposed to us for an example or object of emulation, we have in either case obeyed you, Quintilian, but in a different sense than you intended. You recommend clearness of language for our imitation, but we imitate dismal actions, and our fervent efforts are all applied to this single study.

14. Would that all imitators of good, if there are such, rivaled their leaders in as short a time as the imitators of evil overtake theirs. As far as we are concerned, the advice given for excellence in oratory has been applied by us with the worst kind of addition to the vices of conduct, and the examples of errors left to us by our fathers we are with great zeal transmitting to posterity; and then we wonder at the accumulated heap of madness, to which something is added by each generation and from which nothing is ever withdrawn. I rather wonder that anything is yet lacking to complete the sum of insanity when so many minds are concentrated on a single object with such earnest emulation of their masters.

§III. Of the luxurious imitation of the vulgar and the changing fashions of those who live in cities

15. And though the imitation of actions and of life is more dangerous where important matters are concerned, yet the madness shows itself flagrantly even in small things. Whence now come those strange and absurd fashions of costume and carriage changing from one day to the next? A garment which one day reaches to the ground and the next exposes more than is decent, sleeves which now sweep the earth and now are too tight at the elbow, a belt which oppresses the breasts or flows loosely beneath the body? Whence the variety in musical melodies which, according to Plato, was fraught with so much danger to the state? Whence, finally, comes the

---

[9]   *Inst.* 10.2.9–10.

frequent transformation in literary style and even in everyday speech? It is nothing more or less than imitation, reckless and persistent, and not content with any limits that may be imposed on it, that has brought in these distasteful and disagreeable caprices, and having brought them in continues to nourish and foster them.

16. How indeed can men be expected to maintain a consistent course of life when they do not submit to be ruled by virtue, or reason, or the advice of their friends, but allow themselves to be whirled about by the madness of strangers and the wild caprices of fools? In short, those who so put off their own nature and discard the manners of their fathers and worship only what is foreign and far-fetched must needs be changing every time that something arrests their wandering gaze. There is no limit to their changes because there is no principle in imitation. They like everything that is foreign and dislike everything that is native. They would rather be anything but what they are. In this feeling they would be justified if it arose from a serious consideration of their condition instead of mere volatility.

17. There is a certain Aruntius in Seneca who is laughed at as an imitator of Sallust.[10] But among us every town has its Aruntius, nay, many Aruntii, who ape not only the language of other men but their behavior as well. No one is of a clear mind as to his costume, his speech, his thought—in short, as to what sort of man he would like to be, and therefore every man is unlike himself. Youth, walking with too great docility in the footsteps of abandoned old men, has with great spirit arrived at the very apex of folly; the second generation easily surpasses the first, the third the second, and so on indefinitely. It is difficult for the mind to conceive how great will be the madness, thus augmented in transmission, when it reaches our descendants, although it may be that it has reached its limit and fulfilment in us, as many ages ago it was said,

> Vice is at stand and at the highest flow,[11]
> so that it was impossible to carry things further without ruin.

18. Perhaps some will think that I have harped on this point with more insistence than is needed. But if they knew the first and greatest of my griefs, springing from my pity for humankind and especially for Italy, from which once the patterns of the virtues were diffused and which

---

[10]   *Ep.* 114.
[11]   Juvenal, *Sat.* 1.1.149 (Dryden's translation).

now, alas, I behold corrupted by the imitation of outlandish practices, and overflowing with extravagances where once it teemed with the spoils of conquered peoples, perhaps they would only wonder that my sorrow was compressed in so brief an outcry. For I know not who would endure it in silence. Whence arises this unworthy and disgraceful aversion for our own manners, whence is born the more disgraceful admiration and the more unworthy reverence for foreign practices?

19. This was not the way of our forefathers, whose descendants I wish we deserved to be called. They could and did take satisfaction in what was their own. They did not explore the valley of the Rhine or the branches of the Danube to get possession of silly toys with which to degrade Roman decency to foul barbarism, but they marched abroad with the ambition of expanding their empire and gaining glory, with armed hosts and flying banners, meaning to bring back not some ugly substitute for their native costume but triumphs and renowned names.

20. And yet they were not so much infatuated with their own as to despise indiscriminately all that was foreign. They respected all things according to their true worth equally among enemies and friends, among strangers and neighbors. Wherever there was virtue, wherever there was distinction of manners, wherever there were arts of war and peace, wherever the accomplishments of language and intellect were more elegant, or doctrine more highly developed, they eagerly conveyed it as a possession to their home, thinking none of their spoils more sumptuous. Nor was their judgment mistaken, for no riches are more secure than those that are treasured in the mind. But wherever there was anything disreputable, it was their concern to chastise or shun it.

21. Our glorious posterity, however, thinks it has accomplished something notable if some young fellow or, what turns my stomach even more, some old fop puts on the vile mantle of some unknown visitor or the ridiculous garb of a hireling soldier, or returns home from some journey with a coat cut short above the breeches, as though he were disfigured for some notable jest and submitted to suffer of his own free choice what David inflicted as a severe punishment upon his servants. If the grandfather of this harebrained mimic should come to life, he would stare in amazement and pity upon his grandson.

22. I do not know why I look upon these things so mournfully, as though the dishonor or the glory affected me personally. Ever since I began to take note of them, I admit, my mind has been strangely worried

and I have been waiting to see what would be the limit of these revolutions and where the thing would stop.

23. I am living in this generation, yet I would rather have been born in any other, though no age was ever lacking in causes of complaint. And though time, which in such things is not, as Aristotle says, a good discoverer and collaborator[12] but a mischievous one, has already made stale the monstrosities, it has not yet been able by its slow processes to give definite shape to wholesome manners. For it is certain that our first ancestors, as we have all heard, dealt in virtue and glory, which are laid up for them in the everlasting memory of men, while we, as anyone may see, traffic in undying infamy and empty bubbles.

24. Of this I have complained often, I remember, both in speech and writing, but in vain. Still the wrath of God hovers over us and his just vengeance pursues us. Like an earthly master the Almighty takes vengeance when he is offended; the former visits punishment on his graceless servants, the latter upon the proud rulers of the earth.

25. I long to cry out, "Whither do ye tend, unhappy mortals, where is your utter frenzy driving you? Pause in your career, stop, and look where you are rushing. You have forsaken the footsteps of your fathers and are walking in the ways of the enemy. You are overcome by the errors of those whom you have conquered in the field. Return to the customs of your fathers and abandon those of strangers, that you may live not only more honestly but more happily, and learn sometimes to have one wish for which you are not indebted to anybody's whim but to your own natural reason." This is what I should like to say and whatever else anger and grief might dictate in the present conditions, if I did not think that the minds of men had become sensible and matters were in a hopeless plight.

§IV. The reasons for some of the errors and waste of time of dwellers in the city

26. We who were wont to show the right road to others, now like blind men led by the blind—a token of impending ruin—we are being rushed along dangerous ways, revolving in the orbit of strange examples, not knowing what we desire. For it is ignorance of our aim that produces all this evil, whether it is peculiar to ourselves or common to all people. The misguided know not what they do, therefore whatever they do turns to

---

[12] *Eth. nic.* 1098A7.

disgust as soon as they have begun it. For they do not do what demands doing but look for things to do and go hunting in the densest thickets for occasions of perplexity and trouble. Hence discussions without end, hence strife in the middle of the street, beginnings rejected before they mature, and nothing fully accomplished.

27. They look for devices with which to cheat the day, and, as though the sun did not hasten sufficiently to its setting, they assist its speed with their ingenuity. And how common is the expression of such people: "Let us chase away this day, let us do something to make the day pass." The day ought to be slowed and not urged on in its course. For them, however, the day is too long and the night still longer, and life itself distastefully long. Not only do they pray for summer in winter and for winter in summer, but in the morning they pray for the evening and in the night for the morning, although they will make little account of either when it comes.

28. In them is literally fulfilled what is written in Scripture: "As a servant earnestly desireth the shadow, and as an hireling looketh for the reward of his work: so am I made to possess months of vanity, and wearisome nights are appointed to me. When I lie down, I say, 'When shall I arise, and the night be gone?' And I am full of tossings to and fro, unto the dawning of the day."[13] What Job uttered in his poverty and affliction, our rich men say in the midst of health and prosperity. They complain and are filled with troubles in anticipation. Constantly at strife with the nature of things, they scold the hours for their slowness and spur the dull minutes to headlong flight, though what is needed is not spurs but a curb—if only whirling time would submit to be curbed in any way.

29. But these people, it seems, one moment desire death, the imminence of which they fear above all things, and again they ask for life while they are wishing that it may pass. With such eagerness do they urge on the flight of time as must surely be the cause of death to many of them who, always worrying over the future and bitterly hating the present, are provoked to summon death through weariness of living.

*§V. How the pleasantness of the solitary life preserves
one from these ills and tedium*

30. But you may ask, "Why all these words on this single point of our discussion?" In truth, the pleasantness of the solitary life preserves one from

[13]   Job 7:2–4.

these evils and from this kind of irksomeness. It gladly makes use of present occasions and awaits the future calmly. It does not brood in suspense on tomorrow and puts off nothing to the next day that can or should be done today.

31. And this is reasonable. For what is more foolish than, with a yearning for the future, to hope and crave what is another's or is subject to a thousand chances, and neglect the present which is the one thing safely in your possession? He who waits in suspense for the morrow will never cease from his suspense. For no day except the last will be without a morrow, and every day except the first has been the morrow of some other day. This is the evil of our life—and it hardly has a greater affliction—to be losing life in the hope of living, and like a dog in pursuit of a hare swifter than himself, ever to be catching at empty air with our jaws and not once seizing the game which we pursue. For as soon as ever the morrow comes it ceases to be the morrow, and behold either another morrow is in prospect, or the day has marched stealthily by, and though there be another day, yet it too is a morrow. That is the day we chase after, the day which is always near our grasp yet always ahead of us and baffling us with its proximity, and when we have gotten close to it, it unexpectedly slips from our hold. Snatched from our jaws over and over again and flying steadily before us, it incites us to a pursuit in which we are destined never to overtake. In the meantime, none of those things are done which might be done today.

32. But for the solitary man, who has regulated the entire course of his life and not merely some portions of it, there is no day or night that is too long, though it is often shorter than he would like when he is engaged in his innocent tasks and the light of day is gone before his labor is accomplished. He knows how to join night to day and day to night, and when the occasion demands it to combine the two, and in other ways to interchange the duties incident to each division, acting on all occasions so that the allowance of time, to which he neither wishes to give the spurs nor is able to apply the curb, shall not flow wastefully away. To this he devotes all his deliberation, all his study, on this he concentrates with all the strength of his mind. In short, this is his greatest concern.

33. He removes every evil thought, every annoyance, every feeling of disgust and lives today in the present day, content to live tomorrow if a morrow shall be granted. But in the hope of tomorrow he does not neglect his business, knowing that it is in the habit of betraying many and of telling many falsehoods, but he has faith in today because it gives what the other

only promises. Yet such is the blindness of men that they embrace the hope more eagerly than the actuality.

34. He knows, moreover, what dress, what manner of speech, what habits are becoming to youth and to old age. To these he adapts his mind and makes no change except such as his change in years dictates. There is no one whom he desires to imitate and in following whom he loses his senses; he looks to nature and follows her as his guide and parent. From this it follows, as Cicero says, that, when all the other parts of life have been so well represented, it is not likely that the last act will be negligently treated, as though by some careless poet.[14]

35. I know a man, I am not speaking as Paul,[15] but an actual man in the flesh who is confirmed in the solitary life, content with his rude subsistence and his studies and who, though he lack much of a blessed life, at least has this considerable compensation for his solitude, that his whole year passes happily and peacefully as though it were a single day, without annoying company, without irksomeness, without anxieties. Whereas those voluptuous men of the city, in the midst of their wines and feasts, their roses and ointments, their songs and their plays, saturated with liquor, enervated with sleep, exhausted with their activities, overcome with both their ennui and their pleasures, think a single day longer than a year and can scarcely pass a few hours without grumbling and annoyance.

[14]   *Sen.* 2.
[15]   Cf. 2 Cor 12:2.

10

Temperance and the Solitary Life

§VI. The solitary man should regulate his mind as
good kings do their possessions

1. Thus in the little time at my disposal have I set down partly what I
remember from my observation, partly what this observation permits me
to infer. Of high themes I speak as a sinner hesitatingly, but of familiar
matters more boldly, as one with experience such as is afforded by my
present abode, my devotion to freedom, and my well-known love of literature and solitude.

2. Let me add but one reflection and make an end at last. The governors of provinces and the magistrates of cities when they enter the territory of their jurisdiction are wont to issue a proclamation to malefactors
to abstain from crime. This custom was common throughout Italy in my
youth; whether it still prevails I do not know, for it is some time since I
have been there, and practices gradually decay everywhere. All good practices have a brief life; only the evil ones are undying. We have observed
everywhere upon the arrival of new governors the open flight from the
cities of swindlers, thieves, and barrators.

3. But if we cast our eyes back toward antiquity, the custom turns out
to be of considerable age. A very timely use of it is said to have been made
by the celebrated Scipio with the Numantian army which, after it had been
demoralized by the quarrels of previous leaders and the licentiousness of
the soldiers, he brought to order with severe discipline, and with a single warning from the herald's trumpet expelled from the camp, the very
day he reached it, the cooks, and the procurers, and the great swarm of

hucksters, and all the other elements which catered to that sort of dissipation, together with two thousand harlots who had attached themselves to
an army in the habit of indulging itself and running away. This discipline
is believed to have been largely responsible for the gaining of that glorious
and till then unlooked-for victory. Other famous leaders have imitated this
course, but let it suffice to have named the most famous.

4. To our lot, who have undertaken to rule and to bring into order neither cities, nor kingdoms, nor armies, but only the state of our breast, a
very small province seems to have fallen. But when the sway of reason
shall come to impose its restraint on the rebellious impulses of our spirit,
then we shall begin to understand what a serious war it is and what a troublesome province, to exercise rule over our self. But what is to be done in
this case? Indeed, if you ask me this question, I shall recommend what I
have told you of the practice of governors and commanders.

5. In respect of numbers I admit their problem may be greater, for they
are entrusted with large populations and vast armies whereas we have but
the care of a single soul. But as far as danger is concerned, I deny that there
is any difference. What is more dangerous than to die although you die
alone, seeing that some people rather think it an abatement of their misfortune to die with many? We too have to expel vice from our borders, put
our lusts to flight, restrain our illicit propensities, chastise our wantonness,
and elevate our mind toward higher objects, and as Horace finely says,

> If we for sin repent,
> We must this root of greed accurst
> Pluck up; and young minds on indulgence bent
> We must in sterner studies guide.[1]

6. Let some govern the populous city and others rule the army. Our
city is that of our mind, our army that of our thoughts. We are distraught
with domestic and foreign wars. Do we think that there is any government
more restless than the state of the human mind? Do we believe that our
enemies there are weaker than those of Scipio in Numantia? He attacked
a single city and a single people, we are engaged in a struggle against the
world, the flesh, and the devils. See how your enemies appear before you,
how united, how in earnest, how relentless! That great general came, it is
said, to an army that was demoralized. He took the place of commanders

---

[1]   *Odes* 3.24.50–54 (John Marshall's translation).

who had been beaten and put to flight. But how is it with us? Have not we too come into a city sufficiently dispirited and demoralized and crammed with cases of cowardice, our own as well as that of others? What numbers of fallen have been reported to us, what numbers have we beheld prostrate at our feet! How many times have we ourselves fallen, to how many dangers of falling are we still exposed? Everything round about us is full of terrors—our soft and pliable affections, our numerous and unconquered enemies, dangers both great and small, no place for sleep or relaxation. If we desire safety and victory, let us adopt the example of the victorious commander, since we too are commanders of our own affairs, and a similar danger calls for similar precaution. Why do I say similar? Both our peril is greater and our reward. He was called upon to correct only the vices of others while we are required to correct our own as well. He by preserving the situation of a terrestrial country, destined some time to perish, gained earthly glory for himself, but we seek the salvation and everlasting life of an immortal soul.

7. Therefore, if we place great things before small and our own necessity before that of others, let us with the utmost diligence banish whatever hinders this object. And how, you ask, shall this be done? Will you banish your vices into exile, which neither laws nor kings have ever been able to do? Will you enter upon a path so far unattempted in order to untie inextricable knots, and will you wrest away luxury from the rich, their thefts from servants, complaints from the poor, envy from the base, arrogance from the noble, corruption from the court, pleasure from the town, discord from the mob, and avarice from almost everybody?

8. I wish it were possible, but I have no such hope, and I admit that all the sulfur can be more easily drawn out from the entrails of Etna and all the mud from all the swamps, than these evils, these burning crimes, these filthy customs from the dregs of cities in which is to be found the worst marketplace of such wares, among which the happy man lives unhappily, even though his mind has attained its full growth, and from which it is happier to be withdrawn.

9. What then is the upshot? I return to my oft repeated advice, that we should run away from the plagues which we are unable to drive off. And for this purpose I know only of the haven and refuge of the solitary life about which I have discussed so much that I am afraid I may have wearied you and that you may look upon solitude as more infected even than cities with the disease of talkativeness.

BOOK 2

1

Examples from History

§I. Holy Fathers who have practiced the life of solitude

1. I feel that something is yet wanting, and I now perceive that what you are looking for is to have the argument, strong though it is in itself, reinforced with examples. The philosophers and poets who, in order to rise to greater heights, first chose solitude would make a long story. As for the holy men who, condemning cities by their voluntary withdrawal, made solitude splendid with their saintly presence, their tale is even longer and more widely known. If I were inclined to write of these with any fullness, I could not help discussing what is too familiar, for what is there in regard to them that you are not aware of?

2. Therefore do not expect that I shall transcribe for you what are called the *Lives of the Fathers*. This is a title which I believe our writers have borrowed from Marcus Varro whose book, however, was composed from a different point of view, being concerned not so much with arousing minds to devotion as with the investigation of facts.

3. I shall not speak of the cave in which Dorotheus lay concealed for sixty years, nor of how Father Ammon, leaving the wife with whom he had long lived in virginal continence, spent the remainder of his existence alone in the desert of Mount Nitria and at last gave up to God his blessed soul, which was then seen by Anthony, who lived thirteen days' journey from the place, ascending to heaven accompanied by rejoicing angels. I shall not report the manner of life of Pambo on the same mountain, who by some writers is with careful parallels put into comparison with St. Anthony and even placed above him, nor shall I relate that of Anthony, one of his many disciples, who

became so famous for his study and knowledge of sacred literature that it was sought to make him a bishop by force. Seeing himself fairly caught and finding no other way of escape, in order not to be deprived of his solitude he cut off his ears, hoping that this would disqualify him for the priesthood. When this stratagem did not succeed, he threatened those who were pressing him that if they persisted, he would cut off the tongue for the sake of which he was subjected to their importunity.

4. I shall not speak of the two Macarii who lived in happy solitude, one to the age of 90, the other of 100, accomplishing amazing works. I shall not allude to the manner in which Moses, a certain Ethiopian, was converted from a thief into a solitary priest serving Christ, nor to the manner in which Arsenius developed from a proud senator into a great lover of Christ and despiser of himself. It was to him that a voice from heaven called, "Avoid men and you shall be saved," and again, "Arsenius, make your escape, practice silence, and be at peace." I shall not tell how Paul the Simple (he got the name from his habit of life), when he sought solitude as a refuge from life with his adulterous spouse, arrived at such great familiarity and grace with Christ that by virtue of his most pure and efficacious prayer he was able to banish from his troubled heart that chief of the unclean spirits whom Anthony confessed he was unable to drive away.

I shall not explain the temptations of body and mind which were conquered by the ancient recluses Pachomius and Stephen, nor examine the argument by which Paphnutius brought three friends of God from the cities to the desert as to a place of greater safety and proximity to God, nor how Elpidius drew throngs of monks to the solitary life through admiration of his virtue, nor how Serapion by his charity became a servant twice in order to free his masters from their servitude to sin. I shall not relate the piety of the Deacon Ephraem, the firmness of Pior, the sweatings of Adolius, the merciful severity of Innocent, the industry and toil of Evagrius. I shall not investigate in what solitude Malchus pastured his cruel master's flock, nor in what cavern he lurked with his nominal wife when the lioness fought in their trembling behalf and they escaped from the fury of his pursuing master.

5. I shall not set forth the resplendent virtue of John the Egyptian nor his foreknowledge of future events. From him the Emperor Theodosius, though situated at a great distance, sought an opinion when he was in doubt, and being armed with the advice of the poor recluse, he carried on his pious but terrible and amazing wars. From him too another Roman

general of lesser note sought counsel when he had become alarmed by the invasion of a great horde of Ethiopians and by the unlucky conjunctures in a battle he had fought against them. In that situation he approached the man of God and sought his advice, not through an emissary but in his own person, and being encouraged by him with the hope of certain victory, even the day of the battle being predicted, and with the assurance that he should return with all of the enemy's booty, including what had previously been taken from him, and earn the thanks of the emperor, he went forth boldly, fought the battle, scattered the enemy, carried off the spoils, and received his reward of thanks.

6. If any worth is to be attached to what a man so holy and so wise in knowledge of the future has to say from experience about the matter that now concerns us, observe what is his opinion concerning solitude. And lest anyone think that I have changed anything to suit my argument, I report his very words as they were related by those who had them directly from his lips: "An isolated dwelling place," he said, "and a solitary habitation is very beneficial." On another occasion he said, "For avoiding dangers or transgressions and for gaining the grace of God and capturing the imme-diate knowledge of the divine essence, the most advantageous thing is a remote dwelling place and a habitation in the midst of a desert." And that you may see how he gave force by his acts to what he preached in words, you have the evidence of St. Jerome himself, who wrote what I insert here: "I saw John in the part of the desert of the Thebaid which lies close to the city of Ligum living on the rock of a steep mountain. To go up to him was difficult, the approach to the monastery was blockaded and closed, so that from the time he was forty until he was ninety, which was his age when I saw him, no one had entered his monastery, but he had shown himself to visitors through a window."

7. I shall not describe the dwelling place of the monk Elias, which was almost more amazing than any: how frightful the wilderness, how vast the isolation to which no words can do justice, how rugged the cave, how rough and narrow the path, hurting the feet that groped over it and baffling the eyes that strove to find their way; how in that place, with a tremulous frame but a firm spirit, the old man passed seventy years of the hundred and ten which constituted his life. You will form an idea for yourself of how great a master of the life of solitude must have been a man who persisted for so long and uninterrupted a stretch in its pursuit, when in our day persons consider it a great privation to leave, though only for

three days, their ambitions and avarice, not to speak of the city's resorts for eating, drinking, and prostitution.

8. I shall not intrude here that Eutychianus, who lived in the neighborhood of Olympus in Bithynia and who is famous for his friendship with both his heavenly and earthly princes, nor the gentle and modest Theon, a man who took no oath and knew no falsehood, remarkable by his continuous silence for thirty years and by his great learning in nearly every branch of literature. I shall not introduce Apollo, the inhabitant of the Thebaid who for forty years was buried in the innermost depths of solitude, yet could not so conceal himself but that he was in the end brought to light by the splendor of his miracles; nor Benjamin, the old man who gained renown from his dropsy, and who while performing remarkable cures on the patients brought to him showed no concern about his own disease, far-developed though it was, but comforted the others and besought them to pray for his soul instead of his body, making this noteworthy remark: "This body of mine, even when it was sound, was of no profit to me."

I shall not dwell on Epiphanius, first famous as a hermit, whom solitude later gave to Cyprus for her bishop; nor on Aphrates, a poor and ragged old man, whom piety and a zeal for the faith carried from his cave into the midst of cities to confront an impious emperor with stinging and penetrating reproach; nor on Isaac, the monk, checking the impiety of the latter with the threat of the divine judgment; nor on Macedonius living on a wooded summit, a man of unbounded simplicity and steadfastness, and coming down from his mountain top to restrain a fit of wrath in a pious but hot-tempered prince. I shall give no account of Acepsena, who hid himself for sixty years in a cell, always silent, seen by no one, nor of the well-known Ceumatius and Didymus, both of them blind, but fulfilling every pious duty as if they had their sight. One of them indeed gained literary distinction on top of all. I shall also pass over countless others for whose very names books will not suffice.

9. Finally, that you may know I have omitted the most striking examples as being of too common knowledge, I shall not expatiate on how St. Anthony, the greatest of all the monks of the East, penetrated into a wilderness previously inhospitable and known practically only to wild beasts; how, worn out with impatience at the throngs of the sick who gathered with the growth of his reputation to be cured by him, and fearing lest his celebrity should become a matter of vainglory to himself and an occasion of false beliefs concerning his power, he put on a few garments as for a journey, and

while he sat on the bank of the river meditating flight, a voice came to him from heaven. And do you suppose the voice said, "Abandon solitude, live in the city; this is a place of trouble, that a place of joy and repose; seek out Alexandria, return to your country"? Or did it not rather say, "If you would be at peace, Anthony, go now still farther into the wilderness"? Promptly obeying these words, he went on, having a guide from heaven to show him the way. I might go on to tell how, while he stayed in the desert, always in armor and on guard, he overcame all the assaults of the devils; how the boastful title of philosophy and the wisdom of the world was overthrown and trodden underfoot with the force of clear reason by a humble, uneducated old man; how Roman emperors, attracted by the miracle of his fame, addressed letters to him with the reverence due to a father and were immensely delighted when they were accorded the honor of a reply.

10. Or how when he reached his ninetieth year, victorious in so many spiritual battles, with so many hosts of invisible enemies overpowered, and thought that he was the only one who lived in that desert, no human being having anywhere shown himself, it was manifested to him by a revelation at night that he should seek out Paul the Theban, who had been living much longer in an even more remote region of the solitude, how he looked for him and found him, but not without encountering dreadful monsters on the way; how at last when they met and broke their long silence in the retirement of a cave near the bank of a little spring beneath the shade of an aged palm, a single loaf sent down from the sky sufficed amply to still the hunger of these two valiant veterans in the service of Christ, worn out as they were with much fasting; how a few days later with grief at his heart and shedding many tears, the guest buried Paul, being assisted by the claws of lions while digging the earth in this unaccustomed task of piety; in the end how, still concealed in the desert and so far shrinking from fame that he wished even the place of his burial to be a secret, and that no breath of worldly reputation should come to disturb even his cold ashes, he nevertheless obtained great renown and glory. It is the declaration of Athanasius, his heir and biographer, that Christ, as he had promised in the beginning, made conspicuous to Africa, Spain, France, Italy, Illyricum, and to Rome herself, the queen of cities, his humble servant who was buried in the depths of the Egyptian wilderness and hidden as it were in another world.

11. I shall not proceed to recount how Hilarion, the well-known rival in virtue of St. Anthony, also fled into the solitude, having first been aroused by the man's fame and then, when he had observed his life for two months, and

having been stirred by his precepts and the force of his living example, how abiding there continually from youth to old age, he resisted the severities of winter and summer, first in a narrow hut and later in a cell scarcely narrower and having more the appearance of a tomb than of a dwelling place. When he thought of running away from the crowds which were gathered by his fame and from a solitude which had grown restless with the cares of multitude, and his purpose became known, ten thousand men and more obstructed his way. When by abstaining from food in his distress at this he had almost wasted away and the people at last suffered him to go, though sorrowfully trooping after him, he departed into the most profound solitude. And so he came to the habitation of Anthony, which had recently been deprived of the presence of that great spirit, and finding his disciples there, he made eager inquiry about all those matters which to hear were piteous, though pious to relate, and looked upon the little garden and the cot from which the blissful soul had ascended to heaven, and he lay down on the cot in sweet remembrance of that worthy man and often embraced it and kissed it, as though it were still warm from the recent pressure of Anthony, and—this touch I add not from my reading but in reliance on my own feeling—he moistened with his own tears the bed of the stranger.

From this place he went seeking one solitude after another, but his fame, envious of the peace he longed for, always outran him, and even when he had determined to make his way to barbarous nations among which neither knowledge nor understanding draw breath, the same renown still pursued him. First he sailed to Sicily, from there to Dalmatia, and finally to Cyprus, an island very uncongenial to his habits of life but on which he found a rock which suited his austere purpose. There, to use the expression of Jerome, who has celebrated him in writing, having taken possession of this most terrible and secluded spot, he remained; and while everybody was watching lest he slip away by stealth, because it was generally believed that he could not remain long in one place, he there brought to an end the labor of his life, and followed Anthony to heaven as he had imitated him on earth.

§II. The transition from the foregoing examples to those less familiar

12. Having therefore passed over these cases with brief and succinct mention and placed them as it were in a subordinate rank, and having buried in silence the rest, numerous as are the persons to whom a lonely desert was

a heaven on earth, and though the reading of their lives is full of pleasure and variety, piercing and burning, possessing a thread of precious material which, when woven by genius, delights equally by its substance and form, I shall now assemble a few examples not so trite scattered through the more hidden parts of the Scriptures.

2
Biblical Patriarchs

§I. The solitude of Adam, the parent of the human race

1. To begin with the first, there is Adam, that general parent of the human race, who, as long as he was alone, no man was happier, but as soon as he received a companion, none more wretched. Alone he stood up, with his companion he fell. Alone he was citizen of a happy land, with his companion he was a wanderer in unhappy exile. Alone he lived in peace and joy, with his companion in labor and much sorrow. Alone he had been immortal; as soon as he is joined with woman, he becomes mortal. Behold herein a clear and conspicuous token of what posterity may hope from the companionship of women.

§II. Abraham's cult of solitude

2. But not to linger on the threshold, Abraham, the great father of many nations, speaking with God in tents pitched in the valleys (not in palaces and amidst the luxury of cities), deserved to win those promises which are being carried out continuously in this latest generation of me. Would that it were not the worst! And he was sitting not in a chamber filled with vessels and covered with variegated carpets, but on the grassy floor of nature, in the plains of Mamre, according to the text of Genesis,[1] and according to Josephus under an ilex tree, when he was deemed worthy to entertain God's angels; and, not to assume anything that is not expressly in the words, that rural feast was celebrated in the shade of an acorn-bearing oak, not beneath a roof of fretted gold. This most holy of men and most deserving

[1]   18:1.

of divine favor was likewise of such entire obedience that to listen to the command of God he would not spare his only begotten son. Let me pass over in silence the rest of his praises, for reciting which another time and a more fitting place will be afforded.

3. Because of all these virtues, since divine favor so closely embraced him, it is not greatly to be wondered at that his Egyptian handmaiden, when she ran away, was for his merit brought back by an angel, and when a second time she was imperiled and in despair, was once more restored by an angel. Both these incidents, as is in keeping with the fitness of things, took place in the wilderness, one near a spring of water, the other under a tree, and so it is no wonder that the child whom she carried along in her flight, having been preserved in the wilderness, should be mindful of heaven's benefit and later himself become a votary of the wilderness.

§III. The solitude of Isaac

4. What of Isaac, who was sprung from such a father? When his fruitful wife was being brought to him from a distant land, what do you suppose he was doing? Was he by chance in the marketplace, was he pleading cases or giving judgment, was he buying or selling, extending loans or asking for them, demanding settlement or making it? None of these things! What then? He was walking at that time, it is said, on the way leading to the well which is called the Living and Seeing One. Truly living and seeing, living in eternity and seeing all things, not Sol, as Ovid and Apuleius have declared, but God the omnipotent, creator of the sun and the stars and all things, in whom is the well, or as the Psalmist has it, the fountain of life, to which we travel and attain, not by sleeping nor by treading in byways but by walking over the only true way.

5. And the text follows, "For he dwelt in the south country. And he went forth to meditate in the field at the eventide."[2] In these words also there is nothing which I can regard as free from a hidden meaning. "For he dwelt in the south country," in a country that is lowly and toward the decline, and bright and fervent from its nearness to the ethereal sun. "And he went forth"—whence, do you think, but from the house of his own body? He went forth, I say, out of himself and the prison of mortal misery, not for the sake of ignoble idleness but to meditate. For what else, I beseech you, makes the life of man? In what other action does he differ from the brute

---

[2]   Gen 24:62–63.

beasts? Splendidly does Cicero say, "To a cultivated man living is thinking."[3] For this purpose Isaac chose neither the city nor the theatre but the field as a place especially suitable, and the decline of day as the most appropriate time. For no place is more favorable for the meditative man than a rustic solitude and no time of life than that period of tranquilized peace already verging toward the sunset of existence when the heat of youth has passed away and the hour of high noon, if I may use the phrase, has been left behind.

§IV. *The solitude of Jacob*

6. What of Jacob, the greatest of the patriarchs, the son of Isaac, and the grandson of the great Abraham, when he saw the ladder reaching to heaven and the angels ascending and descending and the Lord leaning over the ladder? Where shall we suppose that he was, in how large a city, in how fair a mansion, how rich a chamber? Not only was he far from cities, he was far even from a habitation, if I am not to change the very words of Josephus. He would not approach any of the inhabitants of the region because he hated them, but he lay down under the open sky, supporting his head on stones which he placed beneath it. And when he was going back to his country with his two wives and many children, with his servants and handmaidens, and enriched with flocks of all kinds, he was again met by angels. But where, I pray you? In a city, when he was taking his ease? No, but on the road, just after his departure. And before he had ended his journey, there appeared to him that nocturnal wrestler from whom he received the new name which has remained illustrious to posterity; and he appeared to him not in a public amphitheater or amidst crowds of men, but at the crossing of a brook when Jacob had been left there alone.

[3]   *Tusculans* 5.38.

3

Prophets

1. Where was Moses, the man who was closest to God, when, holding talk with God, he obtained the law, when he procured the safety of his people, when by himself, far from the field of battle, he gained that memorable victory with prayer for his sole weapon? Indeed, he was not in any of the cities of Syria or of Egypt, but in forests and on the summit of a high mountain. He was in the wilderness when he forced the bitter waters to grow sweet by throwing into them a single stick, and when he performed all those wonders which even to read of them taxes our powers, let alone recounting them. It was not from a golden throne but from a frightful wilderness that he looked after that immense host which contained so many evildoers and ingrates toward God and men, and in their greatest need procured for them a wonderful abundance of life's necessities, when the people, being hungry, gathered in their camp, the quail actually dropped from heaven, and being thirsty, drank their fill of sweet water from the rock he had struck with his staff, when for forty years they enjoyed in the desert that divine and miraculous food which was subject neither to avarice nor parsimony and which was not to be obtained in cities or from the public caterer but was sent down from heaven. Do you see how favorable solitude is to divine benefits, to engagement with God, and to meetings with angels? And so I am less surprised that when this man of exalted life was about to depart from among men, a solitude was assigned for his glorious death, as it had previously been done with his brother, and God's words to him were not, "Get thee to this or the

other city," but "Get thee up into the mountain and die."[1] These words, if I mistake not, ought to receive particular attention from us in every deliberation of life and death.

§VI. The solitude of Elijah

2. Why should I unfold the details? Every part is full of examples. Where was Elijah when he dazzled with his portents of superior brightness; when, hiding in the wilderness, he was fed by the thoughtful ravens at the command of God while the people were perishing of hunger in the cities; when, lying prostrate on the ground, from the top of Mount Carmel he relieved with an unlooked-for rain the three years' drought which had been afflicting the land and the population; when on the same Mount Carmel by the test of the sacrifice, with God as judge, he overcame the 850 false prophets and with the approval of the people slew them by the brook Kishon? Withdrawing on this account from the threatening fury of the queen, he sought the concealment of the desert, and when he had fallen asleep under the shade of a juniper tree, he was roused by an angel and admonished to eat food of mean appearance but of such good virtue that in the strength of it he performed fasting a journey of forty days and as many nights. After this, while dwelling in a cave he is visited by the voice of God and sent to anoint kings and prophets; sitting on the top of a mountain, with unimaginable confidence he orders the fire to descend from heaven on the royal troops of fifty and is promptly obeyed; with the touch of his mantle he divides the waters of the Jordan and crosses over dry-shod, the elements themselves paying reverence to the saintly recluse. Where was Elijah when he did these things? In the wilderness, no doubt, from which he was finally snatched up to heaven in a chariot of flame.

3. Where was Elisha when he obtained a double portion of the spirit of his translated master; when he restored to his grieving friend the iron hatchet, causing it to float in contradiction of the law of its nature; when he came to the assistance of the three kings and their armies and filled their riverbeds without the aid of any rain, that they might not perish of thirst? The first two incidents took place on the banks of the Jordan, the third in the wilderness of Edom. It is superfluous to ask where he was when he divided the waters with the mantle of his master and by himself crossed over the dry hollow of the Jordan as he had previously crossed it in

---

[1]   Deut 32:49–50.

the company of Elijah. Where in short were so many prophets when they were illumined with visions faithfully forecasting events to come? To treat of these singly is for the present too long a proceeding. And not only the prophets, but the sons of the prophets also, those monks, as Jerome calls them, of whom we read in the Old Testament, built themselves huts near the streams of the Jordan and deserting crowds and cities sustained their life on barley and wild herbs.

§VII. The solitude of Jeremiah

4. But Jeremiah, too, ought not to be passed over in silence, since he offers so clear a testimony in favor of this kind of life when he says, "It is good quietly to wait for the salvation of the Lord. It is good for a man that he bear the yoke in his youth." And as if to make it clear that this can be done only in solitude, he adds, "He sits alone in silence, because he hath borne it upon him."[2] In these words I am aware of the blessed patience of one who waits hopefully, I am aware of the endurance of the Lord's yoke which is better than any freedom, I am aware of the peace of sitting still and of silence not limited to one occasion but regarded both in the beginning and the end. In short, I am aware of all things being comprised within the single idea of solitude.

§VIII. Incidental, in praise of the solitary life

5. O life truly peaceful and most like the life of heaven! O life excelling all other lives, free from trouble and endowed with great blessings, where salvation is expected and the yoke of the Lord weighs lightly, where one sits in silence, and having sat, rises up again! O life wholesome to man, dreadful and hateful to evil spirits who, were it otherwise, would hardly afflict with so many kinds of temptations the bodies of those they entered. O life that rehabilitates the soul, repairs our manners, renovates our affections, washes away pollution, reconciles God and man, restores the ruins of innumerable bodies, refines the intellect, moderates reckless passions and stimulates dull ones, parent of generous thoughts, nurse of virtues, conqueror and bane of vices, a ring for wrestlers, an arena for runners, an open field for soldiers, a triumphal arch for victors, a library for readers, a cell for the studious, a shrine for worshipers, and a mountain for the contemplative! And what shall I call it but all things in one—a blessed

---

[2]   Lam 3:26–28

life suited for every good work, the life for a philosopher, poet, saint, and prophet, a life not without reason described as singular, and if I dared to utter what I think, a life so singular as to be the only true life. To all other lives we may apply what Cicero says, and after him Augustine, that this which we call our life is really death. It is a life in short that is unknown except to those who have tasted it, most precious to him who enjoys it, and to be desired above all things by him who has it not.

6. This, too, is the opinion of Jeremiah, following whom we arrive at these commendations of the solitary life which have to be added to what has gone before, when in the great public calamity he yearned for a flow of pious tears and a wilderness suited to weeping. "Oh that my head were waters and mine eyes a fountain of tears."[3] And knowing that this fountain does not gush forth brightly amid cities and crowds, he follows it up by adding, "Oh that I had in the wilderness a lodging place of wayfaring men."[4] It is very easy to imagine what is needful in our case when a man who was everywhere near to God and filled with God, wishing to perform that honorable duty (worthy of such as he) of mourning for the slain of his people, prayed for solitude and piety at the same time, as if he could not expect one without the other. He deserves to be most attentively heeded when in uttering his wish for a lodging place in the wilderness, he adds, "that I might leave my people and go from them, for they be all adulterers, an assembly of treacherous men." To think of these things, to say nothing of uttering them, fills the mind with horror. But so peculiarly applicable are his reproaches to the people of our time, so little, nay, such nullity is there of faith, such nullity even of truth of security, in short, of any human quality at all (though they are called men and are in form human), that to my mind they form clearly a sufficient cause, or at least the principal and most reasonable one, why solitude should be cultivated and cities avoided.

[3]   Jer 9:1.
[4]   Jer 9:2.

4

Saints

Silvester to Augustine

§I. On the solitude of Pope Silvester

1. But let me not in my reverence for antiquity appear unmindful or contemptuous of later examples. Silvester, the first of the wealthy popes, sought retirement on Mount Soracte, having a situation in harmony with his character and a name in harmony with his situation. And if there be no shame in hearing the truth, it is from a simple and barbarous wilderness that there flowed those riches (would they were a means of good!) which now cities can scarce contain. From here came the gilded shoe, from here the ivory crosier, curved in the manner of a shepherd's staff, recalling its rustic origin by its rustic decoration, from here the mantle glowing with brilliant colors, from here the diadem set with carbuncles like stars, from here the snow-white steed, the golden throne, the purple canopy for the reverend head, from here in sum the whole triumphal array, the whole institution of the church militant, as it is here called, whose rule now extends far and wide. Kings are amazed that this should have issued from a forest, and if one will regard the matter earnestly, I do not know how he will deny that a solitude which has given rise to an institution so revered is itself worthy of reverence. But I proceed.

§II. The solitude of St. Ambrose

2. Ambrose, having been appointed by divine will and compulsion to the charge of a numerous population in Milan, though from his consciousness of so serious a duty and obligation he did not dare to lead a life of entire solitude, whenever he could and in what way he could, he gave evidence of

his desire. He lived where the circuit of the wall now runs in a remote corner of the city, where his holy body resides to this day and where stands the sacred church established by him, renowned for its sublime worship, and attended by huge throngs of people. At that time, as may be inferred from definite indications, the place was quite out of the way and solitary in the extreme. Whenever he was free from his episcopal cares and eased from the severe and endless labors which he sustained in repelling the Arians from the church, whenever for a little while he could withdraw and steal away from his business, this holy man used to betake himself to a more private solitude in this quarter. There was a wood which though not far away was nevertheless suited for meditation; in the midst of it was a little house, capacious enough for a man who, though surely great, was also humble, and which, small as it was, was converted into the form of a temple with greater appropriateness than once the house of Pythagoras in Metapontum. The wood is now destroyed, but though the character of the place is changed, its name remains. It is commonly called Ambrose's Wood toward the left on the steep side. At this point the stream, which is noted throughout its course for its great turbulence and violent commotions, with a frenzied impetus taking a wider sweep, shuts it in between the city proper and the outer enclosure. In this place, as I hear, and as I might infer, he strewed the honey-filled flowers of the books, of which the taste today is most sweet and the odor most fragrant throughout the domains of the church.

3. If I may adduce a single passage in evidence of this man's style as well as of his deeds, he says in a certain letter to Sabinus:[1] "I shall continue to speak with you more frequently in my writings and when I am alone." Then, converting to his own use an expression of Scipio's, of which I shall speak later, he goes on to say, "For I am never less lonely than when I seem to be alone, nor less idle than when at leisure. I summon whom I wish according to my pleasure and attach to myself those whom I like best and whom I consider most congenial. No one interrupts, no one interferes. On such occasions therefore I retain you in particular and converse with you about the scriptures, and together we chop words at great length. Mary was alone when she talked with an angel and when the Holy Spirit descended upon her and the power of the All-highest overshadowed her. She was alone and she effected the salvation of the world and conceived the Redeemer of all mankind. Peter was alone and he learned the mysteries by which the nations

---

[1]   St. Sabino of Piacenza (d. 420), friend of St. Ambrose.

throughout the world were to be made holy. Adam was alone and did not go astray, because his mind was faithful to God, but after he was joined with woman he could not stay faithful to the divine commands."

§III. Incidental, no virus is so fatal to the life of solitude as the company of women

4. If I may intrude a little on Ambrose's discourse, I would not pass over in silence what everybody knows, though many pretend not to. There is no virus as fatal to those who would follow this life as the company of woman. For the attraction of women, the more fascinating it is, the more dreadful and baleful, to say nothing of their dispositions, than which there is naught more fickle or more inimical to the love of repose. Whoever you are that desire peace, keep away from woman, the perpetual source of contention and trouble. Peace and a woman rarely dwell under the same roof. The satirist says,

> The bed that contains a bride is forever filled with quarrelling
> And mutual recrimination; there's not much sleep to be got.[2]

Nor is a concubine's bed any more peaceful; there is less fidelity and greater dishonor, but the quarrelsomeness is the same.

5. The sentence of the famous orator is well known, "The man who does not quarrel is a celibate." And what is better than not to quarrel? And what, I pray you in the name of Jesus Christ, what, I say, is more blessed than solitude, especially at night, or than silence, and peace and the freedom of your own couch? Nothing is more blessed than celibacy, but for celibacy nothing is more appropriate than solitude. Whoever you are, therefore, that would avoid strife, avoid also woman; you will hardly escape the one without running away from the other. Even though her disposition be most gentle, which is a rare thing, the very presence of a woman, her mere shadow, so to speak, is an annoyance. If I am deserving of any trust, everybody who seeks solitary peace will avoid her face and her tongue no less than, I will not say a serpent's, but than the gaze and hiss of a basilisk. For not otherwise than a basilisk she slays with her eyes and infects before she touches. To whom, do you suppose,

---

[2]   Juvenal, *Sat.* 6.268–69 (A. S. Kline's translation). Zeitlin had used Dryden's much more provocative rendering of the passage from Juvenal's *Satires*. See Poetry in Translation online, https://www.poetryintranslation.com/PITBR/Latin/JuvenalSatires6.php.—SHM

Just seeing a female little by little tears at his strength
And consumes him, nor do her seductive charms allow him
To remember the groves and grassy meadows.[3]

Truly, in saying that merely by a look the forces of body and mind were devoured and consumed, he might have been alluding to all whom that disease emaciates and inflames, but if in adding that the same mischief erases the memory of grass and meadows, he had said it of men as he did of horses and oxen, whom else would he seem to have meant than us who find a special pleasure in groves and meadows?

6. Hence I proclaim that the allurements of woman should be avoided and shunned by all whose purpose it is to guard their pledge sacredly and honorably, and most particularly by ourselves. And whosoever neglects this warning, let him know that he must be banished from the paradise of solitude, for the very same reason that the first man was expelled from the paradise of delight.

7. After this interruption, I return to Ambrose who, concluding the letter to Sabinus, says, "It is clear from these instances that when we are alone we dedicate ourselves to God; then we open our mind to him, then we take off the garment of deceit." Thereupon our first parent again recurs to his memory, and he says, "Adam was alone when he was placed in Paradise, but he was not alone when he was cast forth from Paradise. The Lord Jesus was alone when he redeemed the world, for it was neither a legate nor a nuncio but the Lord himself who brought about the salvation of his people, though he is never alone in whom the Father always is." Finally, wishing to close the letter with an admonition, he says, "Therefore let us also be alone, that the Lord may be with us."[4] Let not this counsel accrue to the benefit of Sabinus alone; I pray that we may apply it to ourselves and make it ours.

§IV. The solitude of St. Martin of Tours

8. Of St. Martin we know that he somehow conceived a longing for the condition of the solitary life even from childhood, and that, as soon as his years and unavoidable military service allowed, he embraced it with such zeal of spirit that even when he became bishop, he did not leave off the

---

[3]   Virgil, *Virgil's Georgics*, trans. Janet Lembke (New Haven: Yale University Press, 2005), 3.215–16, p. 47. Virgil is here referring to why "stockmen send a bull far away to isolated pastures."

[4]   *Migne* 16.1155.

habit he had formed in private life. Our authority for this is Severus who has described the whole course of his life of which he was himself in part a witness. We learn that at this time Martin was accustomed to complain that before getting his episcopal charge he had been more virtuous. This is remarkable, for although it is not to be believed that that man was ever anything but the acme and perfection of virtue, yet it seems that when he was bent beneath the pontifical burden he recalled a certain something in himself when he was less embarrassed that was more elevated and of clearer perfection, a memory of the time when being alone he was more free, so that it need be no occasion of surprise that he should have frequented in his earlier freedom the solitary places which he continued to resort to whenever he could while serving in a difficult office.

9. Not to trace his steps throughout, which would be a long and difficult matter, it is reported that he had formerly passed a considerable time in that very city of Milan where, as is well known, he erected the first of the many monasteries which were founded by him in different places, having his dwelling close to the house of Ambrose and the city walls, a place which even now is lonely and remote. Ambrose, who was already bishop, being rejoiced at such a guest, used to go to him alone and in secret and to linger in his company with great fondness as long as he might. Good Jesus, what a pair of men they were, what sighing, what talking! The dictates of princes, the deliberations of consuls, the edicts of praetors, the statutes of lawmakers, the speeches of the populace, the disputations of philosophers, the declamations of rhetoricians, the quibblings of sophists, when placed beside that holy and peaceful conversation, I should not fear to call the merest trifles. The poet Horace was at Sinuessa, when Plotius and Varius and Virgil came to visit him, a brilliant fellowship of learned men bound by ties of mutual friendship, and so he exclaimed,

> O what embraces, what delights were ours.[5]

I believe it indeed, and I do not doubt that between such men there was for the time a great deal of witty and elegant discourse, but I am inclined to believe that the embraces were sweeter and the joy more holy in Milan between Ambrose and Martin. The place is pointed out where, according to report, they were in the habit of meeting and conversing. I would rather have been present at these meetings and conversations, if I might,

---

[5]   Horace, *Sat.* 1.5.43.

than at the counsel-boards of all the kings, whatever it is that they contrive with their minions when flown with wine and greed and cruelty. Blessed therefore is the solitude which earned the honor of harboring two such inhabitants at one time and which, though not so scorched or savage as the wilderness of the Thebaid, is perhaps not less glorious.

§V. *The solitude of St. Augustine*

10. We may not yet be permitted to depart from Milan on account of that other great inhabitant of the same city, Augustine, whom an affectionate Father turned over to Ambrose infected with evil errors, as he might entrust a son to a learned physician, in order that the latter might wash him in healthy waters and restore him healed to God. Though ignorant of all that the divine kindness was working in his behalf when he came to Milan, where the holy Ambrose was then flourishing, he had decided at last to change his way of life, and so abandoning the city, he sought the loneliness of the country, in order that, having been mad with the multitude, he might regain his wits in solitude. He calls this country place Cassisiacum and its name is preserved to this time.

Indeed, finding himself in the city on the very day on which he was enkindled with his holy longing, he relates in his narrative what he did and how he conducted himself in the storms of an agitated mind through which the bark of his counsel, under God's guidance, attained to the land of the living and the haven of salvation. Verily he did not issue out in public nor summon a popular assemblage by trumpet call and explain what he was going to do, but he sent away his most faithful companion, and arising, because, as he says himself, loneliness was suggested to him as fitter for the business of weeping, and retiring so far that even the presence of so dear a friend might not be burdensome to him, he used for his solitude a secret corner of the garden as the only refuge which the conditions of place and time permitted. There, holding bitter converse with himself, amid sobbing and weeping, tearing his hair and beating his forehead, and clasping his knee with clenched fingers and with whatever other signs a great and holy sorrow expresses itself, he at length once and for all came to that resolve concerning himself which was to be the occasion of his rejoicing ever after.[6]

[6]   *Conf.* 8, end.

11. Finally, throughout his life he took pleasure in quiet and solitary places, such as the retirement of Monte Pisano, where he is believed to have passed extended intervals in the condition of a hermit; there is a certain book inscribed with his name to the monks of that place. For the rest of this matter, since there is no leisure for turning over the endless writings of this man, I shall be content with a single short but clear testimony that occurs to me from his pen. In expounding the Gospel of St. John he says, "It is difficult to see Jesus in a crowd; a sort of solitude is necessary for the mind. God is seen in a kind of isolation of the attention. A crowd is a noisy thing; that vision calls for calm privacy." Do you observe how careful he is to say that for seeing God there is need not for any other kind of application but that of solitude, meaning thereby that as long as the human mind is filled with its inner disturbances and conflicts, physical solitude is in itself of no avail for purifying and sharpening the eyes to behold that great light? But having now treated of these three very great men, I shall allow my pen to depart not only from Milan but from Italy as well.

5

Saints

Jerome and Some Virtuous Women

§VI. Of St. Jerome, the marvelous worshiper of solitude

1. I shall now pass in silence over Basil who has proclaimed the praises of this life, and also over the great Gregory of Nazianzus, but I shall not pass over the illustrious disciple of the latter. Jerome, forsaking the city of Rome and scorning its wealth, being allured by a hope and longing for the eternal homeland, and, as he himself confesses, on account of the fear of hell, betook himself first to that vast wilderness which provided a savage dwelling place for monks and which, in the letter to Eustochium on virginity, he described in a phrase of Sallust's as burned up by the ardors of the sun. After he had passed a number of years in that place in a severe campaign against the assaults of the untamed flesh and a soul which secretly abetted the tempter, he was victorious. Yet he did not return from the field of battle to Rome for a triumph as if secure in his virtue, but in great haste he sought refuge in the retreats of Bethlehem.

§VII. Of St. Paula and certain other devout women
who embraced the life of solitude

2. In that retreat was living the saintly, pious, and celebrated Paula, a true Roman matron, to say a great deal in a few words, and the most excellent example of feminine virtue in her time. For the sake of dying near the Lord's manger, she forgot the place and quality of her birth. Jerome himself has described her illustrious life and blessed end with such pointed brilliancy, that after him it would be more modest for me to hold my peace. For what am I to say that is worthy, in this casual way, and what am I to

include in so confined a portion of my little book when a man of his great genius found himself at a stand, though at the dictation of love and sorrow he filled up the measure of a true volume? However, I know, as Jerome too is aware and makes no pretense of overlooking it, that there were not wanting those who snapped with spiteful tooth against the peaceful life of both and did not shrink from committing their venom to writing. There is scarcely any virtue so lofty or so concealed that it is not accessible to the darts of envy; but vulgar breath does not shake the solid truth. Yet whatever may have been the opinion of others concerning his solitude, the solitude of a wise man is appraised by Jerome when he writes against Jovinian: "A wise man can never die alone, for he has with him all the good men who are or have been, and he projects and transports his free mind according to his pleasure, and what he cannot compass with his body he compasses with his thought. If there should be a dearth of men, he speaks with God, being never less lonely."

3. But what way shall I now turn? I am confused by numbers and am solicited in different directions by the array of those who occur to my mind. The name of Paula, however, admonishes me before all to award a share of the glory of solitude to the same nation and sex. I shall therefore select a few of the many, and I shall have no fear of being called excessive in my praises of Roman matrons, in which I have no hope of being adequate.

4. I omit Eustochium, the daughter of Paula, renowned through Jerome's commemoration, and Marcella, and Asella, and Fabiola, and Blesilla, and other virgins and widows of illustrious name. But what shall I say of you, Melania, most excellent and glorious of women? I shall not put apart with my pen such fellow citizens and neighbors, who are united by time and courtesy, by faith in Christ, by piety and virtue. You shall sit at Paula's side. The daughter of a Roman consul, the mother of a Roman praetor, you have by your own virtues raised yourself above the family and riches and honors of your father, and by your great devotion to chastity and your works of mercy you have conferred such grace upon the state of widow-hood as almost to transcend the praises of virginity. Forgetting pedigree, forgetting children, forgetting power, and remembering only Christ, put-ting off affection for country, respect for parents, love for those that belong to you, and the care of your body, by the advice of Christ hating your soul in this world that you might guard it for the life eternal, with wondrous pains you sought out the holy fathers in the desert wildernesses, and fol-lowing them even into exile, provided for them holy service with your

labor and pious sustenance from your means—honorer of saints, rescuer of the erring, mother of pilgrims, guardian and counselor of your fellows in Christ! For when with blessed liberality you had distributed your vast patrimony for the nourishment of the needy, and, like some inexhaustible fountain of benefits, never failed in your overflowing bounty, and when, having no other aim in life, you had gone on for thirty-seven years, your means still unexhausted and your charitable spirit unwearied, being now past the age of sixty, a desire came upon you, not earthly in quality but spiritual and divine, to revisit your family. And so returning to Rome, you directed into the way of Christ and the love of the solitary life your son, your daughter-in-law, your granddaughter (who inherited your spirit and mission as well as your name), and, to put it briefly, all your kin, but not before they had distributed their substance according to your example.

5. It is amazing to recall what gold and silver, what silken garments, what sums of money that splendid granddaughter of yours, zealously following in your footsteps, gave away to churches and poor members of religious orders throughout the world, how many thousands of her slaves she set at liberty for the service of Christ, what possessions she sold not only in Rome but in Aquitania, and even in Gaul and Spain, using the money for charity, and keeping the lands that she owned in Campania, Sicily, and Africa (so extensive was this woman's fortune) for no other end than the use of the poor and the continuous exercise of her piety. Besides, at what an age she did this, being in her twentieth year when, influenced by your admonitions and example, she renounced the world and gave up the purple flower, as it were, of life, and a brilliant marriage, and great riches and pleasures!

6. That their holy resolution was assisted from heaven is indeed clear from this, that the huge sum realized from her great possessions and all the rest of her treasure were disbursed to the poor by the younger Melania at just the right time, for if she had delayed a little it would all have fallen into the hands of Alaric who was then laying waste Rome and Italy. But she had already freed herself from the great burden of her wealth and converted it to better uses, as if to snatch herself and her belongings from the jaws of the wolf and bestow it gladly upon Christ at usurious interest.

7. But you, happy old woman, having performed with no feminine superficiality all those acts which open the way to heaven, as though nothing remained to be done on earth when the portion of your time was run and the struggle of your work creditably accomplished, within two months from your return to Jerusalem you found an end of the things that pass and

a happy close to a praiseworthy life and left a monastery behind you. Christ showed you great honor in that he seemed for the sake of a single woman to spare so many thousands of men and women and to put off the punishment which he had decreed or sanctioned. No sooner, indeed, did you depart from the country and from human interests than the barbaric irruption and frightful devastation overtook the city of Rome. O great lady, resplendent in your pious exile, and I know not whether more fortunate in such a life or such a death, surely your grave in the solitary dust is more illustrious than if, lacking these virtues, you lay at Rome in a marble tomb carved with empty titles. The house of Christ founded by your hands in Jerusalem for the service of the poor rises much more gloriously to the view than the ancestral palace in Rome, destined to be burned by the torches of barbarians or to fall into ruins with age. But too long, I admit, has the admiration of your virtue detained me in this discourse. Enough now of women and of foreign shores. Let my pen return to men and to my country.

6

Saints

Gregory the Great to Francis

§VIII. Of Pope Gregory the Great as a lover of solitude

1. What then of our Gregory, the great head of the Roman see? Did he not convert his many magnificent houses into solitary temples, and did he not deprive himself of his ancient possessions and give them to Christ? In that way he made a solitude for himself as far as it was possible in the greatest and most populous of all cities, and where his grandfathers and great-grandfathers had received the homage of a dense throng of obsequious persons, he paid a lonely homage to his Lord. And yet the splendor of his fame drew him out of his retreat and set him in a great sea of troubles and at length on the highest pinnacle of honor. This elevation of his he often complains of with melancholy recollection, as when writing on Ezekiel he says, "When I was lodged in a monastery I was able to restrain my tongue from idle words and to keep my mind almost continuously applied to prayer, but since I have placed my heart's shoulder under the pontifical burden, my mind, dispersed in many interests, is unable to concentrate itself steadily upon itself." In the same place he has other things to say against his condition at that time, and much more in the preface to his *Dialogue*. When about to begin that book he declares that he looked for a retired place congenial to his sadness in which he might find a little repose from the storm of worldly affairs. Replying in that passage to his beloved son and cherished friend, he says, "My unhappy mind, afflicted by the wound of its occupation, remembers that it once was in a monastery, that very far beneath it was all the shifting show of things, that it rose far above the revolving spectacles of life, that it was accustomed to none

but heavenly thoughts, that even though it was held back by the body it escaped by meditation from the prison of its flesh, and that it was in love with death (which nearly everybody looks on as a punishment) as though it were the entrance into life and the reward of its toil." Then he turns more sorrowfully to the other side of the picture and says, "But now, by reason of my pastoral care it undergoes the troubles of worldly men, and after so fair a vision of its peace, it is soiled with the dust of earthly activity."

2. It would be long to add all that follows, and not at all necessary. The end is that he declares he is more painfully tortured because of the recollection of his past life and wretched in comparison with those who live quietly, most of whom he describes as finding pleasure in this more retired way of living of which I am speaking. It is no less superfluous to follow what he writes in another work in which, suffering himself, he has expounded the suffering Job, because both of these books are very well known and these things are found written at the very opening of each. I dismiss the other passages, almost fit for tears, in which he tells us that he weeps incessantly because of his elevation and begs his friends to weep with him, if they love him, and intercede with God for him. You may perceive that he appreciated his danger, seeing that he esteemed it a kind of death to have left off the life of solitude, and implored so pitifully the assistance of his friends in that condition. Speaking of this in a letter to Narses the patrician, he says he is so overwhelmed with sorrow that words hardly suffice him. And so it is clear that the pontificate was a grievous burden to him, as it is indeed to everybody who guards it uninjured and unblemished, and that the memory of his solitary life would have been sweet if he had not aggravated the bitterness of his altered state by comparing it with dissimilar conditions.

§IX. *Of St. Benedict, a singular and most devout dweller in solitude*

3. But where does Benedict remain, the chief of the Western monks? Who among Christ's faithful does not know him or has not heard of the holy resolve of his youth? Although as a friend to virtue and an enemy to pleasure he entered on the steep way to heaven at a very early stage in his life, yet in order that he might proceed with greater advantage and safety he abandoned Nursia and Rome, for both of which he had through nature and custom contracted a fondness, having been born in one and brought up in the other. But by the care of his soul, he overcame his carnal affections

and in a happy boyhood sought out not merely a solitude but a desert, and that a vast one, and a cavern made for devotion; whoever beheld it thought he was somehow viewing the threshold of paradise. How he lived there, though I know, I refrain from describing, since the combined evidence of well-known writers and reputation with its free tongue have made it familiar, and proof is afforded by the great foundations of his celebrated order laid in that place. It is enough for me now to confer dignity upon our solitudes by the mere mention of so great an inhabitant and to strengthen my present argument with such a witness.

4. It is long to enumerate, moreover, who were the men and of what sort who followed in his footsteps, the founders of venerable orders who, provoked by the fame of their leader and the stimulus of his example, or by an inclination of their nature, or by divine warning, sought out various places of solitude. As a sign there still exist sacred convents and devout churches amid the forest caverns—Cistertium, Maiella, Carthusia, Vallombrosa, Camaldole, and numberless others. Though the waters of these orders by the growth of heavenly devotion later spread themselves far and wide and covered up the plains, yet if you inquired for their beginnings, you would find that like the springs of great rivers they flowed from the roughest mountains. But among them all the name of Benedict is famous and illustrious. If anyone wishes to learn his story and the manner of his life, I do not bid him search in hidden places, but let him read the second book of Gregory's *Dialogue*, referred to above, which is comprised entirely of his acts and in which the splendor of the subject is rendered even more brilliant by the style.

§X. *Of the solitude of St. Florentius*

5. If the eye, carried along uninterruptedly, should pass over into the limits of the third book, it will behold the crowded miracles of the solitude of Italy. It will meet Florentius who, while living alone in a monastery, requested of God, with whom continuous prayer and great innocence had made him very intimate, some relief for his loneliness. At once a bear stood before him, whom Florentius tamed and made use of as a sort of shepherd to tend his few cattle. When in revenge for the bear's death, which was brought about by the malice of some of the brothers, the curse of Florentius in anger rose to heaven more swiftly than his words, he was overpowered at the fearful punishment with which the offenders were promptly

afflicted, and calling himself eternally guilty and groaning at being so quickly heeded, all the rest of his life he was never free from lamentation and sorrow. I ask, what armies and what kings have with their labor attained to the power which this lonely humility attained through repose?

6. Continuing, the eye will meet Martin, the dweller on Monte Marsico, for whom a thin trickle of water flowed perennially from the solid stone and renewed the miracle of the hard rock which once gave water in the desert. Moreover, he lived the length of three years without injury in one and the same cave with a terrible serpent beneath whose shape was hidden that ancient serpent who is more terrible; but the latter was finally expelled by his marvelous patience and Martin remained victoriously by himself.

7. It will meet another, an inhabitant of Mount Argentarium, who is without a name here but enjoys a name in heaven. When he had rubbed with dust the face of a dead man—behold something incredible and amazing, save that to a believer nothing is impossible—with dust he brought to life the bloodless corpse which soon was to be dust again. It will meet the solitary Maenas, a man of such great innocence and trust that by the awe of his name and reputation he not only pacified the barbarians who were then harrying the neighborhood, but with the small stick which he was in the habit of carrying, he chastised as though they were household puppies the huge bears from the adjoining forest, who attacked the beehives of the holy man, and drove them away in terror.

§XI. On the solitude of St. Francis

8. It would be laborious, I admit, to include all the cases, nor is that now my concern, for I came to compose this book not with the idea of writing a history but of gleaning distinguished examples from all sources, and by no means all of those, but only such as I might gather in passing while keeping the main road in the work which I had undertaken.

9. Shall we suppose, then, that any of these men would have arrived at such glory in their own country, or that Benedict would have done so in Nursia, or that Francis, if he had remained in Assisi, would have had either his audience of birds, or the seraphic ardor of an ecstatic mind, or that amazing proof of the holy stigmata of Christ, or the limbs that gave evidence of the wound of his mind, or so great an increase of offspring born from so brief a marriage with poverty? It may be, as people say, that after consulting the divine will and receiving a revelation from heaven, he

chose in this place his post, not so dangerous to himself as to his soldiers, for the sake of keeping watch over the safety of great numbers in the wars of human life, yet he was himself a great lover of solitude and a votary of the wilderness.

§XII. Of triple solitude, an incidental chapter,
and of the solitude of Blasius and others

10. Solitude is considered threefold, if I grasp the matter rightly: that of place, with which my present discourse is specially taken up; that of time, as in the night, when there is solitude and silence even in public squares; that of the mind, as in persons who, absorbed in deepest contemplation, in broad daylight and in a crowded marketplace, are not aware of what is going on there and are alone whenever and wherever they wish.

11. I know of no one who had recourse to all these kinds of solitude at the same time more commonly than St. Francis. He traveled through wildernesses, he often passed the night in half-ruined temples, by day and among crowds he was often snatched away from the perception of present objects and, while his body was thrust hither and thither, in collision with men, his mind remained fixed on heavenly thoughts. Hence that sense of security amid however great a throng which was afforded to him by his extremely fervent love of Christ and a body marvelously submissive to the spirit. This was the reason, I believe, that he accepted a post for himself and his followers in populous places, thinking that what was possible for him would be easy for everybody, because his soul was sublime and unbounded in abasing itself and, having been cleaned of all earthly impurities, could not be separated from Christ by any kind of disturbance. What he experienced in himself he assumed would be much easier in the case of others, so far did his humility deceive him in his judgment of the rest.

12. To this view I am forced by the opinion which the holy man had of himself as the greatest of all sinners: we read that he made this reply to one of the brothers who asked him what he thought about himself. Yet in spite of all this, I have often heard his followers, men endowed with learning and religion, sighing in their inmost hearts for a life of solitude, if only the regulations of the father had permitted it. How much he himself always loved solitude is proved by his life as it is recorded in literature, and by the rules of living which he first dictated for himself and later generations on a mountain, and when it was lost rewrote in solitude. It is proved finally by his peculiar habitation, for his place is also pointed out like that of Bene-

dict as one among many. There is scarcely anywhere a spot more out of the way; its name is La Verna.

13. Into both these men, it seems, solitude struck a very sharp spur and goaded their minds, already disposed toward high endeavors, and so, while they were shrinking from notice and scorning the glory of the world, it made them widely known and illustrious over the whole earth.

7

Saints

Remigius and Bernard

1. Among those whom the wilderness has ennobled, the martyr Blasius must not be passed in silence, who is said to have lain hidden in caves and been visited by wild beasts and fed by birds. Nor should we overlook the brothers Leonard and Liffardus, both monks and both recluses, nor Veridimius the famous hermit.

2. Nor his companion Egidius who, though sprung, as it is reported, from a royal family of Athens, considered his pedigree, his country, his wealth, and his Greek literature, in which he was richly versed, of less account than Gallic poverty, despising everything in his zeal for solitude. Here he burst forth in miracles, such as that of the gentle deer by whose milk he had been nourished and which he rendered inviolable to the huntsmen's dogs. Being affected by such a miracle, the king of France journeyed to his cave, which was overgrown with brambles, but not without much toil on the part of his soldiers who had to open up a passage with their swords. Thereupon being much moved by the venerable form of the old man's appearance and by the sight of his sustainer lying beside him, the king sent away all his retinue with the exception of a single bishop and approached the old man. Finding his great gifts magnificently scorned and recommended to other uses, he was so impressed that he acted on the old man's advice and built a convent which is still celebrated in that region, and afterward often came to visit him, setting aside all regal pomp. It was not the splendor and equality of his origin but the honor and sanctity of his solitary life that won this man to him.

§XIII. Of the solitude of St. Remigius

3. What shall I say of Remigius, whose fame attained such splendor that it imposed upon him at a precocious age the pontifical burden, which he is reported to have supported with distinguished virtue and industry for more than seventy years? By grace of this fame, he was the first to convert to the faith of Christ the king and nation of the Franks and to anoint the king with an unction said to have been sent down from heaven, which is the origin of the solemnity of anointing kings prevailing there to this day. Whence, I pray, if not from the very humblest beginnings of the solitary life did he attain to these results and this elevation?

4. What of Narcissus, Bishop of Jerusalem, an illustrious and a wonderful man who was driven into solitude both by persecuting insults and the desire for a retired life, and who, passing many years in deserted places, not only turned aside the slanders of his persecutors but fulfilled the highest duty of a true philosopher?

5. What of William, a brave man and of ancient stock, who, when he had given up the flower of his life to military service, preferred to grow old in a desert and to die in consecrating the last fruits of his life to the heavenly service? What of the other William, alike not only in name but in ambition and rank, originally conspicuous by his worldly pomp but later by his monastic humility, who abandoned and spurned an opulent town and satisfied a wish for solitude, poverty, and silence? For though he was lord of Mount Pessulano, he became a monk in a great forest, and, rescued from the tempests of life, cast his anchor in that convent as in a haven—a man magnificent in the world, as someone truly writes about him, but more magnificent in his flight from the world.

§XIV. The solitude of the Blessed Bernard

6. What of Bernard, all whose deeds are fresher and better known, who, being noted for his physical beauty and good birth, in the very flower of his youth reflected on the fruits of his soul and entered upon solitude? And he was not content to do it by himself but drew his five brothers into the same way of life, in connection with which the following things are worthy of report. When one of the brothers, Gerard, showed an aversion to the fraternal admonitions because of his interest in the military career, and mocked at the better plan, and opposed it, Bernard, being stirred with heavenly zeal, predicted that before long a hostile dart would pierce the

exceeding hard breast that was inaccessible to the warnings of God, and he put his finger on the spot threatened by the wound, saying, "Here, here, shall you be struck; but at least along with the pain to your body there will steal in the salvation of your soul." This happened as it was prophesied, and when his mind had been tried by misfortunes, his soldierly severity was softened to a monastic tenderness, so that soon he was yearning for what he had previously been ridiculing.

7. Another, the youngest of the family, when, being himself at the time probably busy with boyish games, he saw all his brothers departing for solitude, and when the eldest was saying to him amidst his parting caresses, "To you, Lunardus" (for that was the boy's name), "will fall the entire possession of the land which should have belonged to all of us," he spoke up beyond his years and said, "That is not at all a fair division, that you should all possess heaven and I the earth." To this answer he shortly gave effect with deeds, being the last of the brothers to walk the path, and by giving up the earth to seek heaven through solitude. And so not a single one of them remained attached to the lands.

8. For this outcome the pious mother ought without doubt to be considered in part responsible. From infancy she so brought up her sons that their manhood might find them content with the most sparing nourishment and more inclined to the life of religion and solitude than to the pleasures of the city. With such habits and such domestic training the offspring grew up in striking resemblance to the mother, a truly noble and saintly family, generous shoots of a fertile vine, which would have been so esteemed even if they had sprouted elsewhere than among the Allobroges. But though they were all fervent and all eager for the ascent to their heavenly home, yet was Bernard preeminent among them all, who, being third in the order of his birth was first in the resolution of rebirth, and at the last drew after him his aged father and only sister.

9. I shall omit the praises of his eloquence and his abstinence since they are known to everybody, but I cannot pass over that excellent and brilliant observation of his which is so strikingly in accord with what I am here discussing. He was accustomed to say that all the literature that he knew (and I know of no one in his time who was better equipped) he had learned in the woods and fields, and not with the aid of human instruction but with prayer and meditation, and that he had never had any other masters than the oaks and beeches. I like to cite this, because if I am permitted to claim

any knowledge myself, I should wish to say—and unless I deceive myself, I can say it truthfully—that the same thing was true in my case.

10. Arnulfus of Metz, the noble solitary and bishop of that city, might, I think, hold a place here of right, and so might Eucherius who, conspicuous first by noble blood and the dignity of senatorial rank and even more illustrious later for his religion and solitude, lived most perseveringly in a savage cave in the region of Lyons and finally was elevated to the bishopric of that city, neither through his own ambition nor the suffrages of men, but because of his compelling merits and of a surprisingly glorious revelation by angels. That you may know it to be truly a land of saintly solitudes, it was in this region that Romanus and Domitianus first lived as lonely hermits and then flourished as celebrated abbots. And, if I may mix up an example from across the seas with those from across the Alps, Ursacius, known originally for his military activity, afterward abandoned that and became better known as a soldier of Christ and led a life of solitude famous for its miracles as well as its saintliness near Nicaea in Bithynia. But we have wandered long enough among foreign haunts of the solitary, we must return to those of Italy.

8

Saints

Carloman to Celestine V

§XV. The solitude of Carloman

1. Who does not remember Carloman, the uncle of that Charles who is called the Great? While sharing the throne with his brother Pepin, he withdrew both from kingdom and kingly cares and journeyed to Rome with the idea of resting. There he assumed the monastic habit and sought the refuge of Silvester on Mount Soracte. But when he had spent two years there in the peace he desired, at last the place appeared to be unsuited to his wish, growing daily less solitary, because of the frequent and excessive gatherings in his honor of pilgrims from his country, seeing that the spot is known, and visible from a great distance to those who travel to Rome along the road. He therefore removed to the more retired and distant Benedictine convent of Monte Cassino, and there, while his brother and nephew were toiling for a perishable throne, he enjoyed what he longed and looked for, a peaceful seclusion and a tranquil ending to his life.

§XVI. On the solitude of Romuald

2. After him in time comes another who in merit, however, is before him—Romuald, a noble citizen of Ravenna, sprung from a distinguished race of warriors. Though swelling in his early age with the insolence of wealth and youth and rank, and devoted to the fascinations of the world, his mind was so aspiring that in the midst of the pleasures of that time and his youthful pursuits he was always sighing for a saintly solitude. Often in his hunting when he came upon the silent recesses of the woods, he would stop as though suddenly transfixed by a heavenly yearning and say

to himself, "O what a delightful spot! How peaceful, and how suitable for those who desire to serve God! How much more happily the friends of God may live here than in the cities!" And so the high-spirited youth who had gone forth into the forest to capture wild beasts, his piety not yet ripened though already beginning to blossom, reflected on the business of capturing souls for Christ. Nor could such a thought long remain unfruitful, for he who is fed by the Holy Spirit must grow in power steadily.

3. In the very flower of his age he abandoned fame, pleasure, riches, father, country, and everything in the world, and escaping from the man that he had been in order to find the new man he was to be, he applied himself entirely to cultivating the solitary habits of a hermit's life. His first step when he left the world was not a long one; he settled at the monastery in Classe, a short distance from the walls of his native city. After nearly three years there, being shocked with the vices of the brothers, in the most devout humility he made his way to a certain Marinus, a man as saintly as he was simple, who was leading the life of a solitary in the territory of the Venetians and whose reputation had reached the ears of Romuald. He endured the authority and discipline of this man, which was marked more by earnestness than by prudence, with the greatest patience, and received not only his rebukes but his blows with such an even and submissive spirit that he finally extorted the admiration he deserved. Subsequently, for important and honorable reasons they crossed over into France, it being a question of the salvation of the soul of Pietro Orseoli, the Venetian doge, who was giving up his sovereignty and leaving the world in their company. Not long after, Marinus, observing the growth in Romuald of spiritual powers, felt no shame in becoming the disciple of one who had but now been a disciple to him, and in yielding obedience to one who had been receiving his commands.

From this place, to the great sorrow of the people among whom he had spent a considerable time, he escaped by feigning madness. This subterfuge was necessary, because the veneration of the natives for him was such that they had thoughts of killing him, wishing if they could not keep him in their midst alive at least to retain his body like some treasure to provide for the greater security of their country. The motives for his return to Italy were not less legitimate, but rather more so, than for his departure. He wished to be in time to rescue his father Sergius from the danger which was threatening his soul.

4. The latter, having taken the cowl and been received into the monastery of St. Severus near Ravenna, was thinking of withdrawing his neck from the religious yoke and returning to the world. When tidings of this reached Romuald, he sought out his father and, finding he could produce no effect with words and entreaties, he ceased to regard him as the parent to whom he owed duty and looked on him as the monk over whom he had spiritual authority. He confined his pernicious cravings with health-restoring chains, exercising a pious severity toward his earthly father in order to save him from the severity of the eternal father. The outcome was happy, for Sergius, being roused by these harsh measures, experienced a change of heart, and accepting his punishment as though imposed not by a son but a father, he altered his purpose with wondrous repentance and showed such a transformation that soon with his tears he had washed away his sins, and refreshed with the beatific vision, he gave up by a sacrificial death the weight of the body he had loved and the snares of the world he had longed for.

5. It is a long matter to treat of the laborious campaigns of this man in the service of Jesus Christ and of his zealous expeditions not only throughout Italy and beyond the Alps, but overseas as well. So frequent and toilsome were these that they are with justice excused by his biographer; for to this man vainly desiring concealment, there flowed wherever he happened to be a numberless multitude of those who wished to serve God from among the distinguished as well as the humble, so that he had no sooner by his exhortations supplied one place with a company chosen for Christ and appointed a superior over it, than, completely innocent of sloth and unacquainted with rest, this most saintly shepherd of souls felt impelled to move to another spot in search of a new flock for his master amid new pastures. It would be long, moreover, to give the names of all the famous men whom in the course of his travels he acquired as disciples for himself and servants for Christ, among whom were dukes and counts and sons of counts and even the Roman Emperor Otho, although the last because of his delays and postponements was prevented by death from fulfilling the vow which he had made to the saint.

6. It would be long even to speak of the places in which he lived, of the hermitages which he filled with his holy followers, of the deserts he frequented, the churches he built. Among his undertakings the hermitage of the Camaldolese in the province of Arezzo enjoys the greatest celebrity, an order and a settlement which he established and presided over, performing

all his duties with such great devoutness, mocking his appetite with such severe fasts and such abstinence from delicate food, praying with so many sighs and tears and such intensity and fervor of spirit as no style could ever do justice to. And with this solicitude, moreover, so continuous, so anxious, so indefatigable to the last, that like Caesar, but with a different ambition, thinking nothing done as long as something remained to be done, he had scarcely brought to completion these holy edifices than he was beginning in haste to lay new foundations, as if he had quite decided to convert the whole city into a hermitage, and all men to monks. And in the midst of it, what annoying persecutions he endured, not only from devils but from men, particularly his own followers, and with what patience and fortitude! In adversity what alertness and gaiety he had—a great proof of a substantial mind—and in all circumstances a brow marked by its constant serenity, such as is attributed to Socrates and Laelius, to whom our saint is comparable in evenness of temper but superior in piety and religion. And what authority there was combined with this cheerfulness of countenance, and something divine in his expression, at once venerable and awe-inspiring, so that good men loved and bad men feared him, even though they were great and powerful, and trembled before him as if they were in the presence of God.

To such a degree that the Roman emperor, Otho the younger, visited him in friendship and reverence and reposed at night in his chamber. Another emperor, Henry, when the holy man, having yielded to his entreaties and those of his disciples, appeared before him, promptly rose to meet him with a cheerful and respectful manner, and with a pious sigh broke out into these words, "Would that my soul were in your body!" And the company of the imperial knights, surrounding the man of God and bowing humbly before him, with devout importunity vied among themselves, not without great sorrow to him, in tearing shreds from the garment in which he was then clothed in order to carry them back to their country as precious and holy relics—so did the great repute of his sanctity soften even those barbaric spirits! Moreover, Raynerius, the Marquis of Tuscany, declared that he did not fear the countenance of the emperor or of any mortal whatsoever as much as that of Romuald, and that in his presence neither tongue nor brain was of any value to him.

7. Finally, what miracles were performed by heaven through him in life and after death which, it is clear from many celebrated evidences, were accomplished through the power and grace of God's presence! There are two cases in particular; one is of the brother of a certain Gregory whom he cured

of an intolerable pain in the head just by breathing on him, and he expelled not a mere pain but actual madness from another with a single kiss. On being restored, this patient affirmed that no sooner had the man's holy lips touched him than he felt issuing from his mouth the breath of a more intense air, and being promptly filled up, therewith he recovered his former health. What else should I believe that it was but that Spirit which blows where it chooses, with which this man most acceptable to God was truly filled?

8. These matters, I say, are long to recount and not at all necessary, since a book has been published about them by the historian I have mentioned before, a contemporary and fellow citizen of his, a man of remarkable saintliness and learning and himself a recluse, of whom I shall treat in the next chapter.

To give the sum of the matter, therefore; of the 120 years to which his life extended the first twenty were spent in the world, three in a monastery whose rule he accepted under constraint and laid aside voluntarily, and in the remaining ninety-seven he led the eremitic life in constant vigilance, never pausing, bringing forth fruit everywhere, and, as it is written of him, impatient of barrenness, and therefore at all times and in all places anxiously bent with his whole body and soul on no other end than the profit of souls. At the end, being worn out with sickness and age, he hastened as a tired wayfarer toward evening to an inn, to a familiar part of Italy in the region of Picenum or Umbria and to the monastery of Val de Castro which he had himself erected and where he predicted that he would die before the lapse of twenty years. And there, after performing the most extended labors, he found a happy repose and closed his solitary life with a solitary end, which I have not read, to my knowledge, of any save the first hermit, Paul. For when he felt that the last hour of that day and of his life was at hand, he ordered the brothers who were present to go away and to return the next morning, deceiving them with a pious fraud in order that, having served Christ in solitude, he might go to him in solitude to claim the reward for his service, and he drew himself together, both his blessed spirit and worn-out body, and so, unaccompanied by men but having the companionship of angels, he departed from here into the life eternal.

§XVII. The solitude of Peter Damian

9. We come next to Peter who bears the surname of Damian. There is great disagreement among those who treat of the life actions of this man, some

conveying him from the retirement of solitude into the cares of ecclesiastical business while others on the contrary withdraw him from the very arena of those cares and the turmoil of affairs into the peace of a silent leisure. Yet either version redounds to the praise of this life, since either solitude made him worthy of so great a responsibility or seemed itself so worthy as to be preferred to so great a dignity.

10. Others combine the accounts, for when, in searching more precisely for the truth, I sent men to the monastery in which he had lived to report to me all that they could find, I learned from the statements of the religious inmates of that place that in the beginning he had indeed been a solitary, that he had then been raised to a high place and finally returned once more to solitude. If this is so, then it is clear what his final decision favored, and at the same time we have a single example of solitude which unites in itself the twofold honor of fitting such men for the world and receiving them back in this way.

11. And I am persuaded to believe it by certain letters of his which, after hearing these statements, I recalled particularly to my memory. His expressions vary according to the condition of life in which he found himself at different periods; one time being engaged in affairs, as it seems to me, he sighs for the peace of his lost leisure; another time, while enjoying leisure, he recalls the disquietude of the affairs he has been through. The recollection of this is at present clear to me. Leaving out the other things, therefore, as aside from my purpose, this Peter, as far as I can infer from his last writings, occupied a high place in Rome, not without commendation, being scarcely less brilliant in eloquence than in rank. But you shall now hear what resolve he came to. Leaving that office and the shows of the world to his associates, he deemed preferable to these perishable honors the most quiet isolation in the middle of Italy on the left slope of the Apennines, about which he has written a great deal and which still preserves the ancient name of Fonte Avellana. His retirement there was no less glorious than his previous conspicuous life at Rome, and it was no dishonor to him to have exchanged for a rough covering the glittering ornaments of his lofty station.

§XVIII. The solitude of Pope Celestine, who was called
Peter before his rise to the Papacy

12. The extreme rarity of the thing would have rendered this Peter's [Damian] scorn of rank illustrious, if his example had not been dimmed by the more

recent and more splendid scorn of another Peter, a Roman pontiff who was known as Celestine [V]. He laid down the Papacy like a deadly encumbrance and retreated with such eagerness to an ancient solitude that one would think he had been freed from the shackles of an enemy. Let anyone who chooses ascribe this action of the solitary and holy father to meanness of spirit, for it is permissible to have not only differing but opposite opinions on the same subject according to the variety of our minds. In my view, it was advantageous both to himself and to the world.

13. For both, his elevation might have been perilous, uncertain, and troublesome because of his inexperience in human affairs, which he had neglected in long meditation on the divine, and because he had long yearned for solitude. As to the way in which the act appeared to Christ, there is proof in the miracle which God revealed through him on the first day which dawned after his renunciation, which surely would not have happened if the deity had not approved what he had done. Moreover, I regard it as the action of a mind highly exalted and emancipated, knowing no yoke and truly celestial, and so I feel that it could have been performed only by a man who estimated human things at their true value and trampled beneath his feet the proud head of fortune.

14. This passage has need of the support of Ambrose, particularly of the book in which he encourages the holy virgin Demetria to the observance of true humility. "It is not," he says, "as the lovers of this world think, the sign of a poor courage or a low mind to despise earthly riches and to disdain frail honors and not to seek glory in places where the sinner is approved in the desires of his soul and he who does injustice is blessed." Therefore, if that contempt of present things is rightly understood in its tendencies and aspirations, nothing will be found more upright, nothing more lofty than minds of this order, which reach beyond nature in their most hallowed longings, and whose solicitation is not directed toward any creature, however powerful or admirable, but to the Creator himself of all things visible and invisible, to approach whom is to acquire splendor, to fear whom is to rejoice, to serve whom is to rule.

15. Who, I ask, in any place or any time was more worthy than Celestine of being celebrated with such praise? Some men left their boats and their nets, some their small possessions, some the gathering of taxes, some even kingdoms and the hope of kingdoms, and following the Lord Christ were made apostles, were made saints and friends of God. But who in any age, especially since it began to be held in such great esteem, ever scorned

the Papacy, than which there is no loftier station (a thing so much sought after and so admired that they derive the word from wonder and amazement), as did that Celestine with so wonderful and exalted a spirit, being anxious for his original name and place and for a poverty congenial to the moral life, and unmindful of earth as he turned his gaze on heaven? Who that has read the account, worthy of another pen, of the marvelous works which he performed, as it is divided into the three periods—before his elevation, after his descent, and while he was on the throne—does not perceive that he was equally pleasing to God in any condition?

16. But what wonder that the virtue of works was not lacking in him, when the tenor of his mind was single and his life without change even where conditions admitted it? On the highest peak of the world and in the stately chamber of the pope, he lived meditating on his narrow, eremitic cave—lowly on an elevation, solitary amid the throng, poor in the midst of riches. Besides, from the very beginning he attempted flight with a certain disciple of his, Roberto Salentino, then a young man; being surrounded by a sudden and unlooked-for multitude and seeing no hope of escape, he turned to his disciple and asked whether he would like to follow him to the exalted place, dragged and constrained in that way. But the other, who had learned from his master to despise the world and to love Christ and the things by which Christ is reached—virtue, peace, silence, and solitude—replied, "I ask you to spare me the toil and danger, and that you would be pleased rather to make me your successor in a barren cell and a secure leisure than a sharer in glory with its riches and cares." And so it was settled. For he stayed while the father went to Rome, and it is said that not long after he saw his soul ascending from its twofold prison to the starry seats, and being ignorant of the facts and amazed at the miracle, he asked whether he was commanding him then to follow or to do something else. The other encouraged him to remain in the solitude, and so going up toward heaven he disappeared as he spoke. But the disciple remembered the advice, and living down to our own time, he departed a few years ago, full of days, after his master, and left behind him a great reputation of holiness and the fame of marvelous works.

17. But I come back to Celestine, whose descent from the throne by its joyousness and spontaneousness made it clear how sad and how contrary to his will had been his elevation. I have heard those who saw him tell that he fled with great joy and with marks of spiritual cheer in his eyes and on his brow when he was running away from the sight of the Council,

restored at last to himself as a free man, looking not as if he had withdrawn his shoulder from a flattering burden, but his neck from the fatal axe, and that in his countenance there shone a kind of angelic light. And not without reason, for he knew what it was he was trying to regain and was not ignorant of what he was giving up. In truth he was going back from toil to rest, from mad disputations to divine intercourse, and was leaving the city and going in imagination (and if the arrogance of his successor had not hindered him, he would have gone actually on foot) to a mountain, rugged and steep I admit, but from which he had a smooth path to heaven.

18. Would we had lived with him! And this I say particularly of him among so many followers of the solitary life because the wish was never closer to the goal of its desire. For we are parted by no great interval, and it was only necessary either for him to linger a little while or for us slightly to accelerate our pace in order that we might perform together that journey which he performed with our fathers.

And how many sacred monasteries of the order were established by him in a short space of time through the whole extent of Italy, even as far as the Alps! Already, as I hear, the pious work in its diffusion has crossed beyond the Alps. His religious succession endures and will continue to endure. The children he has brought forth in solitude are alive, while those that were born in the palace and whom he raised either to be cardinals of the church or to its other honors have all long since perished, so much firmer are the foundations of holy solitude than of the world!

19. They may therefore mock who saw him, to whom holy poverty and the rude scorn of wealth seem a base thing in comparison with the splendor of gold and purple, but I shall admire this man and count him among the rarest, and call it a loss not to have seen him, for his sight might have afforded great profit and a brilliant example to such as were attempting the rugged ways of the higher life. For the rest, his present renown and consecrated name give countenance to his admirers and give the lie to his detractors. But God be thanked, we have become so high-spirited that we may hope these two Peters are destined to be without rivals and that pusillanimity like theirs will be without an example in our time.

9

A Digression on the Loss of the Holy Land
and the Cowardice of Our Princes and Popes

*§I. Peter the Hermit, a particular lover of solitude, in connection with whom
the complaints here referred to are introduced*

1. But here I am, contrary to my expectation, recalled once more to France,
and while I am going about amongst the famous solitaries, I seem to hear
from afar a third Peter, as though he were crying out at my back that he
ought not to be passed over, and so I am constrained to stop. This is Peter
the Hermit who once led the solitary life in the region of Amiens, where,
however, he did not remain hidden.

2. For when Christ was beginning to grow indignant and wrathful at his
own inheritance having been so long trampled upon by his enemies and
ours, he did not reveal his wishes to any of those Christian kings enamored
of comfortable sleep on down and purple, nor to Urban, the pope of Rome,
who, though an earnest and accomplished man, was preoccupied, but to
Peter, a poor, inactive solitary, sleeping on a humble cot. He first inspired
him to gird himself in haste for the voyage across the sea in order that by
a direct view of the miseries he might be made more eager for the pious
business. When he had arrived at the place to which he had been ordered,
Peter was shocked by the wretched servitude of Simeon, who was then
Patriarch of Jerusalem, and of the other faithful ones, and by the sad defile-
ment of the holy places. Groaning and praying and passing nights in vigils
on the naked floor of the church, he was at length overcome by sleep. And
when he had fallen asleep, Christ again appeared to him, ordering him
to rouse the pastors and Catholic princes for the vindication of his name.
How devotedly he undertook so great a mission and one so far beyond

his strength, how energetically and how faithfully he carried it out, Christ favoring his pious exertions, and how fully he succeeded, it is not now time to describe, especially as the thing is known even to the general public through two volumes of considerable size written in a passable style in the vulgar tongue. And since I observe that in the case of this man too the minds of writers are variously inclined, I follow in doubtful points those whom I judge more worthy of trust and whom I think to be influenced by an attention to facts rather than persons.

3. It is certainly to be wished that the immediate issue had been the permanent result, that the vengeance of Christ had been as enduring as it was fortunate, and that there had been no return because of men's sins to former miseries after so victorious an event. It is all the more disgraceful, inasmuch as to have lost again what was ours is more discreditable to us and more creditable to the enemy than not to have recovered it; it serves to diminish our hopes and to increase theirs for future control and is the occasion of their cruelty toward us. But now why do I weep or why do I complain over the manger, over Mount Calvary, the stone of the Sepulcher, the Mount of Olives, the Valley of Judgment, and all the other places, singularly beloved of Christ, where he took humanity upon him and was brought forth into the light, where he cried on being born, where he crawled as a child, where he played as a boy, where he taught as a man, where he gave up his living breath for us, where he lay in death and came to life again, whence he descended to hell, whence he rose to heaven, where at last he shall judge both the living and the dead with an irrevocable sentence? And now shall the Egyptian dog hold this land which was promised to our forefathers and snatched away from us, which was destined for us if we were men—the center of our hope, the pledge of our eternal home? Alas, what besides groans and complaints is left for a miserable man, when even our kings love nothing but pleasures and our popes nothing but riches, when the people either weep in their bondage or rage in their freedom and everybody seeks his own interest, no one that of Christ, whose special patrimony is being destroyed while we are sitting idly by and looking on? What do I say, or why do I speak of these most active persons as idle? Verily while we are raging and meditating foolishness, while we are rolling about in filth and taken up with our pleasures, striving to keep them in our grasp as they flit by, while we are counting and hoarding the money of the poor, while we are building useless and tasteless towers in the latest Babylon so that our pride, in preparation for its fall, may mount

to heaven, there is no one who will guard or vindicate the humble seat of Christ. Finally while we are laying siege against our brothers, we offer our side unguarded and unarmed to the impious enemy and supply him with an approach to the chamber of our king—an enormous crime and a lasting shame to our armies before which we impudently advance the banner of Christ in order thus magnificently to avenge the insults to him which he in fact might himself with a nod avenge, and is perhaps avenging with a hidden justice, looking down meanwhile from on high upon our faith. But we are either listless or consumed with the passions of our minds.

§II. *The rebuke of our kings and princes who apply themselves to sleep, pleasure, disgraceful gain, despoiling of subjects, and other vices, while none of them are moved by the loss of the Holy Land*

4. Behold now how with insatiable lust and flaming hatred the kings and princes of the earth quarrel about some narrow strip of profane and barbaric soil. But suppose that they were in agreement, what public good were to be hoped from that? Never shall Herod and Pilate agree unless against the Lord and against Christ and his command. Probably they shall take their ease, and apply themselves to sleep and pleasure, and chase after disgraceful gains, and despoil their subjects in civic guise as they despoil them in military guise, for what is a necessity in time of war shall become a privilege in time of peace. Everyone shall love his wife and children, no one God and his neighbor. There shall be as much thought for the body as disregard of the soul. They shall accumulate gold, jewels, and valuable furnishings, but they shall despise the ornaments of the virtues. They shall love their own fields, for these they shall not fear to fight and contend and die; but no one shall be moved by the loss of the entire Holy Land. Why, I ask, unless because what I have said is absolutely true, because the former seem to be matters of individual concern while the latter concern Christ? And so, despising the glory of our creator and redeemer, we seek our own, nor does it enter our minds that Lucifer once fell from heaven through the very conduct by which today we hope to ascend to heaven.

5. But if you are loath to put your faith in words, you will at least believe the facts, which, as it is said, are not in the habit of lying. Look about you, I pray, and survey the countries and ask what is happening among us. The Frenchman and the Briton are quarreling. Twenty-five years have revolved since Mars and Bellona, instead of Christ and Mary, have held sway over those kings, and although the iron on both sides is already growing soft,

their spirits of iron are not at all assuaged and the rain of blood does not allay the great flames of their wrath. Though it happened unexpectedly even among us, among our grandfathers and great-grandfathers it was unheard of that a much inferior enemy should drag away in chains one who but now was by far the greatest of our kings, as if fortune could no longer bear the weight of so great a kingdom. But for all that there is no end to the matter, for the eldest son of the captured king is again making trial of arms. Therefore, as you see, the war now rages with special fury, the royal armies now join battle afresh, and the blood which should have been shed for Christ is devoted to hatred.

The greater Spanish lord out of cowardice permits his brothers within his territory (alas, the shame!) wickedly to blaspheme the majesty of Christ on a narrow rock. The one who occupies our seacoast thirsts for and thinks about nothing but the gold in Venice and the blood of Genoa, being at the behest of avarice the satellite of one and the enemy of the other, bound by one party with gold, conquered by the other with steel. But the remotest of the kings has been deafened by the sound of the ocean waves advancing and receding, and from his great distance he does not hear our sighs but, being buried in the extreme west, has no care for what the East is doing.

§III. Accusation against the Roman emperor and the pope, in addition to the Germans and Greeks

This Caesar of ours[1] snatched a crown and went away to Germany, content with his obscure land and the mere name of the empire whose lowest members he embraces while disdaining the head. The man who we hoped would recover what had been lost does not dare to preserve his own, and running away from the holy embraces of his spouse, though no one is pursuing, he shudders at the face of fair Italy, as if anything fairer existed under the heavens! I confess that my warm and headlong faith, which has not been afraid to inveigh against the very greatest, holds him blameworthy. He excuses himself and swears he has vowed to the church not to spend more than one day in Rome.

6. O infamous day, O shameful compact, O ye hosts of heaven, is this a vow, is this religion, is this piety? A Roman pontiff has so deserted his

---

[1]   Holy Roman Emperor Charles IV. Petrarch repeatedly appealed to and rebuked Charles IV for his refusal to unite all of Italy. Francesco Petrarca, *Selected Letters*, vol. 2, trans. Elaine Fantham, ITRL (Cambridge, Mass.: Harvard University Press, 2017), 188–203, 220–39; *Fam.* 10.1, 23.2.—SHM

Rome that he does not wish it to be visited by another and bargains about it with a Roman emperor. I do not know what to say here, and if I knew it would be prudent to hold my peace, but there is one thing which in my silence the facts should proclaim, that he who removes the dweller from the city would bring in the ploughman there if he could. Let him see how just is such a desire. Germany has no other aim than to arm mercenary brigands for the destruction of the state, and from her clouds she showers down a continuous rain of iron upon our lands. It is deserved, I do not deny, for it falls upon an abject people. Italy ruins herself with her own laws, and when she does draw breath, the love of gold, more potent than the love of Christ, seizes on the minds of its people and scatters them over all the lands and seas. Greece, turned away by her own errors or our pride, despises the ancient fold and our pastures.

§IV. How the Catholic Faith was of old diffused through well-nigh the entire world, but is now reduced through the negligence of the great

7. It is a superfluous labor to speak now of other kings and earthly lords and of our Roman pontiffs. It is all common knowledge. Hence, indeed, results the present state of Europe and hence it is painful to proceed further in the description. But it behooves us to touch the wounds which, though they are not at all far from the head and vital members, have putrefied from their location and long neglect.

8. Augustine, though he was born in Africa, says in his *Confessions* that Homer was hard for him because of being written in a foreign language while Virgil was easy because he wrote in his own, that is, the Latin language. But measure Africa now and roam over it on the wings of thought from the bosom of the Nile to the Atlantic Ocean, and I believe you will not find anyone there who understands or loves our literature, unless by chance he is some pilgrim, or merchant, or captive. Jerome, writing to Evander, also affirms that besides France and Britain, countries of our region, Africa and Persia and the East and India and all the barbaric lands worshiped Christ alone and observed the single true rule of life. How far this holds at present it is not even expedient to mention.

9. To touch on a later witness of our dishonor, does not Gregory somewhere give thanks and rejoice that in his time all of Asia adhered to the faith? Now, alas, you may go through all the extensive windings of the oriental shore from the left bank of the Tanais to the right bank of the Nile, and you may examine the entire tract, its territory and its men, that

lies between those far distant limits of the world and the surface of our own sea, and though someone may still be found there who has the name of Christ in his mouth, I believe there is no one who has the true faith of Christ in his heart, unless he belongs to the class of those that are held there by pilgrimage, traffic, or imprisonment.

10. But let a fourth witness now come to the support of the clear truth. An authentic letter of Athanasius, sent to Jovinian Augustus, testified that in his time all the churches agreed in this true religion of Christ, not only those established in Spain and Britain, to begin from the remotest, but in France, Italy, Sardinia, Cyprus, Crete, and Dalmatia, and also in Cappadocia, and Mysia, and Macedonia, and in all Greece, and in addition throughout Africa, Pamphilia, Lycia, Isauria, and in all Egypt and Libya and Pontus, and in the entire Orient, except for a few Asian sectaries. And in this, he himself declares, he is not following rumor but reporting actual investigations, having by examination informed himself of everyone's opinion, and possessing written proof as well as the assurances of men.

11. But if, perchance, the matter calls for additional witnesses, Ambrose, in the second book of the *Vocation of All Gentiles*, and after him Augustine himself, *On the Ninety-Fifth Psalm*, place the boundaries of the Christian faith more widely than those of the Roman Empire, observing in that connection that the yoke of a people ruling with iron could not have reached as far as the faith of Christ ruling by the cross. Inasmuch as they agree in saying this in relation to the real empire and not to what is now only the image and shadow of an empire, I could wish it might be true in our time as well. Then would not all Africa be sick, nor Persia, nor Syria, nor Egypt, nor well-nigh all of Asia, nor finally, what is more serious still, the greater part of Europe. For the ancient Roman Empire, as famous writers testify, lacked only a small portion of the East, while we, alas, lack nearly everything except a small portion of the West.

12. I believe there is no person so wanting in faith and so dull that he does not realize how much credit and authority attaches to these writers individually as well as to them all collectively in the matter of this particular complaint. And what they all say, with something to boot, is compressed in very few words by Augustine not far from the beginning of his book *Of True Religion*. "In every part of the earth inhabited by man," he says, "the holy Christian practices are handed down": a brief saying, but fraught with tears for us, by which we may easily measure all the vastness of our loss.

But why do I lean on the evidence of individuals? Let the ecclesiastical histories be reread. By how many names do we meet there of Catholic leaders who assembled a thousand years ago from the furthest north and east and south to strengthen and popularize the holy teaching of Christ, where today there is not only no bishop but no Christian living! To pass over less serious cases and to be silent about other cities which had the same beginning and a similar end, the venerable town Nicaea itself, where the foundation of the faith of the Apostles was compacted and strengthened with the mortar of powerful reasons by so many and such holy old men—workmen in behalf of truth—and all Bithynia as well, of which it is a part, are now possessed by the enemies of the faith. Is this the way we are ruled? Is this the care our princes have for the state? Is this how we crave for others' possessions, that we may lose our own?

13. I might easily console myself in other respects with silence and forgetfulness, but what shall I say to you, betrayed and forsaken Jerusalem? Let us carry this wound, continually fresh, in our eyes and faces; there is no way in which it can be covered up and disguised, and we bear rather more easily the burden of injury than of shame. Besides, is this our hope of salvation? Is this our pursuit of glory? Are the holy places thus being trampled on? While our members are inactive, is our head being thus mangled with impunity by the Egyptian dog, and are impious feet insulting the sanctuary of Jesus Christ, while he himself because of our dishonor is suffering his injuries with patience or, as I have said, perhaps avenging them in hidden ways?

§V. Of the high virtue of the ancient Romans when
compared to the kings of today

14. Amid so many and such general misfortunes, is there anyone who dares disparage the glory of the ancient Romans and to pollute his mouth with such falsehoods? Alas, deeply unworthy that we are! For us provision has been made by the great favor of heaven, though our deserts are naught! O truly gratuitous gifts of God! Tell me, Father, for here, when I am seized by the agitation of my sorrow and the fever of my mind, my grief grows bold and my indignation eloquent, and abundant matter of complaint issues forth.

15. Say, Father, for it pleases me to put the question, if Julius Caesar should come back today from the lower regions, bringing with him his former spirit and power and if, living in Rome, that is, his own country,

he should acknowledge the name of Christ, as he doubtless would, do you think that he would any longer suffer the Egyptian thief, "the multitude so effeminate of Pelusian Canopus,"[2] as the poet calls it, to possess not only Jerusalem and Judea and Syria but even Egypt and Alexandria, when he remembered that he had once wrested kingdom, spouse, and life from a legitimate king, and that at his own peril he had conquered those lands in order to make a present of them to Cleopatra? I do not inquire into the justice of the performance, but I admire his force and energy of spirit and declare it necessary to our own time. For with what ease would the action of the believer have restored his own to Christ, knowing he had received from him his soul and was destined to receive eternal glory, when he gave to a concubine such a prize for adultery? If Caesar Augustus, if both the Scipios, if the great Pompey, or a thousand others should come to life again in the same city, initiated in the holy rites of the Christian faith, would they suffer the name of their Christ to be held in contempt in the regions associated with their glory—the first one in Spain, where by the majesty of his name he composed the disorders which had troubled it for centuries, the next two in Africa which one of them made a tributary and the other quite destroyed, and the last in the northern and eastern regions where he bound with chains the necks of so many kings? If, wanting the light of true faith, they dared such great enterprises for an earthly country, what do you suppose they would not have dared prosperously, with Christ as leader, for their eternal country?

§VI. *The character of our princes compared with Muhammad*

16. But our princes and exalted leaders of men, in their chamber braver than lions, in the field tamer than deer, dishonor masculine countenances with effeminate minds, being very alert for nocturnal wars but otherwise pacifically inclined, and spirited in nothing else than the pursuit of luxury and the hatred of virtue. Those whom they are unable to imitate and whom they ought at least to have revered or admired in silence, they persecute and disdain. But there is nothing unusual in finding that models of virtue are annoying to the enemies of virtue or that those who sympathize with Muhammad in many ways, should agree with him also in this. The latter,

---

[2]   The quotation is from Lucan's *Pharsalia* 8.543. Petrarch is referring to Pothinus, regent for Ptolemy XIII, as "the Egyptian thief" and his agents who killed Pompey on his arrival in Egypt.—SHM

as I believe it is written, has blessed Mecca and Jerusalem among cities and cursed Rome and Antioch. It is worthwhile to inquire deliberately into the reasons for his impieties, but I find nothing at all to disturb me in his references to Mecca and Rome. For what novelty is it that an adulterous and licentious fellow should have enjoyed the city of Mecca, the profane dwelling place of all impiety, the worthy lodging of a defiled and incestuous body? There the wicked, infamous robber is buried, though he is worthier to feed the bellies of wolves and crows. And that butcher rests in the midst of his own people in the greatest love and most undeserved respect, while the tomb of Christ, alas the sorrow, is held without reverence by the enemy and is approached only rarely and stealthily by the faithful, not without serious danger and the dishonorable payment of tribute. Moreover, what wonder is it that the creator of a wicked superstition should hate the gracious city that is hostile to his acts and sprinkled with the sacred blood of martyrs, and is the most eminent stronghold of religion and faith, fearing it particularly as the place from where in all likelihood should come destruction to his own poisonous teaching, and recalling at the same time all the ruin and heavy mischances that had fallen from that quarter at different times on the Persians, Medes, Egyptians, Chaldeans, and his Arab forefathers? The hatred inspired in him by fear and distress is almost reasonable.

17. I rather wonder that the wilderness of the Nile did not move him to hatred, where he had heard of so many miracles and so many virtuous deeds performed by the Anthonys and the Macarii through the sole name of Christ. Indeed, I have no doubt that he did hate them, being an accomplished voluptuary and an instigator of every obscene lust. What does puzzle the mind is the reason of his love for Jerusalem and hatred of Antioch. But I am inclined to surmise that he remembered the first as the city in which his adversary Christ—clearly an adversary, though perhaps he did not dare to abuse him openly because of the majesty and glory of his name—had endured so many indignities, so many lashes, so cruel a death, and he was glad to love it as the place which shared his hatred and envy of Christ, even though the love which Christ's death instilled into his savage breast ought to have been extinguished by the glorious resurrection. But that the unreasonable and impious fellow, blind with the lust of rule, failed to see. He hated Antioch, on the other hand, because there the designation of Christianity first arose, as is shown in the Acts of the Apostles,[3] and

---

3   Acts 11:26.

there the Apostle Peter, the friend of Christ and the leader and standard-bearer of the Christian band, ascended the first pontifical chair. It would seem then that one city disturbed him in that it approved Christ and the name of Christ, the other in that it supported the name and the vicar of Christ with renowned reverence. No place was more hateful to him, I suppose, than Bethlehem. Yet he does not mention its name, being cunning with a native shrewdness of wit, though perhaps untaught, in order not to appear to betray too openly the reasons for his hatred. Thus much I may be allowed to offer as a diversion not unpleasant to myself and agreeable, I imagine, to the reader. It is time to return to the point of departure.

§VII. The denunciation of Catholic princes, because
they neglect the special concern of their country

18. Goaded by the sting of sorrow, I have with a glowing and flaming point impressed this indelible mark of infamy, which was all I could do, upon our peoples and princes who have involved themselves in so many useless, nay, mischievous and impious concerns, and neglect this honorable and particularly obligatory duty to our home—by which I mean to our eternal home, Jerusalem, not the one here on earth but that of our mother which is situated in heaven on high, from which we are now exiled. The former bears but the image of the latter, and if it is estimated with reference to itself, it is not our country and merits the fate it has suffered, and is deserving of more intense hatred, since with sacrilegious daring and wicked unanimity it crucified its God who had come down to serve it in a lowly garb, though from the cloud of his flesh he shone with the splendor of many and great miracles. But that impiety, though destructive to herself, may be of advantage to the world, since by placing him on the cross it revealed him to the peoples for worship as though from a greater elevation.

§VIII. That we are not obliged to fight for every country,
and what country deserves to be fought for

19. Not for any country are all things to be dared, though those who have dared are exalted to the skies with many commendations. Among our own patriots who have shed their blood for their country, praise is given to Brutus[4] and Mutius and Curtius and the Decii, the Fabii, and the Cornelii. Foreigners also meet with praise, for a like virtue deserves a commenda-

---

[4]   Lucius Junius Brutus, who is traditionally credited with overthrowing Tarquin the Proud, ending the Roman monarchy, and establishing the Roman Republic in 509 BC.

tion. Codrus and Themistocles are praised by Athens, Leonidas by Sparta, Epaminondas by Thebes, the brothers Philenus by Carthage, and other citizens by other states.

20. If you ask my opinion about all of these, it is that our love should be for the celestial state, which is not disturbed by the agitations of tribunes, the uprisings of the populace, the arrogance of the senate, the envy of factions, or foreign and domestic wars; whoever sheds his blood for it is a good citizen and certain of his reward. Not that I think one's earthly country should on that account be forsaken, for which, if the situation requires it, we are even commanded to fight, yet only provided it is ruled by justice and lives under equitable laws, as was once the case with the Roman Republic, according to the writings of Sallust, Livy, and many besides.

21. Cicero in particular argues this point acutely and eloquently in his book *On the Republic*. I might easily agree with the writers who maintain that Rome was just even when it imposed force upon the whole world and seemed to be most violent, on the ground that it was to the advantage of those very peoples who were coerced to be coerced, and that it might be salutary, though harsh to the taste, for the world to have a single head for its affairs, especially when it was a head of such supreme excellence. But there is this serious objection to such a view, namely, that while they maintained justice between men by means of those Roman arts described by the poet, assigning to each one his due, engrafting the laws of peace, "forbearing the conquered, and warring down the proud,"[5] and although, as Cicero notably remarks elsewhere, "As long as the empire of the Roman people maintained itself by acts of service, not of oppression, wars were waged in the interest of our allies or to safeguard our supremacy; the end of our wars was marked by acts of clemency or by only a necessary degree of severity; the senate was a haven of refuge for kings, tribes, and nations; and the highest ambition of our magistrates and generals was to defend our provinces and allies with justice and honor,"[6] and though it might be very true that "this could be called more accurately a protectorate of the world than a dominion"—although, I say, I might admit that the conduct of the Romans of that time was actuated by perfect justice and good will as regards men, yet toward God there can be no doubt they were unjust, for they deprived him of something not insignificant, namely of themselves, in the manner of fugitive slaves making theft of themselves from their

[5]   *Aen.* 6.852–53. This is Anchises' charge to Aeneas in the Underworld.
[6]   *Offic.* 2.8.

master, and, what is the most serious form of theft, offering to his enemies the worship due to him, which is doubtless a much greater injustice than if some ancestral estate or property were seized from a neighbor.

22. This passage is examined and curiously discussed by Augustine in his book on the celestial republic [*City of God*].[7] Suppose, indeed, a man should be born into a country corrupted with wicked manners, as are nearly all that you now see. Should he be commended for having shed his blood for such a state? By no means. If, at the risk of life, a man sought to obtain for wicked and dishonest citizens impunity for their crimes, would you say he was deserving of praise and commemoration (though this has indeed happened to many of whom we read), would you say that his life was glorious? I call him wasteful of life and doubly dead, since he has thrown away at once his body and his soul, at once his temporal and eternal life. On the other hand, not to wander too far, if there is any piety or justice in us, what would it not be reasonable to dare and to do in behalf of the heavenly Jerusalem, in behalf of that eternal country which assures us of a blessed dwelling place, without end, without toil, without trouble, without fear, without any vexation, in which there dwells nothing disgraceful, nothing impious, nothing unjust?

23. Truly, I have now journeyed as far from my beginning as Peter [the Hermit] did from his home. The encounter of a single solitary old man gave me this courage to rebuke the princes and peoples of the West with our reproach in relation to the East. Would that my right hand were as effective in this as was Peter's tongue! That this wish is vain I am not at all sure; I rather fear lest I should be thought to have spoken with too much insistence and boldness by those who regard freedom of mind as reckless-ness, truth as madness, and every exhortation as an insult. But however the matter may be received, being now by these words and this digression eased of the heavy and annoying load of my grievances, I return to the path of the original narrative with greater alacrity.

---

[7]   Augustine, *Civ.* 19.21.

10

Most Exalted Examples of Solitary Life

Christ, Mary, and David

§I. Of the solitude of the most holy John the Baptist and of the blessed Mary Magdalen who is on that account preferred to her sister[1]

1. Why should I any longer loiter among lesser figures? The greatest among those born of woman, John, holy in the womb, whom Christ, when he was about to visit earth, sent before him from heaven's height as a king sends a messenger, as a judge a crier, as the day sends dawn and the sun Lucifer, did not think himself safe until he went into the caves of a desert, though of a tender age.

2. Mary did likewise after sinning. She did not choose to be seen long among people or to reside in palaces, but escaping from her country and being conveyed to these regions as into a new world, she remained in constant hiding to the end, and had for her home that base and hollow rock which I think you have seen. It is not far distant from here and the place is hallowed, venerable with a kind of religious awe, and not unworthy to be visited even from great distances. I remember having been there often myself and once spending three nights and as many days, with quite a different satisfaction from what one is accustomed to take in cities. There the sweet and blessed hostess of Christ, living and dying, did not use the service of tiring-maids but the ministrations of gracious angels. But, some will object, her sister Martha did no such thing, and yet she is a saint. I do not deny it, but surely Mary, who did it, is much holier. Rightly therefore

---

[1]   In medieval Christianity, "Mary of Magdala" was often conflated with both "Mary of Bethany," the sister to Martha and Lazarus, and with the "sinful woman" of Luke 7. Conflicting traditions assert that she either journeyed to and later died in southern France or that her relics were brought to this region.—SHM

is she praised by that supreme and infallible judge for choosing the better part. If it is true, as the learned declare, that in addition to its literal truth the story of the two sisters cloaks the mystery of the two kinds of life, then there is no room left for doubting that the contemplative life was placed before the active by the judgment of Christ and should be especially preferred by Christ's faithful in making a choice.

§II. The solitude of Jesus Christ, our Lord and Savior

3. Who therefore shall wonder that a sinner, being besieged by so many enemies, should flee eagerly to a safe concealment when he is conscious of his own weakness and encouraged by so many examples, not only human but divine? Though all the cases are powerful, there is one that is irresistible. The Savior himself, the source of all salutary examples, though he was not in need of solitude or fearful of numbers, desiring to furnish forth his teaching with illustrations, went up to the mountain to pray, and prayed alone. In a wilderness he fasted and in a wilderness he overcame the temptation of the enemy, though later of his own will he was destined to be slain by his enemies in the midst of a crowd. Twice in the wilderness with a scant repast—a few loaves and fewer fishes—he fed the countless famished horde, not only with wondrous satisfaction of their appetites but with a prodigious quantity of fragments remaining. To the wilderness as a place of consolation and peace he betook himself when he heard of the death of John [the Baptist]. Moreover, he taught multitudes in the open fields. On a lofty mountain where the voice of the eternal Father thundered over him, he was transfigured. On the mountain he passed the night in prayer and again ascended it to pray and to die, not being satisfied till he had turned away from his followers to seek for his last prayer a spot more and more lonely, teaching by the act that we too should seek solitude in our extremity. Again, spurning the weight of the offered kingdom, he fled alone to the mountain; in the wilderness also he turned aside the danger of death, for which the time was not yet ripe, so that we might be taught to escape into the wilderness from the enticements and menaces of fortune and to despise them from a higher plane.

4. If these things are all true, if they are known by the evidence of the Gospels, shall we, Christian men, so far hesitate in our opinion of solitude when we know that this was the attitude of our Master and Leader and Lord, that his forerunner, as we said, spent his life in the

wilderness from the very outset, that his friends in such numbers had chosen the same kind of life before and chose it afterward, that his virgin mother finally, when she was heavy with God, proceeded without delay to the mountainous country, carrying the most blessed burden of her sacred womb into the solitude before he should be born? None of the faithful would hesitate to believe that the Holy Ghost was her guide in this journey.

§III. Praising the solitary life by way of epilogue to what has been said

5. By such instances as these and whatever others of the kind there may be (for to include all was neither necessary nor with so little paper possible), does the praise of solitude appear great and serve as a spur and example to imitation. Surely, whoever hears these things, if he has similar aspirations, will act in a like manner, nor will he be carried to the single goal by any other route, especially when there is none straighter nor more convenient. Doubtless, being remote from the populace in our purpose and point of view, it ought hardly to appear incongruous if we are as much separated from them by the remoteness or unlikeness of our situation as by our pursuits. Different habits and distinct dwelling places are proper to different minds. The confusion of opposites is generally unhappy. We should love solitude and admit it to familiarity, and that not only for honesty's sake but for safety.

6. For as luxury is a rare thing in the woods, so is modesty utterly rare in cities. What place can there be for reason and virtue where the power is controlled by evil examples and evil counsels, where everything is determined by false views, sway is given over to custom, and error is prescribed as something pleasant and seemly, where no one asks what is actually true but what is usually done or what the majority thinks, than which there is no test more misleading. Believe me, therefore, whoever you are that pursue virtue or fly from vice, lingering among people is dangerous for you if you are to hold on to the former and not be held by the latter. For what shall you see there save strife, adultery, fraud, injustice, theft, rapine, and murder? These are the arts that will greet you on the very threshold of the city, these shapes of things will fly about your head, these examples will clamor about your ears. Though you were at first quite unlike all the others whom you shall find, it will be very hard not to become as they.

§IV. Of King David and certain patriarchs who loved the solitary life

7. Lest by chance you should now be flattered by a better hope, thinking to hear or see things of another nature or to stand with firmer footing among slippery places, learn from the example of a more innocent age and a greater man what you may expect. David surely was a king both holy and wise and a prophet, and yet when weighed down with sorrows and afflictions, overwhelmed with the terror of death and with fear and trembling, overcast with shadows, what else did he see in the city but violence and strife, to use his own words, iniquity upon its walls, sorrow and wickedness in the midst of it, deceit and guile not departing from her streets.[2] Therefore, though himself the ruler and servant of such great peoples, he fled to a distance for his own safety and remained in the wilderness awaiting the Lord, who saved him from the tempest of his mind.

8. For he remembered that it was in the wilderness that the kingdom had been offered to him by God and that he had been placed not only over his brothers in the city, who were older, but over the king of Israel, who was on the throne by divine will. This same king, who implacably persecuted him, had twice been delivered into his hands in the wilderness and in caves, and twice he had allowed him to escape with such clear tokens of his innocence that when he displayed from afar the skirt of the king's robe and his spear, he constrained his spirit to tears, and, fierce though it was, subdued it by the sense of the benefit. And he pondered thereupon that whereas in solitude he had twice triumphed over his great enemy and twice been victorious over his own spirit, than which there is no victory more splendid, in Jerusalem on the other hand, he had been overcome by lust and had combined mean deception and cruel manslaughter with disgraceful adultery, a crime unworthy of the majesty of a king. Reflecting on his own lot in the city, he compared it with the solitude of Isaac, considering how the latter, having gone forth to meditate in the fields at the close of day, met with a happy and chaste spouse, as he was strolling along the road, while he himself, promenading voluptuously after his midday relaxation on the roof of the royal palace, had been visited with the impious and arrogant desire of defiling another man's wedlock—an occasion of misery and penitence to himself. He was right therefore to run away from the dangerous and ill-omened city and to hasten to safety and happiness in solitude.

[2]   Ps 54:10–11.

9. But if we understand it, as some would have it, to be spoken of Christ, it becomes an even stronger argument in support of our contention, inasmuch as Christ is greater not only than David but than all persons whatsoever. Not without reason indeed to attach the end of this discourse to the beginning, may we suppose that it was written about Abraham himself that the Lord "brought him forth abroad and said, Look now towards heaven,"[3] for in my judgment whoever wishes to look up toward heaven and meditate on heavenly things should be brought forth abroad, because in cities the mortal gaze is dulled and obscured by the interposition of many evil objects. And so, I say, he should be brought forth abroad, but brought forth by the Lord, otherwise he is nowhere safe, for our sins follow us into the deserts and cross the high seas with us.

10. That is why some, following not God but their own impressions as their guide, have come to grief in the wilderness. I am not unaware that Lot was a just man in Sodom and sinned on the mountain. Though he did not know what he was doing, as Jerome says, and though there was no element of deliberation in his offense, yet there was a fault involved in his sin. However just and upright he may have been in other respects, there is yet this one particular in which he cannot be excused, that he suffered himself to be so overcome by wine as to leave an opening even in ignorance for a shameful act that he would have shuddered to think of in his conscious and sober state. He went up to the mountain, one may say, with his left foot, and would have done better perhaps to stay in Zoar, which was the place he had chosen of his own accord as a home suited to his weakness.

11. But truly it is too clear and evident a matter to require such a host of examples, that those who aspire to heaven do not yearn for the clamorous assemblage of cities but for silent and tranquil solitudes, where God is constantly over their heads and the world and human affairs beneath their feet.

[3]   Gen 15:5.

11

Non-Christian Examples

§I. Of the life, customs, and rites of the Brahmans and the solitude of the famous Calanus

1. It is time I made an end; the intended limit of my work is exceeded and I am summoned by other tasks, while you have been already too much distracted by this discourse from attention to a greater duty. But I am unable to restrain myself from touching on a number of examples drawn from another class of men who ingeniously contrive the substance for a rarer fame.

2. I shall be silent about the Gymnosophists, who, it is reported, are accustomed to philosophize while wandering about naked (which is precisely what their name denotes), through the remote, shady wildernesses of India. I shall pass over the Brahmans, about whom some persons show a book inscribed with Ambrose's name. They live in the extreme East on the other side of the Ganges in a most healthy climate and an isolated region, which, as far as I can ascertain by conjecture, is not far distant from the place where the earthly paradise is believed to be, and they, too, wander naked through the woods. I should have said that they did not differ from the Gymnosophists either in principle or customs, or in anything save perhaps in situation and name, if it were not that Bardesanes, a Babylonian, and therefore worthy of credit, at least from his nearness to those parts, divided the Gymnosophists among the Hindus into two schools, one of which he calls Brahmans and the other Samarians.[1] Jerome, writing against Jovinian,[2] makes mention of this, so that it appears that

---

[1]   *Samaneans* in Jerome.
[2]   *Jov.* 2.14.

Gymnosophist is a generic name and Brahman a specific one, although I am not unaware that quite a different conclusion might be reached from what the same Jerome recounts in his preface to the Holy Scriptures. But lest this trifling difficulty should interfere with my undertaking, let me drive past it and follow rather the line I have begun.

3. There is, then, a tribe of Brahmans, as they say, distinguished by continence and purity and by contempt of riches, and greatly to be respected for their severe silence, in the midst of which the chief delight of their ears is not, as with many, in old wives' tales. Nor is this silence violated for them by the roaring of men or instrumental music, but their whole desire is for the song of birds and the sound of hymns, which is the only exercise they have for their tongues. Their entire hope is fixed on life in a future world. Their food consists of herbs and wild berries, their clothes, if they have any, are made of leaves, their roof of branches, their beds of flowers. They drink water from the springs.

4. The well-known Calanus, who is reputed to have written a letter to Alexander [the Great] of Macedon, was a member of this sect. When, according to the custom of his people, he was going voluntarily to his own death and the pile of wood was already kindled, he playfully predicted the impending death of Alexander. Both the Greek writers and ours make mention of this. But though famous among us, he is held infamous among his own people because, deserting as it were the more severe discipline of his native morality, he took refuge in the verbose philosophy of Greece and in luxurious delicacy. For this he is attacked severely on all sides, but more severe than all is the invective of the naked old sage, Dandamus, his contemporary, who was not himself tainted with foreign customs or far-fetched doctrines. I find among the writings of others a letter of his also—I don't know whether it is more spirited than verbose—addressed to the same king.

5. As for the letter of Calanus of which I have spoken, lest there be any doubt concerning it, Ambrose has placed it among his own letters, but of the other, it is not a letter that survives but a conversation with the king himself, quite long, and free on both sides, in the book about the life of the Brahmans which I have referred to above as inscribed with Ambrose's name. It does not fully savor to me of the style of Ambrose, yet it appears in the midst of his writings in a huge, venerable, and antique volume of his library which is guarded in the archives of the Ambrosian church in Milan. As far indeed as I can conjecture, on no random suspicions, the book is the work of Palladius rather than Ambrose.

6. But whoever the author may be, his account is surely one which it should not be unpleasant to hear. He reports that the king sent him presents of gold, silver, clothing, food, and oil, and that the philosopher disdained all but the last, because the gold and silver, he said, was so lacking in value that far from captivating the mind of a man, it even lacked the power to draw a sweeter song from any of the birds that were flying about. The clothes he not only rejected as superfluous but shrank from them as a hindrance to freedom and a bondage; at the food he mocked as though it were the remains of a fire. But in order not to seem disdainful of all the king's gifts, he reports that he took the oil, and lighting immediately a great pile of wood, he poured it over the fire, and when the brilliant flame burst forth, he offered thanks to almighty God, very briefly as always, as though this were a kind of sacrifice to him. But enough now of this solitary old man.

7. What should be my general judgment on him and on all the usages of those people, I do not know. For I do not like the habit of going naked, however great the gentleness of the elements, since the respectability of a modest garment is ordained for decency as well as protection against cold; however, it is written that though otherwise naked they were in the habit of covering their loins. I do not like their inhuman disregard of food and sleep, for in avoiding the extreme of the solicitous life we may well lapse into the opposite extreme. What I like, in this regard as in most, is the Ciceronian moderation: "We must besides present an appearance of neatness—not too punctilious or exquisite, but just enough to avoid boorish or ill-bred slovenliness."[3] The same principle is to be observed in regard to dress, in which, as in things generally, the middle way is the best.

8. This, I repeat, is the manner of life that I like. Let your sleep be short, your food light, your drink simple, your garment plain, but there should be some difference in dress and bed and food between men and cattle. I do not ask for the spoiling of rich houses nor golden ruins, I do not ask for tables loaded with chased silver and steaming dishes; I am not so forgetful of myself. But in all things, I ask for measure. I do not object to reclining occasionally or taking a nap on the ground, lest I should seem to reprove my friend who says in his Epistles,

Sup lightly, sleep on grassy river-banks.[4]

[3] Off. 1.36.
[4] Horace, Ep., i, xiv, 35 (Hovenden's translation).

But to spend one's whole life in the open air I judge to be more proper for bears than for men, although the poet glories in having the sky for his roof and the whole earth for his couch. But I fear you will say that these observations are too frivolous to be brought into a comparison with serious matters.

9. Their perverse custom of anticipating death is a mark of unsoundness, in that they claim the right whenever they wish of abandoning the post of their body without the command of God, as though their life came only from themselves. This is condemned alike by Christian faith and by the most celebrated of the philosophers. Moreover, it is a sign of grievous arrogance that they declare themselves to be without sin, thereby deluding themselves and charging with falsehood the Holy Spirit which through the mouth of John the Apostle beat down this insolence, inviting us to confession and repentance. These are the things which offend me in the sect; that old man who with such great freedom resisted Alexander to his face would, if he were here, doubtless make a magnificent reply to me also on behalf of his heresy.

10. On the other hand, however, I like their contempt of the world, which cannot be too great in a right-minded man. I like their solitude. I like their freedom, which no people enjoys to an equal degree; I like their silence, I like their leisure, I like their repose. I like their habit of fixed contemplation, I like their self-possession and assurance, provided it be not reckless; I like the even temper of their minds, their undisturbed brow, their fearing nothing and desiring nothing; I like their choice of a habitation in the woods near a stream, which, as appears from that book, they were accustomed to drink pure and undefiled, as though it were the breast of mother earth. I am affected, too, I confess, by the grave conversation of the Brahmans in general, but particularly by that colloquy of Dandamus with Alexander, which I mentioned a while ago, in which not Alexander alone but practically the entire human race is upbraided with a mass of innumerable crimes—the insatiable thirst for gold, inhuman savagery, universal hate and contempt of God, puerile admiration of riches and effeminate adornment of men, swelling of the mind, trembling before death, inconsiderate appetite for glory; add to these a slippery tongue, empty chatter which is often harmful even to the speaker, a philosophy which is all in words, an understanding which is in the lips, conversation which is contrary to life, heedlessness in action which is close neighbor to repentance, an unlimited craving of material objects induced by avarice,

strife among the feelings within and a great conflict of the members without, much perversity of morals, and above all, the love of slaughter and
passion for war; besides, excess in our domestic life, deep drinking and
gluttony which is enemy to itself and the ruin of the body it feeds, the
absurd quest for all kinds of food, and particularly the eating of meat, in
which he very bitingly says we are not like oxen or horses or deer but like
wolves and lions, and with even more burning reproach calls us living sep-
ulchers of dead bodies.

11. Into this digression I have led you not unwillingly, O father, dear to
my spirit, for though you have heard that I do not approve all the practices
of Brahmans, yet I do approve their solitude and solitary life, and in writing
on this subject I did not feel that I could pass over those who, I had heard,
were accustomed to glory remarkably in this life above all other men. But I
depart from here as from a suspected region, lest by dwelling too long on
such distant matters I should by chance mix up falsehoods with the truth.

§II. Of a certain solitary among Hindus

12. Even now, as I am writing this, there are found some among us, than
whom no nation is more curious in exploring the earth, who assert that
there is a man among the Hindus of this character, of amazing purity and
learning, whom the people and the kings of India approach with something more than humility and supplication, to see him and to beg of him
intercession with God and answers to their doubts and advice on the conduct of life, and whom they venerate in all ways with almost divine honors,
while he, aged, naked, reclining on the ground and not rising even before
kings, makes brief reply with scarcely a movement of his lips. His utter-
ances are received as oracles and act as a great comfort in every misfortune
and as a refreshment after the longest journeys.

13. Kings themselves, it is said (and this agrees well enough with what
we read of Alexander's conduct), when they come to the wood in which
he lives, are accustomed to dismount from their horses and take off their
purple robes and put down their crowns and rings and amulets and scepters and, after sending away their minions, to approach him alone or with
a very few chosen men, not without a certain awe, and to prostrate themselves at his feet and to regard it as a cause of eternal glory if they are
honored even once with his conversation. I might suspect this as quite
fabulous if it were not that Bardesanes, whom I mentioned shortly before,
and after him Jerome, said something not out of keeping with it, though

more briefly expressed, namely that there were men there whom the king was accustomed to worship when he came to them, believing that in their prayers lay the peace of the country. If there were in the past numbers of such men, what prevents the existence of one today? Many more things might be said of them, but they are too long to go into.

§III. Of the solitaries beyond the North and the Rhipean Mountains and the Hyperborean race and the remaining islands

14. But inasmuch as it seems worthwhile in speaking of the individual friends of solitude, to touch also upon nations of solitaries, so to speak, I shall recount a rumor of a Hyperborean race in a far different region of the world, beyond the North and the Rhipean Mountains, where, because of a necessary principle of the heavens, they say the whole year consists of a single day and a single night, each lasting six months. These Hyperboreans are said to have almost the same habits as the men of India, except that on account of the more inclement sky I do not believe in their going naked. But they have the same obnoxious practice of voluntary death, though the manner of dying is different. For while the Hindus enter the flames, these people, when they are invaded not by weariness but the satiety of life and the desire of death, adorn themselves with wreaths and go forth as to a joyful and festive ceremony and hurl themselves from a steep rock into the nearby waves of the ocean. Such an ending to life is with them most glorious, such a burial most distinguished.

15. In other respects, however, the race is the purest and most upright among mortals and enjoys a long and happy life, being innocent of wars and unacquainted with strife, always enjoying peaceful leisure and living amid groves and solitudes. Pomponius Mela in his books of Cosmography and many others have made mention of this people. Pliny the Elder and Solinus, who are very curious investigators of such matters, refer also to a people living near them and greatly resembling them whom they call Arimphaeans. Their dwellings are in the woods, and they subsist on berries. They are described as a serious and gentle race. They live where the peaks of the Rhipean Mountains terminate and are considered a holy people. Their influence is so great that in the midst of so many savage nations they are not only themselves safe and inviolate, but whoever takes refuge with them enjoys sanctuary as though in a temple. Among them hair is thought improper and both sexes shave.

16. Turning from here to the West, I pass over the philosophers of the Gauls, of whom frequent mention is found among writers. The Druids, they say, are accustomed in caves and distant ravines to instruct the noblest men of the nation in wisdom and eloquence and natural science and the motions of the stars and the mysteries of the gods and the immortality of the soul and the state of the future life. I pass over Thule and Hibernia. The former, though it is far famed through a variety of writers, is actually unknown, but the latter is very well known. I have learned that its people despise riches and the objects of civilization and moreover neglect the tilling of the soil but live in pastures and woods. Leisure is their luxury and freedom their greatest wealth. I should call them a happy people if I were not restrained by a certain ill repute, which may not be well founded, imputing viciousness to their character.

17. I pass over the Fortunate Isles which, being situated at the extreme west, are nearer and better known to us, but are as remote as possible from India and the North—a land famed through the writings of many men but chiefly through the lyric song of Horace, and whose repute is both very old and quite fresh. For within the memory of our fathers the warships of the Genoese penetrated to them, and recently Clement VI gave a prince to that country, a man of noble stock mixed of the royal blood of Spain and France, whom I once saw. You remember how, on the day when he went out to display himself in the city with crown and scepter, a great rain suddenly poured out of the sky, and he returned home so completely drenched that it was interpreted as an omen that the sovereignty of a truly rainy and watery country had been imposed upon him. How he succeeded in that dominion situated outside of the world I have not learned, but I do know that many things are written and reported in view of which its fortune does not appear fully to square with the designation of the Fortunate Lands. For the rest, its people enjoy solitude beyond nearly all other men, but are without refinement in their habits and so little unlike brute beasts that their action is more the outcome of natural instinct than of rational choice, and you might say that they did not so much lead the solitary life as roam about in solitude either with wild beasts or with their flocks.

18. But I have wandered enough in this curious quest through the widely separated corners of the earth. The responsibility for the truth of all these matters rests with the original authors and not with me. I only report what I have read or heard. But having now run over them, I shall proceed to more illustrious and more familiar examples.

12

Philosophers and Poets

§I. Of philosophers and poets who took refuge in solitude

1. What of the philosophers and poets? When I speak of philosophers, I do not refer to those who were fittingly named by the man who first dubbed them "professors," for they are philosophers only in their profession, in their actions they are foolish; they teach others but are the first to act in opposition to their own teaching, the first to disregard the laws they themselves have handed down. Proclaiming themselves the standard-bearers, they are the first to desert the ranks and to rebel against the commands of virtue. I therefore do not mean these, but those true men who are always few and at this time scarcely to be found at all, who give evidence of their love and devotion to the wisdom which they profess.

2. And by poets I understand not such as are content with the spinning of "verses void of substance and sonorous trifles,"[1] as Horace describes them, with whom we are replete to the point of disgust, but those who, if we may trust Cicero, were ever more rare than philosophers themselves, true poets I mean, and using Horace's language once more, those who have genius, "a soul of heaven's own fire, words that grandly roll,"[2] to whom the honor of this name is deservedly assigned. Would not philosophers and poets of this kind, of whom I am not able to point out a single one but might imagine many as existing in our own age or destined to exist in later ages, would not these, I say, shun the cities and run after solitude? It is known to be the case with the philosophers of the past.

---

[1]   *Ars* 322.
[2]   *Sat.* 1.4.43–44 (Conington's translation)

3. Question Plato, and I think he will prefer his Academy to the greatly admired Athens. Question Plotinus, whom Macrobius calls with Plato the chief of the teachers of philosophy, and he will answer that with the whole world before him he chose leisure in Campania. Though his end was unfortunate, his choice was glorious. Inquire of Pythagoras and he will tell you that he sought out not only agreeable seclusion but even vast and frightful wildernesses, and often went on toilsome journeys in deserted regions in his zeal for investigating the truth. It is certain, too, on the evidence of Jerome, that the Pythagoreans who inherited his name and teachings shrank from engagements which exposed them to the agitations of the pleasures and were accustomed to live in lonely and deserted places. Ask Democritus and he will admit that he tore out his eyes in order to see the truth and avoid seeing the mob, which is the enemy of truth. Examine Parmenides and Atlas and you will find that they left their names in the mountains which they inhabited. And if the truth of the matter is looked into, Prometheus too will not deny that the occasion of the fable in which he is bound to a peak in the Caucasus and exposed to the gnawings of an insatiable vulture was that he had taken possession of the solitude of that mountain and applied himself with the greatest concentration of mind to penetrating the inner mystery of things, which is surely exhausting to the mind of the student.

4. The place often provides a spur to the intellect and therefore it is to be wished that it were conveniently free and adaptable to those who must apply their minds to lofty things, seeing that the numberless forms of vanity which prevail where people are assembled serve to lower the mind's tone and to dissipate it, and death, which is bound to come in, finds a thousand ways through the windows. Impelled by these reasons, many of the philosophers, as I read in Jerome, not only forsook the haunts of cities as the chief seats of restlessness and trouble, but even their little suburban gardens, which were rendered suspect, most likely, by an excessive development of luxury and close proximity to riotous cities. Therefore, many considerations lead me to believe that, in the case of Socrates and Aristotle and some others, there were accidental circumstances which always stood in the way of their desire for solitude, whether it was the authority of their royal disciples or the commands and requirements of the state.

5. To these examples of antiquity I shall add a later one not very far removed from our own age, that of the famous Peter Abelard, a man whose orthodoxy is by some, I know not with what justice, suspected, but whose genius was surely not slight. In the long account which he gives in the

History of His Calamities he records how, yielding to the envious, he penetrated the hidden solitude of Troyes. Even there, however, he was not free from the immense concourse of students from all parts whom the great fame of his teaching had assembled from many cities to sit under him in his solitude, but had to live without the longed-for peace of which inveterate and persistent hatred and malice had deprived him. From this point we must return to antiquity and to another form of intellectual activity whereby the argument we are aiming at may be confirmed.

§II. Of the ancient poets who chose solitude

6. What shall I say of Homer, who is the father of poets, since of his forerunners like Orpheus, Linus, and Musaeus, whether we regard them as poets or musicians or, as some would have it, both poets and musicians because of the kinship of the two arts, only the bare names have come down to us? Homer has so well described the lonely places not only of Greece but of Italy, that what, according to Cicero, he did not himself see (for tradition makes him blind) he has made visible to us, so that we behold the painting, as it were, of his genius and not the poetry. But shall we believe that he would have been able to do this if he had not before growing blind carefully observed those places and faithfully retained their memory?

7. And what shall I say of our Virgil, who ran away from Rome, where he was basking in the admiration paid to his genius and in the friendship of the prince who ruled the world, and while seeking the freedom of loneliness encountered on the way a premature death which rescued him from all such cares? In his own judgment he had need of the assistance of solitude in order that his divine poem might be perfected. Death envied the genius of the Latin tongue and was intent on doing it greater injury but was hindered by the piety of a prince distinguished for his mildness and devotion to literature.

8. Horace openly avows that it is not royal Rome that he likes but quiet Tibur and unwarlike Tarentum, and he means by these words nothing else than solitude and peace, having made trial in Rome of the opposite of both. So earnestly does he enumerate the annoyance arising in that city from the great assemblage of people that you may easily see his feelings are speaking. The last of his Epistles is written to Florus, whom he asks more than once, in order to express himself as explicitly as possible on a clear point,

> Think too of Rome: can I write verses here,
> Where there's so much to tease and interfere?[3]

Then, after inserting an elegant account of these vexations, he concludes ironically

> Go now; abstract yourself from outer things,
> And hearken what the inner spirit sings.[4]

But this not being enough, he asks again

> And how should I, with noises all about,
> Tread where they tread, and make their footprints out?[5]

Nor is he satisfied till he once more puts the question

> Here, in this roaring, tossing, weltering sea,
> To tune sweet lyrics, is that work for me?[6]

And lest you suppose that he is content with angry questioning and ironic observations and says nothing distinctly about people, he gives a rule which is short but of the broadest application, to the effect that

> Bards fly from town and haunt the woods and glades.[7]

Imitating him and likewise restricting the meaning to poets, I have remarked in a certain epistle,

> The forest is dear to the muses, the city is an enemy to poets.[8]

The same Horace, whether captivated by the weather of the Gulf of Baiae, or loading with many praises his woods and his little field inhabited by five families,[9] or sighing in the midst of oppressive and hateful business for the aspect of his favorite farm, infallibly condemns and scorns residence in the city. On this subject he disputes with his friend and likewise with his stew-

[3] *Ep.* 2.2.65–66 (Conington's translation).
[4] *Ep.* 76.
[5] *Ep.* 79–80
[6] *Ep.* 84–86.
[7] *Ep.* 77.
[8] Petrarch's *Poetic Epistles*, bk. 2, epistle 3 (Bernardo Ruthenensi S.R. E. Cardinali).
[9] *Ep.* 1.14.

ard and slave, so that taking everything together no one can doubt what his feeling was. In one of his satires, referring to his domestic leisure, he says

Here you see a careless life, from stir and striving free.[10]

How greatly he valued it, he has expressed in his *Epistles* where he says,

Give me a country life and leave me free,
I would not choose the wealth of Araby.[11]

9. He praises solitude, therefore, and prefers leisure to great wealth, and so it is that the works of his leisure remain, and the place preserves the memory of his solitude. It is still called Horace's Field, and after having changed so many owners, keeps the name of its more famous master to this day. Among poets I believe I shall scarcely be able to find anyone to oppose him, since to no class of men has solitude been so needful and so friendly, except it be Ovid alone, or perhaps those who imitate him or whom he imitated.

10. Ovid strikes me indeed as having been a man of great genius but of a lascivious, unsteady, and extremely effeminate temper, who found pleasure in the company of women to such an extent that he placed in them the sum and apex of his happiness. Writing his *Ars Amatoria*, an unwholesome work and in my opinion justifiably the cause of his exile, he not only teaches that the city of Rome, as being very fruitful in matrons and maidens, should be sought by those who to the natural excitement of that madness add the provocation of a certain art, but he also distinguishes the places and the holidays with a view to providing more abundant material for passion. I shall be silent about that disgraceful wish, which it is even indecent to recount, though it comes from the mouth of a desperate and abandoned man, which he was not even ashamed of setting forth in writing for the knowledge of all ages, defining the happy man as one relaxed in the act of venery. He even dares to praise death in that state in which life is most disgraceful and useless and desires of the gods that this might be the cause of his own extinction. To be sure, as he himself says, it would be appropriate to him and to his life, but in itself it is the most wretched form of death and worse without a doubt than death itself. If he had not been of such morals and such a mind, he would have had a brighter reputation

---

[10]   *Sat.* 1.6.129.
[11]   *Ep.* 1.7.36.

with serious men and he would not have come to his exile in Pontus and the solitudes of the Ister, or he would have borne it with greater composure. But I pass over to the example of a firmer intellect.

§I. The solitude of Seneca, a citizen of Cordova and a Roman senator

11. Seneca of Cordova, when already a Roman citizen and a senator and more famous in Rome than was compatible with regard for safety and assurance of concealment, in a certain tragedy recalls his solitude in Corsica with no little tenderness of mind, and with reason puts the humiliation of his leisured exile above the glory of his active life of that time. Read the passage and you will understand from his comparison of the opposite conditions which of them you should regard as preferable. Moreover, what his opinion was is sufficiently indicated by that advice which he gave to Lucilius, which I mentioned earlier. But in that view he is so harsh that even I, who have always liked solitude, do not like his counsel of solitude. And though the last end of this man does not admit of any doubt in the matter, though it is clear that in the deserted solitude he enjoyed entire freedom and undisturbed study of philosophy, while in the royal city not even his life was safe from the relentlessness of men. Yet there is something quite amazing in the fact that in a passage of his tragedy he should so far in advance have foreseen and put into writing his fall and grievous ruin.

§II. The solitude of Cicero

12. I am aware of only Cicero in this class of persons who did not bear loneliness with sufficient equanimity, and this, I believe, was because he not so much hated the thing itself as the ruin of law and justice which was the occasion of it. That is what is suggested by the tenor of his own complaints. Moreover, in addition to being a student of philosophy he was the greatest of orators, and when one seeks, as he unaffectedly did, to acquire glory in this special branch of literature, one naturally cannot meet with it save amidst populous cities. That is why, when he had to defend King Deiotarus before Julius Caesar, he complained at the case being conducted in a private chamber and not in the presence of the Roman people.

13. It is peculiar and appropriate in the case of orators that in proportion to the greatness of their own powers they should take satisfaction in great cities and crowded assemblies, that they should feel a loathing for lonely places and a distaste and hatred for silent tribunals. And there-

fore, just as the lesser men each had a great desire for his own city, so did Cicero for the city of Rome, not solely as for his own country, all the more precious to him for the greater care and trouble he had spent for its safety and reputation, but as for a country adequate to his genius. In saying this I might lean on the support of Seneca, who dared to declare that no voice but that of Cicero was really alive, although by an error of popular speech the phrase has been used of many others, and to affirm that no genius but that of Cicero was on a level with the power of the Roman people. But more trustworthy than any witness whatsoever is the manifest assurance of the facts themselves, which show that as in rule and glory absolute sovereignty belonged to the Roman people, so in intellect and eloquence it belonged to Cicero.

14. For the rest, it is well known what advantage Cicero derived from solitude, though it was unwillingly. It transformed the greatest of orators into a great philosopher, and there is not a student who does not know how magnificently Latin studies were enriched by this circumstance. In such an outcome Cicero himself found the consolation for his grievance when he said, "As I am kept by force of armed treason away from practical politics and from my practice at the bar, I am now leading a life of leisure. For that reason I have left the city and, wandering in the country from place to place, I am often alone. . . . I have accordingly," he adds, "written more in this short time since the downfall of the Republic than I did in the course of many years, while the Republic stood."[12] In truth he was not mistaken, for who is able to set forth and appreciate the splendor of this man's intervals of leisure and the fame of his retired dwelling places in Arpinum, in Cumae, in Pompeii, in Formia, in Tusculum? In one place he projected a system of laws, in another erected an academy, in another equipped the orator, or defined the duties of men, or described the shapes and qualities of the gods, or attacking divination dug up that root of manifold errors, or established the bounds of good and evil, or composed a magnificent exhortation in favor of philosophy, which Augustine, the illustrious champion of our faith, frankly admits was his guide in the imitation of life and the pursuit of truth. Finally, lest I should seem with a lover's infatuation to have gone astray in the wake of a single man out of the many that I treat, it was in that retirement, I say, that he learned to despise death, with patience to triumph over physical pain, by reason to banish illness and grief, to

12   *Off.* 3.1.

eradicate affliction and the causes of affliction, and what, to use his own expression, gives the greatest luster to his philosophy, he there taught that virtue was in need of no support for the attainment of a good and happy life but was sufficient unto itself, an opinion contrary to that of some great men. Moreover, what others deliver with dry and insipid utterance, he has treated in a style of great eloquence and beauty, so that an element of pleasure might be added to its usefulness and a fitting stateliness of language not be wanting to such majestic thoughts.

15. It is clear that isolation kindled the genius of this man. And if it surprises you that it operated in this way even while it was disliked, what do you think would have been its effect if it were freely chosen? Or how greatly do you think it is to be desired when it is of so much benefit even to those who embrace it with reluctance? But whatever the manner of life which he would have preferred for himself, he is very positive in setting the kind which should be chosen by philosophers, in the book in which he describes the duties proper to every class of men. For he says that many in their craving for repose gave up their public cares and sought refuge in leisure, and among these were the noblest of philosophers, preeminent in their calling, and also certain men of grave and austere character, some of whom, being unable to endure the conduct of the people and of princes, lived on their farms in the enjoyment of their domestic goods and had precisely the same idea as kings, though they did not live by the same practices, wanting no other man's possessions and subject in their freedom to no other man's will. Although in making the comparison he affirms that the active life is more profitable to the state, which in a measure even I will not deny, he admits that the retired life is safer and easier, less burdensome and vexatious than other modes of life, and therefore he not only sanctions it for those who have some fair reason for embracing it, but especially commends it to those who excel in intellect and learning. And although he himself, as I have said, was at first impatient of this kind of life, in the end when he was depressed with many sorrows and overwhelmed especially by the death of his beloved daughter, he came to long for it, and, writing to his friend Atticus, said, "I now reject everything and consider nothing more tolerable than solitude,"[13] and again, "Solitude and retirement are my proper sphere; indeed, I avoid the city for many reasons."[14] In another

---

[13]   *Att.* 12.18.
[14]   *Att.* 12.26.

place he says, "I cannot endure to be in a crowd,"[15] and yet again, "Nothing is more pleasant than this solitude, in which I am free from all company. I bury myself in the dense and wild woods in the morning and do not issue from them till it is evening."[16] As often as I read this sentence, I mentally fall in with it as though I myself and not another had written it, for the same thing often happens to me.

16. But to take leave of Cicero at last, there is that passage in which he flatters his dear friend by remarking, "After you I have not a greater friend than solitude," and then adding, "In it my only converse is with books."[17] I shall not collect every remark, for from those which I have presented you may see how that lover of the city and the Forum came to hate what he had once loved and placed literary leisure above all things.

§III. The solitude of Demosthenes

17. In this particular I surmise that Demosthenes was of the same mind with Cicero, and, unless a reason should appear for changing my opinion, such as I have not yet met in my reading, his feeling was consistent where that of the other wavered. For the calling of both was alike, and Demosthenes was besides rather vain, as Cicero himself points out,[18] deriving pleasure from hearing old women whispering at his back, "That is the great Demosthenes." And yet it is well known that it was in a lonely place that he specially drilled those oratorical powers which he so effectively wielded in the city. Hence Quintilian says of him, "Demosthenes, though so great a lover of seclusion, used to accustom himself, by studying on the seashore, where the breakers dashed with the loudest noise, not to be disconcerted at the uproar of public assemblies."[19] Do not be confused by what I formerly said about Demosthenes[20] being accustomed to choose a spot that was free from all disturbance to ear and eye, whereas here I speak of his seeking the sound of the waves and the open sea. In one place he sharpened his wit, in the other he exercised his voice, but he did both in a lonely place.

18. These men studied in privacy that they might traffic in public; they meditated in the woods that they might make a display in the cities. Their

---

[15]   *Att.* 12.26.
[16]   *Att.* 12.15.
[17]   *Att.* 12.15.
[18]   *Tusculans*, v. 36.
[19]   *Inst.* 10.4.
[20]   DVS bk. 1, tract 5, ch. 1.

profession was their excuse, since their object was the same, whether by speech or by silence to increase their substance. Though I recall nothing of the sort in the case of Cicero, it is well known, as appears from the *Attic Nights*, that Demosthenes put a price even on his silence. As for us, in whose hearts nothing venal should enter and nothing be a matter of display, but all things should tend to salvation, to the law of life on earth, and the hope of the life to come, we must study in solitude what it remains for us to practice in solitude; we must live in solitude and die in solitude. This is my earnest wish, and if God will look affectionately upon me, I dare even make it my hope.

§IV. *Of Anaxagoras and other illustrious men who loved the life of solitude*

19. My impression that philosophers have always in this respect differed in their attitude from orators is derived from observing the difference in their habit of life and above all in their aim. While the mind of one class is fixed on capturing popular applause, the toil of the other, unless their pretension is hypocritical, is occupied in the knowledge of mind introspectively turned upon itself and in contempt of empty fame. For what sort of man shall we suppose Anaxagoras to have been, or Xenocrates, that most austere of philosophers in his steadfastness and abstemiousness, as Cicero reports, or Zeno, the father of the Stoics, or Carneades, the most industrious of them all, whose complete absorption in studious thoughts, as we read, often made him quite forget himself while he was reclining at table? Shall we suppose that it was amidst the turmoil and distractions of men that a mind could preserve such firmness and fixity beyond the ninetieth year, rather than in solitude where there is no one to distract it from its object?

20. I for one should not easily be persuaded, though I had nothing to support me beyond my own conjecture, that any of these men lived in the city. Nor should I believe that it was in the streets of a city that Chrysippus had his house or Diogenes his tub, seeing that the former was annoyed by the greetings of men and the latter by the shadow of even the greatest king, were it not for the statement of Jerome, who is nearer to them in time, that Diogenes lived in the doorways and porches of cities. The authority of Jerome and his wide and various reading compels me to believe what I should not equally accept on any man's word, for he surely would not have

set down such a thing if he had not found it in a trustworthy writer. Of these men I have now said enough.

21. There is, however, Solon, whose name is the most celebrated among the Seven Wise Men of Greece. Though in the beginning he was the legislator of his country and its chieftain and ruler, yet in his last years, as Plato's *Timaeus* indicates, he devoted himself to other pursuits. He must be reckoned with the lovers of solitude at the moment when he left the country that he had furnished with its laws and in his eagerness for knowledge went to unknown lands, getting special pleasure from his travels in Egypt.

13

Emperors and Military Leaders

§I. Of Julius and Augustus Caesar who loved and wished for solitude

1. What wonder it is that men of studious pursuits should be fond of solitude when even emperors and generals of armies were fond of it, which is a real cause for wonder. I shall pass over Julius Caesar, who though a very young man when he decided to withdraw from the struggles of public life to the peaceful atmosphere of Rhodes and devote himself to literature, was prevented at that time by the attacks of pirates and later by the storms of domestic and foreign wars and was unable to attain to the object of his wishes.

2. I do not include in the number of the solitary the name of Augustus Caesar, in whom was reached the summit of mortal power and human greatness, even though I find him sometimes living in the country or strolling by himself in the woods, because this was a privilege which the burden of his private and public duties, I suppose, enabled him to enjoy but rarely, but I am not afraid to name him with the admirers of the life of solitude. For he was constantly longing for the restfulness of this kind of life. All his thoughts and all his words terminated in repose, this was his comfort in present toil, this his compensation for labors past, this his expectation for time to come. By comparison with this state every privilege of wealth, every burden of power had a mean flavor as of something troublesome and despicable. In short, being exhausted at the height of his enjoyment of all the honors which can fall to the lot of the most fortunate man, he drew breath at the mere naming of the solitary life. Of the truth of this a number of writers have spoken, and it is also witnessed by a letter of his to the Senate which has come into my hands.

3. How great, then, do you suppose would have been his pleasure at attaining the condition on which he had fixed his mind's eye with such tenderness? And it was not only by letters that he appealed to the Senate to allow him at last to live and, if the condition of the state warranted, to spend his old age as a private citizen, but on occasion, as Suetonius reports, he summoned the Senate and magistrates to his presence and turned over to them the imperial reckoning. He continued, however, to exercise power, whether because, as the same historian has it, he thought he could not live privately without danger and that it was rash to entrust the state to the power of numbers, and so kept his wishes in restraint for the sake of his own and the public safety, or whether, as we have a right to believe, he yielded to the entreaty of the Senate and the people, since it is a fact that no prince was ever more loving toward his subjects. Or perhaps he was not at all influenced by any entreaties or any fear for personal or public welfare but was troubled by a natural human weakness. For to one sitting upon the highest peak of fortune as lord and ruler of the world, the descent to the humble and lowly position of his desire must have seemed very abrupt as he mentally revolved it, and, as the expression goes, a kind of vertigo may have taken possession of him in fear of the dizzy height, and so, after weighing and considering the matter well, he stuck to his place and never descended from it till his death.

4. Therefore, as I have said, though there is no place for this great and active prince among those who actually enjoyed solitude and leisure, yet it was impossible to omit his case in a discussion of the theme because there is no witness through whom the great charm of this blessing may be more clearly recognized. Caesar, who could give everything, desired only this *gift for himself; elevated over all men, he saw only this lifted up above his throne.*

§II. Of Diocletian and Antoninus Pius as lovers of the solitary life

5. What was a wish to Augustus became an actuality for Diocletian, the first of our emperors who ordained that he should be worshiped as a god and who, putting pearls on his shoes and garments and coming out loaded with jewels, seemed to convert the habit of the Caesars from a Roman and human one into something Persian or godlike. He had shortly before celebrated a triumph with captive standards borne in front of his chariot and the booty of the Parthians carried in advance, but afterward he grew

weary of the turbulent court and the costly encumbrance, of troops of attendants and of general servility, suddenly changed his mind, and conceived a desire to be alone and poor and free, and to swim out from the sea of imperial cares into the haven of a humbler life, naked like a pilot from a great shipwreck.

6. We admire Celestinus, though that holy man did for the sake of an eternal life what this great sinner had already done for the sake of the very short and uncertain remainder of his old age. And when out of his longing for the utmost peace he surrendered himself to the lot of a private citizen, he did not fix on Rome for the abode of his changed life, lest he should be disturbed by the smoke or the smell of the power he had resigned, but preferred to go to his native town of Salona in Dalmatia, and not inside the city either, but to a place near his native walls where he died in a country house which he had perhaps built with that very end in view. By his solitary and humble life, he felt that much serenity had been added to his old age without any diminution to his highest honors. He is the only private citizen, according to the statements of Eutropius and Eusebius, to be reckoned in the number of the gods. However, what Diocletian did after laying down power had been done by Antoninus Pius before the assumption of power. Julius Capitolinus, the historian, records that during his whole private life he lived most commonly in the fields and was famous in all places.

§III. *The solitude of Numa Pompilius, the second king of Rome*

7. But I go too fast, I must retrace my steps. I shall omit the Quintii, the Curii, the Fabricii, the Serrani and others the greater part of whose life was spent in the fields and shall show that from the very outset and even before the beginning of the Roman Republic, the wisest and best of the kings enjoyed this form of life.

8. Numa Pompilius, the second in order among the kings if one regards sequence, the first in justice, being as a foreigner summoned unexpectedly to power, when he had applied his whole mind to the care of the civil and religious laws in order by his genius to control and soften a people passionate and imbued with the ferocity of its first king, was often, according to report, accustomed to seek for the purpose a dark and solitary place, which I have seen with my own eyes, distant from the city fifteen miles, or not much more. In that place at the base of the hill of Aricia there is a hollow and shaded rock from which a spring flows perpetually, with ilexes all

about, a dense grove and a profound silence. There the king, a very learned man for that time, had formed the practice of discovering human laws and divine ceremonies, or perhaps of giving them a sanction after having discovered them elsewhere. There he sat alone in long silence, and after a great interval he issued forth alone in meditation and brought the written laws with which to control a people as yet rude and untrained but soon to become the ruler of nations.

9. In order to bind their new and untamed spirits with a sort of religious noose and the curb of fear, he sought acceptance for his plan by imitating, it is said, the example of the Cretan king Minos and pretending with the boldest fabrication that he enjoyed nightly meetings and converse with the gods. This fiction along with the other sacred mysteries (supposedly) discovered by him, he deplored at his death, issuing books in Latin and Greek by which he might point out as well as he could to those learned in either tongue that for the temporary assistance of truth he had used the support of falsehood. But when the authority of the laws introduced by him was already standing on its own foundation, he did not care to have the people involved in superfluous errors. After the lapse of many generations a Roman praetor with the concurrence of the Senate ordered the burning of these books which had been found next to the king's tomb, although I do not know whether it was because he found them dangerous to true religion, which reason he is in fact said to have alleged, or whether he merely sought this pretext, as I am more inclined to believe, and was really concerned lest the people being liberated from fear should shake off the yoke of their nobility.

10. I shall say nothing of the vanity or impiety of the act. For the moment it will be enough to have pointed out that solitude is the source of many excellent things and that from it also flowed the origins of the Roman laws.

§IV. Of Romulus, Achilles, and Hercules who loved solitude

11. Romulus was more fiery and violent than his successor, yet he also trained his mind to affairs in the woods and in a shepherd's hut, so that none but a solitary architect may be regarded as having been fitted for the founding of the greatest empire. It is difficult to conceive: the harshest solitude of all gave to the queen of cities its material, its name, its ground, and its founder. We read that Achilles learned in solitude what soon made him terrible in the cities of Asia and famous in those of Greece. Hercules too

attained in solitude that wholesome plan of life which I have mentioned in the preceding book, when, hesitating long and much as though at a parting of the ways, he ultimately spurned the way of pleasure and took possession of the path of virtue, and marching indefatigably along its course he was raised not only to the apex of human glory but to a reputation of divinity. Although the fame of this man extends its branches high and wide, if you look for its roots your mind must turn back to solitude.

§V. Of the two Scipios who particularly loved solitude

12. But whither shall we dismiss the two Africani, by far the greatest of all military leaders? Truly they are the two thunderbolts of war, as Virgil says, and I am surprised that some persons take this to refer to anybody else. The first of them, as we learn in Livy, from the time that he put on the dress of manhood never any day performed a public or private action before going to the Capitol, entering a temple, sitting down, and spending some time there in secrecy. This habit was maintained during his whole life. Thus did that singular man, whose celebrity does not come from Greek legends and superstitions but from celebrated Roman judgments, and who also gained the reputation of divine origin because of his admired virtue, depend upon religion for the beginning of his enterprise and reckon solitude as the best abode for religion. From that starting point, he was accustomed to assail the business, whatever it was, with more than human confidence and to promise a prosperous issue of his undertakings to himself and his followers; and in fact he never failed.

13. Besides, not to separate two so closely allied and so much alike, it is a familiar fact that both of these men, each in his time, were as much lovers of solitude as of virtue, and after the exertions of war, after the victories and triumphs, were accustomed to remove to Liternum or Formia or Caieta and to rest there, alone with a few friends. O excellent spectacle, transcending the pomp and scepters of all kings, to see such men, the preservers of the state, the liberators of the citizens, the defenders of Italy, the conquerors of nations, their task successfully performed, the victorious people dismissed free and rejoicing, their bodyguard left in Rome, their triumphal habit put off and the insignia of their rank eagerly restored, strolling alone, at leisure, and unconscious of depressing cares, over the hills and along the shore, and often picking up little shells or sea pebbles of different sorts, both white and black. I find in Cicero, set down with the

greatest respect and reverence, that they used to grow incredibly childlike when they flew out of the city to the country, as though they had escaped from chains.

14. But surely, beautiful thoughts followed in the train of that solitude, and in that leisure some quality of greatness always appeared. And so Cicero himself, in the passage in which he mourns his own solitude, admires that of the elder Africanus and, relying on the evidence of his contemporary and rival, Cato, he inserts Scipio's utterance, a magnificent one, as he calls it, and worthy of a great and wise man, that he was never less idle than when at leisure, and never less lonely than when alone.[1]

15. Strange to say, Ambrose tries to wrest the glory of this saying from his fellow citizen, but there is never wanting civil strife where Romans are concerned—they fight even in their books. Now it is in the third book of *de Officiis* that Cicero bestows this praise on Scipio, and to make the matter quite obvious, Ambrose, who imitates Cicero not only in many of the details but in the title and the number of his books as well, in the corresponding portion of his work, that is, at the very beginning of the third book, strives with laborious argument to transfer the honor snatched from Scipio Africanus to the prophets of the Lord, Moses, Elijah, and Elisha, on the ground that long before Scipio they were active in leisure and enjoyed companionship in solitude.

16. I shall not contend with Ambrose, for I know that he speaks the truth, and even if I did not know it, he would crush me with his authority much more effectively than Plato crushed Cicero. For his authority is great with me, and not undeservedly, since I believe the Holy Spirit speaks through his mouth. How should I dare to suspect that Moses was ever alone, who was not only always with himself, which is the very quality of a wise and learned man, but with whom God spoke face to face as a friend with a friend? And how should I think him idle when, sitting silent and unarmed, he cried out to the Lord and was heard as far as the heavens, and when, with difficulty and by the assistance of another lifting up his weary hands, he overcame by himself the strong hands of so many enemies, which armed legions could not do without his help? How should I think Elijah lonely, with whom likewise God and angels conversed, and how think him idle when he commanded the rain, and with a word provided an unfailing barrel of meal and an inexhaustible cruse of oil for his

---

[1]   Cicero, *Off.* 3.1.1.

hostess who was in fear of death from starvation, and with a great effort of faith restored her dead son to her alive? How should I call his disciple Elisha lonely when he showed his servant, who was trembling with fear of the enemy, the supporting chariots and horses and angelic troops which were invisible to others? How call him idle when according to his promise he gave to his Shunamite hostess a son by her aged husband and restored that son again by reviving him after he had died in childhood, so that a single boy might serve as proof of his prophetic faith and power?[2] But what is there remarkable in his power of resuscitation while alive, when he is known after his death by the mere contact of his body to have brought the dead to life? Moreover, who will regard him as idle when, sitting in complete leisure, he knew all the attempts of those who were out of his sight and the thoughts and plans of the enemy as though he were present, making report of everything to his adherents? Having this knowledge when he was encompassed with an entire army at the order of the king of Syria, he reduced the legions of the besiegers by the mere bidding of his tongue to blindness and captivity and then with a word freed them again.

17. These are the marks of a dominating leisure and of a very potent solitude. But granted that the glory of the character is of greater antiquity with the prophets, who clearly come first both in time and in merit, is the praise of Scipio any less because someone has preceded him in the same kind of praise, especially since there can be no question of imitation where, as I feel certain, there has been no communication of knowledge? I do not deny that imitation usually detracts and diminishes a trifle of the commendation and fame of human achievements, but surely, whoever may receive the original title for the qualities, the saying, which made me after so long an interval revert to the names of these prophets, is original with Scipio and belongs to him alone, and in that even Ambrose will not contradict me.

---

[2]   2 Kgs 4:32–35.

14

The Nature and Virtues of This Solitary Life

§VI. Explaining, by an interpretation of the saying of the elder Scipio, about what kind of solitude and leisure the author intends to speak

1. The force of this aphorism is to impress in a few words what I have in mind. I mean a solitude that is not exclusive, leisure that is neither idle nor profitless but productive of advantage to many. For I agree that those who in their leisure are indolent, sluggish, and aloof, are always melancholy and unhappy, and for them there can be no performance of honorable actions, no absorption in dignified study, no engagement with distinguished personalities. This then is the sum. I do not admit into our leisure employments that are more inconstant than the winds but only such as have some fixity, whose result is not trouble and gain and dishonor but satisfaction and virtue and fame. The holiday which I ordain is for the body, not for the mind; I do not allow the intellect to lie fallow except that it may revive and become more fertile by a period of rest. For a rest benefits the brain just as it benefits the soil.

2. Furthermore, in my solitude I not only entertain but take pains to summon noble thoughts, than which no companionship can be imagined more agreeable and charming, and without which life is miserable whether in cities or in the woods. Then there are books of different kinds in whose substance and whose authors one has pleasant, unfailing companions, ready at his bidding to go into public or return to his house, always prepared to be silent or to speak, to stay at home or to accompany him in the woods, to travel, to remain in the country, to converse, to amuse, to cheer, to comfort, to advise, to dispute, to consult, to teach the secrets of nature, the

memorable deeds of history, the rule of life and the contempt of death, moderation in prosperity, fortitude in adversity, equanimity and steadfastness in all our actions; cheerful associates, learned, humble, and eloquent, free from annoyance and expense, without complaint or grumbling, without envy or treachery. Add to all these benefits that they do not ask for food or drink and are content with scant raiment and a narrow portion of the house, though they afford their hosts inestimable treasures of mind, spacious houses, brilliant attire, delightful entertainment, and most savory food.

3. Into my solitude I also admit friends—that sweet society of which I have said a good deal already[1]—without whom I should look upon life as deformed and stunted, as a thing altogether devoid of light. Whenever toward night, as may happen, a friendly hand knocks at my door,

> If, on a rainy day, when work is slack,
> Some pleasant neighbor or old friend drops in.[2]

(I think these verses were composed by Horace from a deep experience of the pleasure of friendly intercourse and were drawn by him from the very heart of nature.) Whenever, I say, such a guest happens my way—keeping in mind that the welcome depends upon long separation and that I am free from tasks, lest you should think that I take pleasure in frequent conviviality or in interruptions to my work—then it seems to me that I have found not another, but myself somehow duplicated. Surely they are not two who have a single mind. Love knows how to make one from two, otherwise the command of Pythagoras were impossible that through friendship many should be united into one. From this it follows that any place which is capable of holding one person can hold two friends. No solitude is so profound, no house so small, no door so narrow but it may open to a friend.

§I. How the virtues of the one to whom the book is dedicated and of the friends granted to him by fortune invite one to the life of solitude.

4. In your own case, father, if you but knew yourself and your advantages, there is nothing wanting that can make solitude agreeable and leisure delightful. You have an excellent mind and one moreover well developed by the years, refined with much care, taught in many arts and sciences—a mind to guide and control human actions and holding the rudder of our

---

[1]　　DVS 1.7.19–25.
[2]　　Horace, *Sat.* 2.2.118–19 (Hovenden's translation).

entire life, and with such piloting the voyage ought not to be other than
fortunate. You are acquainted with the illustrious and distinguished men
who have lived—I should like to say with those who are living, but you
see how things go. If, however, there are any such surviving now, they are
indeed not unknown to you. With some of them you can converse only
in imagination, a form of intercourse which neither seas nor mountains
will deprive you of; with some you may also hold bodily converse. Perhaps
you are rich in the latter kind, although there has never been a great abundance of this commodity, and the scarcity at present is conspicuous. But I
believe I ought to insert one name here as a mark of compliment. Among
those whom destiny has granted to you for your comfort in the life of solitude is Ponzio Sansone,[3] who next to you gives most distinction to your
church. Concerning him, since I have known him most intimately from
early youth and think I have even surer knowledge of him now, I shall
speak with particular confidence. I am inclined to believe that the name of
"Samson" did not fall to him by chance but arose from his nature, because
he is as remarkable for strength of mind, refinement, and prudence as the
Jewish hero was for strength of body; in addition he is endowed with no
slight knowledge of literature and with such sweetness of character as can
easily alleviate whatever harshness may pertain to the state of solitude.
Embrace him, as is your practice, with your whole heart; summon him to
share your leisure and retirement. For if I am not mistaken in my guess,
he will follow you willingly, and being tired out with the life of the city will
have no dread of abandoning it.

5. But alas, where am I leaving our Socrates?[4] Or am I deceived? Do I
really leave him, seeing that while the others are only companions, he is an
integral part of us, and while they have to be invited, he is indissolubly joined
to us by love? You know the man, endeared by firm and faithful friendship
and ennobled by familiar association with the Muses. With him your life will
be joyous and pleasant so as never to be wanting in wise counsel, intellectual
stimulus, and mental vigor, with never a cloud of melancholy intruding such
as is sometimes associated with those powers; but that equability of a countenance ever cheerful which we are wont to admire and praise in the ancient
Socrates, we behold and love in our friend as well.

[3]   A priest of the church of Cavaillon. There are two brief letters of Petrarch to him
(*Fam.* 14.8; 15.10).
[4]   Ludwig van Kempen, one of Petrarch's closest companions and the one to whom
he dedicated his *Familiares* collection of letters.

6. However, I shall not pass in silence over our Guido, than whom there is no one purer and more open in spirit, keener in intellect, weightier in judgment, more agreeable in conversation. Let him be admitted as the fifth in our company, not the seventh as his name of Settimo[5] suggests. I cannot imagine anything pleasanter than this society, although others might be available, suited to our wishes and pursuits, were it not that some inequality in our conditions, some obstacle of a general kind, and the inextricable tangle of human affairs acted invidiously against us. But the number of the former will suffice, and Fortune herself cannot restrain us from enjoying the society of the others in imagination. With these men by you, neither grievous sickness nor pressing occupation nor need of occasional journeys can so sunder us as to leave you without someone for a constant companion.

7. Why should I enumerate all the particulars? Nothing will be wanting if only you will be not wanting. You also have means that are freely at your disposal without being in the least burdensome, or to put the same thing in different words, your poverty is neither afflicting nor degrading but honorable and cheerful and, if we would admit the truth, an occasion of envy to many. You have a good supply of books, an ardent love of reading, an understanding and a memory conferred from heaven and strengthened by watching and study.

8. As to what follows, I should have observed silence, for so modesty dictated, if I did not know that the value of things depended on the affection of the one who used them. Therefore I say that I myself shall be in your company, and the work of my pen, of which you are so fond, shall never fail you, offering each day something new the esteem of which, because of your insatiable desire for reading it, I confess would be doubled in my eyes, were it not for the consideration, as I remarked at the outset, that affection, according to the old saying, hinders the judgment. I recall how often you have preferred a book of mine before one of Plato and Cicero, not to mention lesser writers. When you would enter my library (which often you do not as bishop but as friend), eager to read with a thirst that is never

---

[5]   Guido Settimo or Sette was a hereditary and lifelong friend of the poet. Their fathers had suffered exile together from Florence and the sons were educated in the same school. Petrarch reviews in a long letter (*Sen.* 10.2) the incidents of their friendship. In a letter to Boccaccio (*Sen.* 5.1) he refers to him as "another self—such was the accord and harmony between us since our childhood." He studied canon law and attained distinction in the Church, became first Archdeacon and then Archbishop of Genoa, where he died in 1368.

slaked, and I would offer you the divine works of those godlike intellects, you would wave aside what I put before you, turn away your head, and ask only for my own. In this preference there was not necessarily an error of judgment; you might have been actuated by your perfect knowledge of the ancients, which did not require repeated reading, or by the love of novelty in my writings. For though the authority of ancient literature is greater, and it is true, as Horace says, that time improves poetry as it does wine,[6] yet newness has an attraction of its own, and it may please you to discover what progress I have been making with the passage of time, for nothing is more attentive and more inquisitive than friendship.

9. But be the cause what it may, I have often secretly wondered at your enthusiasm. Sometimes, after being away, I have learned of your interest from the mouth of my steward who would greet me on my return with vehement reproaches, asking why I had carried off some paper or other which you were in the habit of demanding to see when you visited my house. I laughed and marveled at the affection of the father, or the fidelity of the keeper, or the innocence of the steward. And so when I went away another time I would play a joke on the old fellow and give him some blank paper, saying that was what you were asking for. When he discovered how he had been tricked he would once more on my return make bitter complaint, but in the end the whole thing passed off in mirth and laughter.

§II. Of the things which the solitary man should always desire and concerning his home

10. But I return to my theme. You have then, in addition, that without which life is, I will not merely say lacking in happiness, but not life at all. I mean a hatred of evil and love of good, a reverence for virtue, a beautiful aspiration for a good name, an interest in what is honorable, a scorn for what is futile. If I call this one of the foundations of the solitary life, I shall maintain that I am speaking the truth. You have a body apt to sustain toil, of matured strength not verging toward the decline; you are in that flourishing age which has attained its freedom from the evils of adolescence, that best portion of life which is neither unacquainted with action nor unresourceful in counsel, but capable of daring great matters. You have, finally, a country in which as citizen and bishop you occupy the highest place in the affection and reverence of the people, enjoying the one because

[6]   *Ep.* 2.1.34.

of your character, the other because of your rank, and both because of your virtue and desert. Fortune has granted you for a country which, though your episcopate dignifies it with the appellation of city, yet apart from its antiquity and designation, has nothing of the city about it—not the luxury, nor the crowds, nor the turmoil, features which render it particularly suitable for the life of which I am speaking.

11. If I am accurate in my calculation, I find that it was already esteemed in authentic writings among the ancient cities of that time, about fifty years before the coming of our Lord, when Julius Caesar was attacking Britain. The appearance of the place is such that as often as we came to visit you there, our Socrates was accustomed to remark with considerable elegance, "Here is the city, small indeed but honorable, which according to the ecclesiastical histories was offered to our Savior Jesus by King Abagarus." In its very midst you can, if you wish, make a solitude for yourself. You do not need a long journey to attain the object which many of those whom I have formerly described sought in flight. The character of your situation is such that you may lead the life of a solitary in your own country and in the bosom of your own people, an opportunity scarcely to be despised. You have that at home which many have looked for beyond the seas.

12. But if your own nest displeases you and you are looking for some freer spot, you may flit to a branch nearby and place yourself in this most pleasant and peaceful abode at the head of the neighboring stream. Within your reach is the Sorgue, that matchless spring to whose murmuring accompaniment I compose these words. Within your reach is the free and delightful seclusion of Vaucluse—the Closed Valley, as the inhabitants call it and as nature meant it to be called, for she has hidden it among the encompassing hills away from every road and every common intrusion and has not permitted it to be seen by any save those that dwell in it. Here you may enjoy in a rare union the privileges of being free and a lord, a dignitary and in solitude. Can you scorn a place which has inspired awe and amazement in strangers?

13. According to Seneca, "a cave, made by the deep crumbling of the rocks and holding up a mountain on its arch, a place not built with hands but hollowed out into such spaciousness by natural causes, will deeply move the soul by a certain intimation of the existence of God."[7] If that is true, where, I ask, is there a cave more suited to inspiring religious awe?

[7] Ep. 41.

2.14.15

And if his next observation is true, that "we worship the sources of mighty rivers," where shall we find a more conspicuous object of worship? I have seen rivers greater in length and in the volume of their waters but none with so splendid a source. A third remark of Seneca's is that "we erect altars at places where great streams burst suddenly from hidden sources," and if that is so, where shall altars be more fittingly located? Such altars, Christ is my witness, I have long thought of erecting, if opportunity should favor my wishes, there in my little garden which lies in the shadow of the cliffs and overhangs the stream, and I shall dedicate them not to the nymphs, as Seneca thought, nor to any of the pagan deities of springs and rivers, but to Mary, whose ineffable conception and fruitful virginity overturned all the altars and temples of the gods. Perhaps she will lend me her aid that I may sometime bring to completion what I have long and, if I mistake not, piously desired.

14. I now resume where I left off. Can you, then, disdain your own place when strangers venerate it—a place most propitious for freedom and peace and leisure and study and virtue, and, not to linger over particulars, for all things, in sum, in which you are interested—a place, even if other things are disregarded, once honored by a great occupant who is an object of special devotion with you?

15. You know that your Veranus, the excellent confessor of Christ, who, I do not know how many years before your time, lived in your province, which is even now uncommonly wild, came here in quest of a peaceful spot for a rest, and after expelling the terrible dragon led a holy and solitary life in this locality. I have not overlooked his name among the friends of illustrious solitude but have only deferred it to the last in order to fix it more firmly in the memory, not so much for you as for others who may chance to read this. For from your memory he cannot be torn because you are daily reminded of him, having always his shrine before your eyes, a witness of your faith, to the completion of which as a shelter for the relics of the saint you have contributed all your zeal and all your wealth, cheating your stomach as the saying goes, giving in fact all the silver and gold you ever had, best of men that you are. Verily here he dwelt while he lived, before the virtue was discovered which caused his elevation against his will to the troubles of the pontifical rank. Here, as in a hostile land which he had conquered and pacified and redeemed for human cultivation, he raised a trophy to Christ, under whose protection and banners he had gained the victory, erecting a fair church in the name of the Virgin Mother, small in

size but elegant. By the labor of his own hands, it is said, he cut through this stubborn flint and made a passage over this mighty mountain, a work of enormous zeal and industry. On this bank he had a cell, being rich in Christ and contented with his little garden and stream. And dying at last far from this place, it was here that he wished to be brought back and buried, as you know, making use of a clear and amazing miracle. The same power which the rod of the living Moses displayed in the crossing of the Red Sea was exercised, if we may rely on faith, in the crossing of rivers by the cloak of the dead Veranus. Enough of this, for though much remains that can be spoken in praise of your countryside, much, too, has been spoken and often, and for this day an end must be made of our conversation.

§III. Whoever wishes to serve God or develop his own powers by virtuous practices or accomplish any other good work, let him escape, lest while he appears to be helping others he incur his own ruin and commit that fault which he reproves in others

16. Therefore, whether our desire is to serve God, which is the only freedom and the only felicity, or by virtuous practices to develop our mind, which is the next best application of our labor, or through reflection and writing to leave our remembrance to posterity and so arrest the flight of the days and extend the all too brief duration of our life, or whether it is our aim to achieve all these things together, let us, I pray you, make our escape at length and spend in solitude what little time remains, taking every precaution that, while we seem to be bringing aid to the shipwrecked, we be not ourselves overwhelmed by the waves or shattered against the rocks of human activities. Finally, what we approve, that let us perform, lest we be guilty of the common weakness with which we often reproach others, and make our words and judgments disagree with our actions.

§IV. We ought not to seek great wealth, for it is a hindrance instead of an aid

17. Let no one deceive us, let no one persuade us that great riches are called for in this kind of life. They are a hindrance rather than an aid; they weigh us down instead of lifting us up. This life is reached by an ascent, and no one will ascend high if of his own accord he burdens himself with superfluous loads or ties himself up with a noose. Nothing is heavier than gold, nothing more binding; except so far as it contributes to our necessities, it is neither to be desired nor liked. For whenever avarice is served, there is nothing which more bows down the carrier,

depresses him, and forces him down to the ground. Nor is it any wonder if, coming from the ground, it is carried back to the ground by its own weight. It is not fitting for a soul of heavenly origin to be buried under heaps extracted from a hole in the ground, to be polluted with filth. Gold presents, to be sure, a brilliancy and softness to the senses which is deceptive to the mind, but it actually brings darkness and thorns and the stings of grievous and tormenting troubles, and the more refined its appearance, the more it is tainted with hidden evils. Riches never come alone but bring with them many and divers ills and endless burdens and occasions of strife.

18. If you do not take my word for it, ask those who are called happy and bid them on their oath not to conceal any of the truth, and you will find that their lives have been filled with tortures, so that what you used to regard with admiration you will come to look at with horror or scorn, and understand that in the life to which I encourage you great riches are of no benefit at all, but often of the greatest possible mischief. Therefore, far from having so many pains spent in their acquisition, they should rather be thrown away if they are excessive, until they reach the measure established by nature and virtue, as is the manner of sailors distressed by a heavy storm who save their ship by sacrificing their cargo.

19. It strangely enters my mind at this point to request and implore you, father (and myself along with you), to submit to a piece of advice useful to both of us, once given by a boy to an old man. The boy was Alcibiades, who later as a man was distinguished for his beauty and genius and is an illustrious example of the vicissitudes of fortune; his uncle was Pericles, himself numbered with the rare spirits, conspicuous for the power of his eloquence and trusting more to the tongue than the sword for the wielding of his great power. Coming to his uncle one day as was his habit, the lad Alcibiades found the old man more troubled than usual and feeling disturbed perhaps at not being received with the customary signs of affection, he repeatedly tried, it is said, to learn the reason of his uncle's sadness, and what had befallen. The old man, being pleased, I suppose, with the boy's wit, did not conceal the true reason from him and said that he had spent a huge sum of money on behalf of the state and with all his brain-wracking was unable to discover a way to render an account of his outlay. Then Alcibiades, speaking beyond his years, said, "You should rather consider how to avoid rendering an account"—a clever bit of advice even if it had been given by an old man,

and a large and evident augury of his riper years. Leaning on this hint, his uncle stirred up a foreign war and so escaped the difficulty of giving an accounting.

20. But I return to the advice, in which I generally approve not the injustice of the action but the keenness and quickness of mind. I am urging the application to our own use of this ripe counsel given by a boy, but not before it has been converted into different terms. For behold, there will come persons who will show us the way to great riches, which is nothing else than to teach avarice—verily a pernicious school, and exceedingly laborious and difficult doctrine, to be learned only with great expense of vigils and toil and destined either to miss its goal or to do injury by its success. To a mind occupied in such thoughts let us say, "Consider, rather, the way to avoid the desire of riches." For that is the more useful, and certainly the easier art, and if the mind is a little slow and indisposed for this lesson, it should be stimulated with additional incentives. Let us prove to it that, aside from the evils of riches concerning which I have just been speaking and which are daily in the mouths of many persons, this art is in our own hands while the other is in the power of fortune.

21. Anyone may despise wealth, to gain it is not so easy. You know that saying of our friend, "Why should I demand of fortune that she give, rather than demand of myself that I should not crave?"[8] And so I think it is better to leave unattempted an undertaking which is difficult and of doubtful issue and which, even if it were of assured utility, would be ill-timed and too late. For lo, shall we perspire and pant and torture ourselves for fear of lacking sustenance in our short and perishable existence when, as I said, we already have means heaped up to the extent of enviable luxury? But suppose even that we want for something, what king is there who does not want for something? At this point someone will say that we should rise aloft with a great impulse and like the gods banish altogether every fear of want for the future. But even if for the moment it is banished, in time it will return with greater force.

§V. That a life anxious with solicitude for tomorrow is not life but preparation for life that avarice should be vanquished and the way to true riches learned

22. Cicero, you recall, writing once to his brother said, "As for your frequent exhortations to me in the past to ambition and work, I shall act on them, but

---

8   Seneca, *Ep.* 15.

when shall we live?"⁹ A brief question but a pregnant one. Similarly, may not any one reply with sufficient point and seriousness to the adviser I have just spoken of? "Your suggestion, my friend, is good, if only it is practicable. But when shall we begin to live, I pray you, whose part it clearly is not merely to begin to live but already to have lived?" For this life of constant anxiety, directed toward tomorrow, is not life at all, but preparation for a life which may never come, and which is well known to be doubtful. Among many observations of the plebeian poet, you may hold this one as not spoken in an ignorant manner,

> Trust me, it is not the nature of a wise man to say, "I shall live,"
> It is too late to live tomorrow, you must live today.¹⁰

23. The advice of Alcibiades is of wide scope and applicable to many things. Vengeance is provocative, appetite is tempting, ambition brings anxiety, love inflames one to carry out what is difficult and to scorn what is easy. Let us teach our mind that the way to the infliction of injury is doubtful and dangerous and that while we seek revenge we often but accumulate the wrongs; that the service of the appetite is vile and the troublesome preparation issues in a disgraceful conclusion; that ambition is always windy, calling for a humble appeal to the people, than which nothing is more distasteful; that love is impudent and domineering, requiring service to many women, than which nothing is more undignified for a strong man, an occasion of idle mirth and of mourning, and often no less when the outcome is happy than when it is sad, so great is the vanity of the thing.

24. For all these temptations there is a single rule. Since in satisfying these desires thought is obstructed, and mortal griefs and causes of misfortune will never be wanting, in order to escape from them and be happy and free, only contempt will avail. Therefore, we should rather consider how to avoid getting into these difficulties than how to extricate ourselves from them. See to what a manly judgment that boyish saying can be applied. But leaving the other things out of account and regarding only what concerns us at the moment, let us by this desire overcome that avarice which dangles great riches before us as necessary for our leisure, and by disdaining mortal inclinations, curbing our passions, and setting a proper value on natural modesty, let us learn the short way to true wealth. For in truth, greed,

⁹ *Quint. fratr.* 3.1.12.
¹⁰ Martial, *Epigrams* 1.15.2.

while it is injurious to all who aim at virtue, is particularly hostile to our purpose, for it has no end, and by heaping up superfluities burdens with a handicap the life to which it promises a support, and which ought not to be heavily encumbered but lightly equipped and mobile. Surely it is well known that many who seemed capable of everything have been hindered in achieving this one thing by the greatness of their wealth and power.

25. But nothing hinders you, unless (which I am far from suspecting) you are in your own way. You can, indeed you can, provided you prefer to cut all the knots at one stroke instead of untying them one by one. We are engaged with a Hydra; there will be no end unless we cut off its ever-sprouting heads in the style of Hercules. I not only know how, but have already begun to lead the life of solitude, and I shall easily persevere in it if I am reinforced on the lonely way by a leader and companion like you, who will be not only a support to my peace but, if I may somehow express what is in my mind, my very peace, not only a comfort in my solitude, but in a way the very soul of my solitude. When I am with you, I shall think myself truly solitary. I have gone before and tried the way; you should at least follow, though you ought to have been the leader. Like one who has crossed a dangerous torrent I call from the opposite bank and bid you pass over boldly: there is not the slightest danger. Where I first set foot, everything was slippery and uncertain; here I can report everything is safe and pleasant. If you hesitate, if you delay, I shall recross and retrace the footsteps which I have marked clearly, as Virgil says, in order that I may take you by the hand, as it were, and lead you to these places. When you have grown habituated to them you will look upon the chambers of kings and the courts of popes as prisons and noisome dungeons.

§VI. *The remedies against a slow progress toward solitude*

26. But if we cannot all at once free ourselves from all the bonds which hold the spirit captive—for this is among the lessons which men begin to teach before they have themselves learned it—let us at least treat solitude in a friendly fashion. Let us transport ourselves to its province with all the little encumbrances of our fortune. When we shall find ourselves able to dispense with these, we shall at last come into our full liberty. Meanwhile, as things are, we shall surely live nowhere more peacefully.

27. I do not plead so strenuously because I distrust you, nor am I trying to persuade you with such a great effort of language as though to some-

thing harsh and difficult, since I know the elevation of your mind and that you have illustrious and familiar guides to this road or even to a more exacting one. For Martin [of Tours], in whom your trust is great and with whom, judging from your pilgrimages and conversations, I have noticed you are most friendly among the friends of Christ, observed this manner of life, as is clear from an earlier passage, embracing the repose of a solitary and retaining the rank of a bishop at the same time, so that Gennadius [of Constantinople] justly calls him both a monk and a bishop. His course is especially striking because he adopted it even before baptism (which is particularly difficult), and during youth and military service, both of which are unfavorable to such resolutions. And he lived in such a way that already at that time, as is set down in the account of his life, he was looked upon as a monk rather than a soldier.

28. Maenas, whose birthday is the same as Martin's, is another who changed earthly service for heavenly, but he lived in the desert instead of the city. To this refuge also came Gregory of Nazianzus when he was distracted from his industrious study, as Jerome reports, and ordaining a bishop in his place, lived in the country in monastic fashion. How great his love was for this kind of life, you may infer from the circumstance that much earlier, shortly after his departure from the school of Athens, he laid his hand on Basil of Caesarea,[11] his famous compatriot and fellow student and also his brother in the flesh, as Augustine, following rumor, declares, and took him down from his lecturer's chair where he was teaching rhetoric with great success, and with the remarkable confidence and the authority of love drew him away to solitude and better studies.

[11]   There is a confusion here between the two Gregories—Gregory of Nazianzus, the friend of Basil, and Gregory of Nyssa, Basil's brother.—JZ

15

Refutations and Commendations

*§VII. The refutation of the arguments of those
who oppose the solitary life*

1. But I hear again, on the other hand, the clamor that is usually raised against this view. For in the first place, they try to stir a grudge against us out of the Bible. "Woe to him that is alone, when he falleth: for he hath not another to help him up,"[1] and "Two are better than one; because they have a good reward for their labor,"[2] and many other things of that kind. But if they paid attention to what I thought and said, they would make no such statements.

In the next place they oppose me with Aristotle's saying that man is by nature a social animal or that one who does not associate with others is either a beast or a god, as if I had been suggesting hatred or prohibiting all association with man, or as if the choice were doubtful whether I should prefer to be a beast or God, I mean a man of beastly or divine characteristics. Moreover, they mutter against me that passage of Cicero in which, not content with having explained once that society has its origin not in necessity, as some have thought, but in the nature of man, he alleges as his best proof for the matter that any man, though he were supplied with all resources and free from all necessity, would yet shun solitude and seek a companion for his study. To all these objections I think I have made sufficient answer in the first book. For if I did not in this fully agree with Cicero, I should not myself say that we should seek for a friend, or even

[1] Eccl 4:10.
[2] Eccl 4:9.

friends, in our solitude and study, and cherish them. I understand the force of these objections and all others of the same kind that are usually adduced against me. I am not unaware, too, that Aphraates, whom I have spoken of formerly, and the famous hermit Julian left the wilderness and went to Antioch, and that the more famous St. Anthony went to Alexandria and other cities, but I know that they did it not spontaneously nor for any frivolous reason but for some grave necessity and momentous decision of faith. For those holy men knew what was appropriate to each season, both when there was need of enjoying peace and when it was necessary to prefer cities to solitude.

2. I know that what they add to the foregoing and what I quite often hear objected in my presence is almost absurd. "What would happen," they say, "if you could persuade all men in general of your design? Who then would live in the cities? Beware lest you speak against the interests of the state." But the facts themselves may reply clearly. If indeed everybody should remove from the city, there would be a definite ground for changing my opinion. The solitudes would have to be deserted, since they would no longer be solitudes, and we should have to return forthwith to the places from which the restless populace, father of all weariness, had departed. But it is all right. The disposition of men at large is not of such a sort: the multitude does not lend ears so alert and wide open to honest advice. I shall be glad if I can persuade the few. It is indeed not reasonable to induce all men to lead one kind of life, particularly the life of solitude, and so I do not speak for everybody, but for you and myself, and for those few with whose dispositions these unusual habits agree. For us, surely, if we follow not the foolish opinion of the crowd but our own nature, nothing is more appropriate.

§VIII. Exhortation to solitude and that cities should be left to worldly people

3. Let us leave the city with no idea of returning to it, lest having put our hand to the plow we should look backward. Let us rather pray that we may never return to the ungrateful crowd which is underserving of the regard of all good men. This is said to have been the action of Lentulus, who under the color of an honorable departure chose a lifelong exile, and it is an example which hatred of the vulgar, at least, should have persuaded us to imitate, if the love of peace was not enough. There is also the less familiar but more religious example of the Phoenician monk Chronius who,

when he entered his solitude, prayed he might never depart from it and
imposed many duties on himself to confirm his resolve and in order that
his prayers might not be ineffectual.

4. We must tear up the roots of our troubles, break the chains which
hold us confined, and destroy the bridges behind us, so that no hope of
flight or return will remain. I shall not say to you what Palladius, the nar-
rator of such instances, reports as the advice given to him by John, that
Egyptian hermit of whom I have already spoken. "You are going to be
a bishop," he said, "and are going to have a great many tribulations and
labors. If therefore you wish to avoid them, do not forsake our solitude; for
no one is going to make you a bishop while you are living in the desert." I
shall say nothing to you about the bishopric, seeing you already have the
dignity which the other was warned to guard against, and that it is no longer possible for you not to have been a bishop, a rank to which your early
ripened virtue raised you before the customary age. But my advice will be
as close as possible to that given by John. For your episcopate is of a character which makes you in dignity equal to the greatest while giving you a
freedom such as belongs to a moderate and humble station.

5. If you fear the burdens of a greater diocese, it would be best to cherish our place of solitude, and if you wish to be freed from the bonds of
immortal troubles, you should seek out this place of rest, saying like that
celebrated Roman centurion when he was returning from his severe campaign, "This is the best place to stop." If this phrase uttered by chance was
inferred for an omen of such mighty power, it should not be held cheap
when deliberately spoken.

Arise, come, hasten, let us abandon the city to merchants, attorneys,
brokers, usurers, tax gatherers, scriveners, doctors, perfumers, butchers,
cooks, bakers and tailors, alchemists, fullers, artisans, weavers, archi-
tects, statuaries, painters, mimes, dancers, lute players, quacks, panderers,
thieves, criminals, adulterers, parasites, foreigners, swindlers, and jesters,
gluttons who with scent alert catch the odor of the marketplace, for whom
that is the only bliss, whose mouths are agape for that alone. For on the
mountains there is no smell of cookery, and it is a torment for them to miss
their customary delights. Let them be, they are not of our kind.

6. Let the rich count their coins and employ therein the aid of arith-
metic; we shall calculate our wealth without science and without art. We
have no cause to envy them unless, which God forbid, we are still children

to be caught by painted figments. "Remove the frontlet from horses that are for sale" is an old caution. No sane man wants to marry a misfeatured girl because she is well dressed. If we tear off the frontlet, or the mask rather, from those who are so gay in their purple, we shall clearly see their wretchedness. Let them have their kind of wealth, their habits, their pleasures. In truth, the riches they would like to keep forever will depart, and the pleasures they would fain hold back by force will escape, but the habits which they disavow will remain and accompany them against their will. Everything that they display for the wonder of the vulgar will vanish in an instant. They live beneath the sway of fortune, and though she should spare them, death will not spare. They who possess the most precious things, if they can be said to possess the objects to which they are enslaved, will themselves soon fall to the possession of the basest creatures, and from them an ungrateful heir or perhaps a hateful foe will receive their ill-gotten wealth. Their bodies will go to worms and owls, their souls to Tartarus, their names to eternal oblivion. On the other hand, however poor he be here below, "the righteous shall be in everlasting remembrance."

Therefore, let not a seeming prosperity and an actual misery stir us to emulation; let the soft and luxurious men of wealth be far removed from our neighborhood. Let them enjoy their hot baths and brothels, great halls and dining places, while we delight in woods and mountains, meadows and streams. Let them enjoy their carnal desires and their lucre from wherever it comes; let us pursue our humane and honorable studies.

7. And if it be thought desirable to mingle some physical activity with our employments, let it be the tilling of the fields or hunting. Although in the latter there is a suggestion of noisiness which is not in keeping with our regimen (for it is an old saying that many words are wasted in hunting), nevertheless I know that some very thoughtful men have considered it favorable to meditation and study, probably because of the solitude and the deep coverts of the woods and the silence of those who guard the nets. This would be especially true if you attached yourself to the party as a spectator rather than as a huntsman and could remain or go according to your convenience with our leave from any of the hunters. That is a privilege sometimes granted to clerics, particularly to such as live in the woods. Nor is hunting of this sort forbidden, provided it is indulged in rarely and with moderation, and for the sake of bodily exercise rather than of dissipation. The same thing is true of the related exercises of fishing and fowling. These are the arts of country life.

8. In short, let the others be constantly in a state of restlessness and agitation, let us establish ourselves with feet firmly planted on the rock; let them be always motionless, let us make some progress; let them in their perplexity be always seeking counsel, let us at length carry wholesome counsel into practice; finally, let them embrace the fleeting world and cling to it as best they can, let us seek the Lord while he may be found, and call upon him while he is near, lest when our bodies are removing from the city, our souls should remove from our bodies. Let us send our souls before us to heaven; when the time comes (which philosophers did not hope for), we shall follow with our bodies.

§IX. The glorious commendation of solitude

9. See how far the impetus has carried my pen. How much I have said about a small thing (as it may seem to most) but to my way of feeling an extremely important one, the source to me of so much satisfaction that as long as I remember to have been chained in the prison of my body, the duration of my life has seemed no greater than the space of my solitude and leisure. If I dared to take to myself the striking saying of the illustrious commander, and if the privilege of such a boast in such a disparity of reputation were not attributed to brazen impudence, I should then not be content with saying that I was never less at leisure than in my leisure, never less lonely than when alone, but I should assert that I was always at leisure except in my leisure, always lonely except when alone.

10. Though I have no doubt, as I have often declared, that the generality will raise a great clamor against these opinions, yet the truth is fearless and unassailable and does not tremble before a vain outcry, as Maro says in describing a generous steed,

Lofty-necked, sharp-headed.[3]

I am not indeed so presumptuous as to assert this idea dogmatically: I only appear as a solicitous inquirer. Though I have always diligently sought for the truth, yet I fear that the recesses in which it is hidden, or my own preoccupations, or a certain dullness of mind may have sometimes stood in my way, so that often in my search for the thing I may have been bewildered by false lights. Therefore, I have treated these matters not as one who

---

[3]   *Georg.* 3.79–80 (Dryden's translation).

defines[4] but as a student and investigator. For to define is the province of a wise man, and I am neither wise nor neighbor to the wise, but in Cicero's words, "a man fertile in conjectures."[5]

11. On the other hand, I know that the chosen few to whom I address myself will be on my side and they are in all respects but numbers superior and triumphant over the rest. I already have the assurance of your judgment: that is enough. If others wish to judge, let them do so at their pleasure, since there is no compulsion by which indefinite and wavering opinion can be reduced to positive truth. Surely when the inevitable day shall arrive and the ineluctable hour of death shall come to dismiss the soul from this life, when it shall profit us not to be pointed out with the finger in the squares and at crowded crossings, to have been a king or a great prelate, to have abounded in wealth and influence and enjoyments, but only to have lived chastely, piously, and innocently, then I hope that even he who now denies it will admit that our advice was at least conducive to tranquility.

12. So great is my love and enthusiasm for this subject that, though I have said so much, many other thoughts crowd upon me. But I must have regard to my studies. I intended to write a letter and I have written a book. Moreover, I ought not to have divided it, since a book on the solitary life ought appropriately to be composed as an unbroken unit. But it occurred to me that I was writing in praise of the kind of solitude which, while it avoided crowds, was not averse to a limited companionship. I was also deterred from my first purpose by the consideration that an interruption in the middle of the journey would relieve the weary and overtaxed reader, and so I divided the book in two.

13. Differing here from the practice of the ancients whom I follow in many things, I found it grateful in this unassuming book of mine often to insert the sacred and glorious name of Christ. If this had been done by those early guides of our intellectual life, if they had added the spark of divinity to their human eloquence, though great the pleasure which they now afford, it would then have been still greater. As it is, the original source of eloquence allures us by clear brilliance of style, but it is without the true light of doctrine. It soothes the ear, but it does not give repose to the mind nor lead it to that highest and most secure enjoyment, that peace

[4]   Augustine, *Against the Academics*, trans. Michael Foley (New Haven: Yale University Press, 2019), 1.5.15, p. 28.
[5]   *Acad. pr.*, 2.20.

of the intellect to which, though wicked and headstrong men despise it, there is no approach save through the humility of Christ.

14. These things I have addressed to you with such affection of mind that every rustle of the branches breathed upon by the wind and every ripple of the waters gushing from the ground about me seems to say a single thing: "You argue well, you counsel uprightly, you speak the truth."

APPENDIX

De vita solitaria

Sections and Chapters according to the Bâle Edition, 1554

7. Of the misery of the busy man and the happiness of the solitary man when night returns and it is time for supper

8. Of the misery of the busy man and the happiness of the solitary man when it is time for sleep

Section 3

1. Summary of the discussion and transition to the unhappiness of those who are engaged in other people's affairs

2. Almost every busy man is unhappy, though there are some few who are worthily employed

3. In praise of the serenity of mind which is granted to those who are confirmed in solitude, and that the mind cannot apply itself to a diversity of interests

4. How from the dangers of the shepherd's life it may be inferred that the busy life is less safe, and for that reason the author himself has chosen the retired life

Section 4

1. The retired life, especially to those unversed in literature, is heavier than death and seems calculated to bring on death

2. Although it would be best that all should recognize in their youth what is the proper kind of life for them, nevertheless if one fails to do it in youth, it is wise that one should at least do it in old age

3. What course is to be kept in the order and plan of personal reformation

4. The praise of solitude

5. On the fourfold distinction of virtues introduced by Plotinus and approved by Macrobius

6. The delight and sweetness of the solitary life and the spiritual conflict of the solitary man

7. The comfort and joy of hoping for the perpetual company of the angels as a reward for the brief withdrawal from men

8. Having Christ for our faithful witness, we need no imaginary witness

9. Of the freedom of the solitary man and of mental employments

10. How divine honors were awarded to the inventors of certain arts

Section 5

1. Reasons why some people blame the solitary life

2. Woods, fields, and streams are of great advantage to the solitary individual

3. The interpretation of the words of Seneca in which he seems to impugn solitude

5. The solitude of St. Augustine

6. Of St. Jerome, the marvelous worshiper of solitude

7. Of St. Paula and certain other devout women who embraced the life of solitude

8. Of Pope Gregory the Great as a lover of solitude

9. Of St. Benedict, a singular and most devout dweller in solitude

10. Of the solitude of St. Florentius

11. On the solitude of St. Francis

12. Of triple solitude, an incidental chapter, and of the solitude of Blasius and others

13. Of the solitude of St. Remigius

14. The solitude of the Blessed Bernard

15. The solitude of Carloman

16. On the solitude of Romuald

17. The solitude of Peter Damian

18. The solitude of Pope Celestine V who was called Peter before his rise to the Papacy

Section 4

1. Peter the Hermit, a particular lover of solitude, in connection with whom the complaints here referred to are introduced

2. The rebuke of our kings and princes who apply themselves to sleep, pleasure, disgraceful gain, despoiling of subjects, and other vices, while none of them are moved by the loss of the Holy Land

3. Accusation against the Roman emperor and the pope, in addition to the Germans and Greeks

4. How the Catholic Faith was of old diffused through well-nigh the entire world, but is now reduced through the negligence of the great

5. Of the high virtue of the ancient Romans when compared to the kings of today

6. The character of our princes compared with Muhammad

7. The denunciation of Catholic princes, because they neglect the special concern of their country

8. That we are not obliged to fight for every country, and what country deserves to be fought for

Section 5

1. Of the solitude of the most holy John the Baptist and of the blessed Mary Magdalen who is on that account preferred to her sister

2. The solitude of Jesus Christ, our Lord and Savior

3. Praising the solitary life by way of epilogue to what has been said

4. Of King David and certain patriarchs who loved the solitary life

Section 6

1. Of the life, customs, and rites of the Brahmans and the solitude of the famous Calanus

2. Of a certain solitary among Hindus

3. Of the solitaries beyond the North and the Rhipean Mountains and the Hyperborean race and the remaining islands

Section 7

1. Of philosophers and poets who took refuge in solitude

2. Of the ancient poets who chose solitude

Section 8

1. The solitude of Seneca, a citizen of Cordova and a Roman senator

2. The solitude of Cicero

3. The solitude of Demosthenes

4. Of Anaxagoras and other illustrious men who loved the life of solitude

Section 9

1. Of Julius and Augustus Caesar who loved and wished for solitude

2. Of Diocletian and Antoninus Pius as lovers of the solitary life

3. The solitude of Numa Pompilius, the second king of Rome

4. Of Romulus, Achilles, and Hercules who loved solitude

5. Of the two Scipios who particularly loved solitude

6. Explaining, by an interpretation of the saying of the elder Scipio, what kind of solitude and leisure the author intends to speak

Section 10

1. How the virtues of the one to whom the book is dedicated and of the friends granted to him by fortune invite one to the life of solitude

2. Of the things which the solitary man should always desire and concerning his home

3. Whoever wishes to serve God or develop his own powers by virtuous practices or accomplish any other good work, let him escape, lest while he appears to be helping others he incur his own ruin and commit that fault which he reproves in others

4. We ought not to seek great wealth, for it is a hindrance instead of an aid

5. That a life anxious with solicitude for tomorrow is not life but preparation for life that avarice should be vanquished and the way to true riches learned

6. The remedies against a slow progress toward solitude

7. The refutation of the arguments of those who oppose the solitary life

8. Exhortation to solitude and that cities should be left to worldly people

9. The glorious commendation of solitude

CPSIA information can be obtained
at www.ICGtesting.com
Printed in the USA
LVHW030727130423
744224LV00001B/3